Lands and Peoples of Central Africa

Completely revised edition with updated statistics

W. D. Michie M.A. (Hons.), Dip.Ed.

E. D. Kadzombe B.Sc., M.Sc., Cert. Ed.

M. R. Naidoo B.A., M.Ed., Dip.Ed.

Longman

Acknowledgements

Ab
2.
950430

The publishers are grateful to the following for permission to reproduce photographs in the text:

A.A.C. for pages 180 and 181; A. Bristow for page 45; British Steel Corporation for page 122 bottom; J. Allan Cash Ltd for page 54 right; Bruce Coleman Ltd for page 21 top right; Department of Conservation and Extension for pages 13 left, 13 right and 15; Department of Information, Zimbabwe for pages 4 top, 4 bottom, 11, 16 left, 16 right, 21 bottom right, 75, 86 top, 86 bottom, 87, 93, 94 bottom, 95 top, 96, 97 top, 97 bottom, 98, 100 left, 100 right, 101 102, 104, 110 left, 110 right, 111, 117, 121, 122 top, 123, 130 and 134; F.A.O. for pages 161 top left, 161 right and 161 bottom left; R. H. G. Howden for page 95 bottom; John & Penny Hubley for pages 133 and 140; Alan Hutchison Library for page 94 top; E. D. Kadzombe for pages 40, 41 top, 59, 60 and 61 left; D. F. Lovemore for page 17; Malawi Information Service for pages 35, 37, 56, 61 right, 62, 64, 68 and 69; A. Malinki for pages 41 bottom, 46 left, 46 right, 49 left and 49 right; W. D. Michie for pages 108 top, 108 bottom, 115 left and 115 right; Ministry of Agriculture, Malawi for page 44; G. Nicholson for pages 18 top left, 18 middle top left, 18 middle bottom left, 18 bottom left, 18 top right, 18 bottom right, 20 top right, 21 top left and 21 bottom left; Picturepoint Ltd for page 163; John Wilson for page 53 and 54 left; Zambia Information Services for pages 151, 156 top, 156 bottom, 159, 164, 171, 174, 182, 185 right and 195.

The cover photograph was kindly supplied by Paul Spearman.

Unfortunately we have been unable to trace the copyright holders of the photos on pages 185 left and 190 and apologise for any infringement of copyright caused.

Longman Group Limited
Longman House
Burnt Mill, Harlow
Essex CM20 2JE, England
and Associated Companies
throughout the World.

© Longman Group Ltd. 1973, 1983

First published 1973
New Edition 1981
Completely revised edition 1983

ISBN 0 582 65548 X
Illustrations by Parkway Illustrated Press
Set in 10/12 point Times Roman
Printed in Singapore by
Selector Printing Co (Pte) Ltd

Contents

What this book is all about

This book may be used by students of O level standard with only a little guidance for it aims to teach, not merely state, the geography of Central Africa. Self-testing questions may be found throughout the text and in Things to Do at the end of each chapter, more questions will be found. Maps, photographs, diagrams and the general layout of the book are all designed to encourage thinking and to present the material interestingly.

There are many features common to the geography of Malawi, Zimbabwe and Zambia and this has meant some repetition. Naturally, this has been kept to a minimum and cross-referencing ensures that no important points will be overlooked. We would strongly recommend that before a study of one country is made, the section on Central Africa be read.

1 Location, relief, drainage and climate

In this book Central Africa has been taken to include Malaŵi, Zimbabwe and Zambia. The three countries are located in central southern Africa and were all formerly part of British Central Africa.

Fig. 1 provides the information to describe the position of Central Africa in two further ways which are likely to be familiar, namely:

1 Location relative to the surrounding countries.
2 Location by latitude and longitude.

Draw your own location map and mark on it these two sets of facts.

Fig. 1 also brings out a most important feature of Central Africa's position, which has a strong influence on the transport costs of imports and exports—the inland position of the three countries.

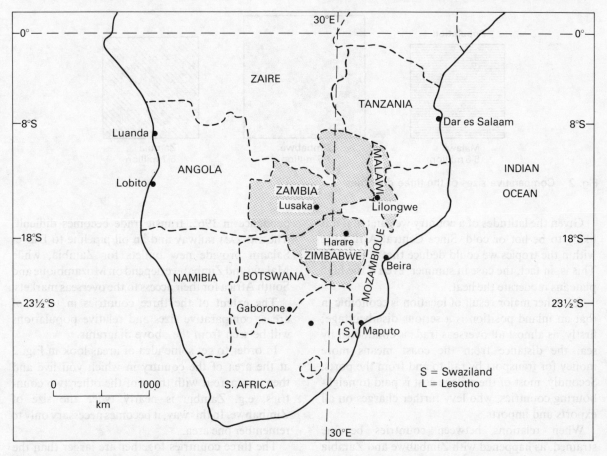

Fig. 1   The location of Central Africa

1

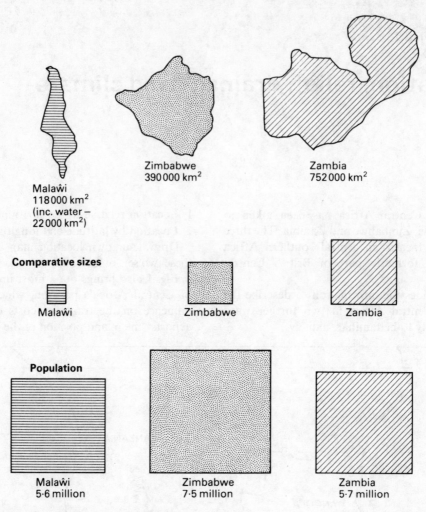

Fig. 2   Comparative sizes of the three countries

Given the latitudes of a country we can tell if it is likely to be hot or cold. Since Central Africa lies within the tropics we could deduce that it was hot. This is, in fact, the case in summer, even if the high plateaus moderate the heat.

A further major result of location is economic in that an inland position is a serious disadvantage; firstly, as almost all overseas trade is conducted by sea, the distance from the coast means more money for transport by rail to and from the ports. Secondly, most of the railage cost is paid to neighbouring countries, who levy further charges on all exports and imports.

When relations between countries become strained, as happened with Zimbabwe and Zambia after the former's unilateral declaration of independence in 1965, transit trade becomes difficult. The TANZAM railway and an oil pipeline to Dar es Salaam provide new outlets for Zambia, while Malaŵi and Zimbabwe depend on Mozambique and South Africa for their access to the overseas markets.

The extent of the three countries in terms of areas, comparative sizes and relative populations will be seen from the above diagrams.

In order to get some idea of areas look in Fig. 2 at the area of the country in which you live and then compare it with those of the other two countries, e.g. Zambia is nearly twice the size of Zimbabwe. In this way, it becomes necessary only to remember one area.

The three countries together are larger than the Republic of South Africa. Compared with the

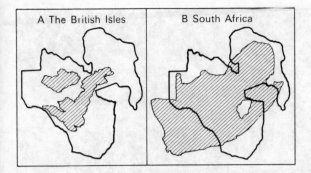

Fig. 3 Central Africa compared to the British Isles and South Africa

British Isles Central Africa is several times larger, as Fig. 3 shows.

If you were to travel from the most northerly point of Zambia to the southernmost point of Zimbabwe, you would cover about 1 600 km; to go from the most westerly point of Zambia to the easternmost point of Malaŵi would be about the same distance. This is roughly equivalent to crossing the Sahara from north to south or to flying from London to Rome.

Distance can probably be more easily understood when thought of in terms of the time which it takes to cover it. Although much would depend on the type of car used and the driver concerned, one could expect to cover roughly 15–30 km more in an hour on the roads of Zimbabwe than on those in England for example where there is much more traffic and more towns.

Many students find it difficult to draw from memory a sketch map which shows the main towns of Central Africa, but the following points will help to locate the main towns in their correct relative positions:

1 Harare and Livingstone are on the same line of latitude.
2 Harare and Masvingo are approximately on the same line of longitude.
3 Lusaka and Zomba are approximately on the same line of latitude.
4 Lusaka and Bulawayo are approximately on the same line of longitude.
5 Chipata is on the same line of longitude as Mutare.

Things to do
1 Using a large scale map measure the distance by rail from Lusaka, Harare and Blantyre to their nearest port.
2 Draw an outline map of Central Africa and insert the capitals and other main towns, using the suggestions made in the previous paragraph.
3 To get an idea of the great distances in Central Africa, measure carefully on a map how far it is in a straight line from Mbala to Beitbridge and from Nkhata Bay to the Zambezi. Then work out how many days it would take you for each of these two journeys, if you travelled 200 km per day.
4 Practise drawing outlines of Central Africa. On the drawings name the surrounding countries.
5 Distance means money to the farmer, to the industrialist and even to the school pupil (well, to his parents). Give examples of the truth of this statement.
6 How far does the shape of the country determine the location of its capital? To help you tackle this question here are a few pointers–the capital of Malaŵi is now Lilongwe: the former capital of Zambia was Livingstone, which is on the border of the country: look at atlas maps to find the positions of the capitals of some other African and some European countries. Shape is clearly not the only influence on the siting of a capital. Can you think of others?

Relief and the Zambezi River

The plateau is the most common landscape in Central Africa. Large parts of the plateau are fairly level, but some areas, such as the Eastern Border Highlands and the Mafingi Mountains, which rise above the plateau, are deeply dissected. Since the relief of each country is described in its relevant section, the causes only are treated here under the headings

1 Jointing of rocks;
2 Faulting;
3 Differential erosion.

1 Jointing of rocks

Jointing is a property of rocks which is responsible for much of our natural scenic splendour. In granite, there are two patterns of jointing; firstly, the rectangular pattern which gives rise to *kopjes*

3

Dwala type of granite formation in the Matopos. Some fine exfoliation is taking place in the foreground. Note the boulders which are the remnants of the old surface.

and the curved pattern which causes *dwalas* or whale-back mounds. It is the dominance of one type of jointing which explains the formation of these very distinctive landforms. Fig. 4.1 should now be examined closely.

In the *kopje* (a pile of rocks) the shape of the boulders is due chiefly to the system of rectangular jointing within the granite. This jointing resulted from the cooling of the original granite-forming magma. Weathering and erosion round off the edges of the blocks and open up any line of weakness, thus creating a variety of shapes.

The *dwala* type of relief shows the dominance of curved joints which are more pronounced than the rectangular set in the granite. These curved joints probably formed when the great thickness of rocks above the granite (remember that the granite magma cooled at great depths) was removed by erosion. Such removal causes the rock below to expand upwards leading to curved joints.

Warping is the cause of many basins occupied by swamps or by *vleis* or *dambos* (marshes). This is simply sagging of the crust downwards, a movement of the earth's crust causing basins.

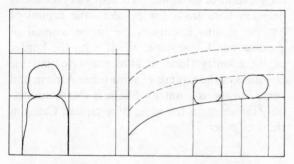

Sketch to show how the rectangular jointing of granite can determine the rough slope of a kopje.

Curved joints as well as rectangular jointing can be seen. This sketch shows how the surface has been eroded, leaving boulders as remnants.

Fig. 4.1   Rectangular and curved jointing

A kopje (Matopos)

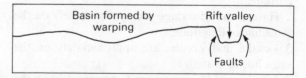

Basin formed by warping   Rift valley

Faults

Fig. 4.2   Warping

Lake Bangweulu and the Lukanga Swamps lie in basins caused by warping.

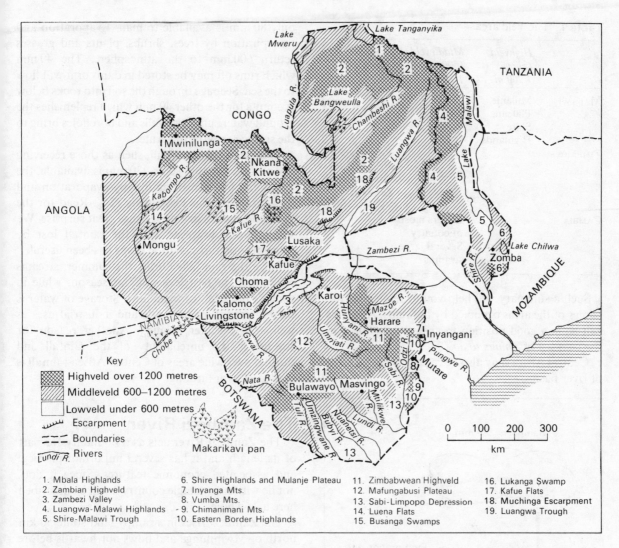

Key

- ▨ Highveld over 1200 metres
- ▨ Middleveld 600–1200 metres
- □ Lowveld under 600 metres
- ⌇ Escarpment
- --- Boundaries
- ⁓ Rivers

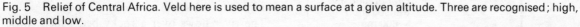

1. Mbala Highlands	6. Shire Highlands and Mulanje Plateau	11. Zimbabwean Highveld	16. Lukanga Swamp
2. Zambian Highveld	7. Inyanga Mts.	12. Mafungabusi Plateau	17. Kafue Flats
3. Zambezi Valley	8. Vumba Mts.	13. Sabi-Limpopo Depression	18. Muchinga Escarpment
4. Luangwa-Malawi Highlands	9. Chimanimani Mts.	14. Luena Flats	19. Luangwa Trough
5. Shire-Malawi Trough	10. Eastern Border Highlands	15. Busanga Swamps	

Fig. 5 Relief of Central Africa. Veld here is used to mean a surface at a given altitude. Three are recognised; high, middle and low.

2 Faulting

Faulting generally causes steep slopes rather than the gentle gradients caused by warping. Contrast the scarps of the middle Zambezi Valley with the slopes around the Bangweulu Swamps. Faulting accounts for the several rift valleys in Central and East Africa with consequent profound influence on climate, development, communications and migrations of people.

3 Differential erosion

The resistance of rocks to weathering and erosion varies greatly. The *syenite* (a rock like granite but

without quartz) of Mount Mulanje and the *quartzites* (rock made of quartz, the mineral in the sand) of the Chimanimani are clearly very resistant. *Schists* (rocks which readily split along cracks) and clays usually form the lower ground as on the gold belts of Zimbabwe where there are rocks of varying resistances adjacent to one another.

Relief divisions

These relief divisions are shown in Fig. 5. Make a copy of this map in your notebook.

Below the map you could describe very shortly the relief of each country in tabular form.

Table 1 The Veld areas

	Highveld (above 1 200 m)	Middleveld (600– 1 200 m)	Lowveld (below 600 m)
MALAWI	Mulanje Plateau, Shire Highlands		
ZIMBABWE			Two large areas in Sabi– Limpopo and Zambezi Valley
ZAMBIA		Covers most of country. Several large swamps	

Such a summary will help you to remember the names of the areas occupied by the velds. Also you will be in a good position to answer question 4 in the next list of *Things to do*.

Central Africa may also be regarded as a number of river basins.

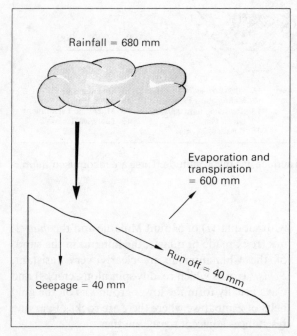

Fig. 6 What happens to an annual rainfall of 680 mm in Central Africa.

Water resources

From Fig. 6 you can see that from a rainfall of some 680 mm, the average annual rainfall of Zimbabwe, only 80 mm is available to man. Evaporation and transpiration by trees, shrubs, plants and grasses return 600 mm to the atmosphere. The 40 mm which runs off may be stored in dams or it will flow to the sea. Seepage through the soil into rocks below accounts for the other 40 mm which replenishes the ground water supplies. Wells and boreholes bring to the surface some of this water.

In areas of high rainfall, such as those receiving 900 mm per annum, some 230 mm is available, the remaining 670 mm being lost by evaporation and transpiration. This loss equals 75%. Read for the first time, figures like these cause great surprise. We should note, however, that the rainfall lost by transpiration through food crops has been useful.

Since the rain falls during the summer, streams reach their highest levels at this season, while in winter only a few of them flow. Storage of water is therefore vital for domestic and industrial uses as well as for winter farming. Another reason for storage is the unreliability of the rainfall and thirdly, over wide areas of Central Africa rainfall is inadequate for farming.

The Zambezi River

The Zambezi River acts as a boundary for part of its length and it has several important physical and associated economic features. Since it does not lie within any single country it will be described here as a whole.

The Zambezi rises in swampy land some 50 km north of Mwinilunga and flows northwards before swinging to the south.

The river flows over a rocky bed which causes frequent rapids until, to the north of Zambezi, it passes from granite to sandy country and begins to show features of a mature stream. The reason for the maturity is that the sand (Kalahari in origin) is much more easily eroded than is the granite and in this sandy area are found meanders, ox-bow lakes and flood-plains. The greatest of these flood-plains is the Upper Zambezi, a large depression which has been carved out of the confluence of several tributaries with the main river. Very likely the area sank along a line of weakness thus initiating the depression. The Upper Zambezi Plain extends for about 175 km and varies in width from 15 to 50 km. It is a fertile alluvial plain which floods annually between February and June. The people living there

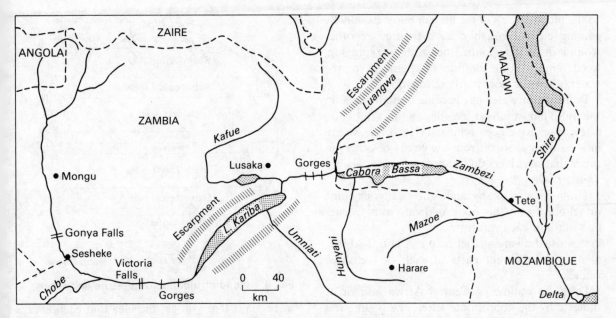

Fig. 7   Sketch map showing some physical features of the Zambezi River.

move from the plain in the summer to their winter farming area around Mongu. Limulunga, near Mongu is the summer capital, and a village called Lealui on the plain is used as the winter capital.

Favourite sites for cultivation on the Plain are the remarkable circular depressions from two or three km in diameter.

The Gonya Falls are the first of a series of waterfalls and rapids caused by hard layers of rock on the river bed. After leaving this rocky stretch the Zambezi enters the Sesheke Plain which is again made up of Kalahari sand. During the flood season the river overflows southwards to the Okavango Swamps, a huge basin of inland drainage.

Between the Sesheke Plain and the Victoria Falls the Zambezi flows over the resistant basalt which forms islands. The Victoria Falls, with its five gorges, which are world-famous, have been carved out of this basalt. Basalt, which is a volcanic rock poured out of fissures, forms six layers, and, although resistant, there are well developed joints in the rock and it is these that the gorges follow in their characteristic zig-zag pattern. The falls themselves have a maximum height of 103 m and a width of 1 708 m. Below the Victoria Falls and their gorges, the Zambezi flows through the long Batoka Gorge and the Devil's Gorge before entering the Gwembe Trough which trends in a north-easterly direction. This trough, now partly filled by Lake Kariba, is a

rift valley which is continued along the Luangwa valley as shown in Fig. 7. The Gwembe Trough is bordered by a zone of escarpments rather than a single steep slope. The dam wall of Kariba blocks a wide gorge below which the river flows generally in a narrow valley to the Mozambique border. East of the border Lake Cabora Bassa stretches some 250 km to Chicoa to another dam wall. The Zambezi widens below Tete as it flows across a broad, fertile floodplain with swamps, to reach its delta.

Conservation of water is one of the themes of this book because in Central Africa it is generally scarce in the winter and sometimes the scarcity occurs also in the summer. The Zambezi River provides many examples of how a river can be used by man and some of these uses are noted later in the book in detail. From what has been written already you should be able to jot down a few uses.

Not all rivers flow during the winter months and this, together with unreliable summer rains, accounts for the many dams on tributaries of the Zambezi.

In Central Africa there is not only the problem of the conservation of water but also that of *bilharzia*. The cause of this disease is a parasite worm which lives in the livers of the snails found in rivers and water storage dams. It transfers itself

7

to the blood-vessels of the human body, usually by gaining entry through cracks, fissures or other wounds in the feet. Control measures, like spraying, weed removal and addition of chemicals to the water, are so far only partly effective.

Pollution of water has become a major issue in the more industrialised societies and in Zimbabwe a few cases have been reported. However, we are in a position to learn from the errors of others in order that our rivers do not become cesspools.

Things to do

1 Draw sketches of any landforms near your home or school. From this book or from your teacher find out how each was formed.

2 Practise drawing a relief map of Central Africa, naming the different parts of each of the three velds.

3 Draw an outline of Central Africa and on it indicate by the appropriate letters the boundaries which follow mountains (M), rivers (R), lakes (L) or lines of latitude or longitude (A).

4 One danger of the method used to show relief

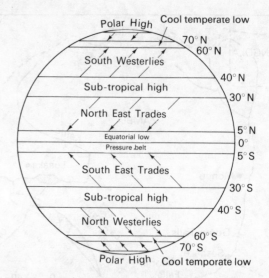

Fig. 8   World distribution of pressure and winds

in Fig. 5 is that you get the idea that each area is uniform throughout. Of course, this is not true, but to prove it to yourself you should examine some 1:50 000 maps of different areas in your country.

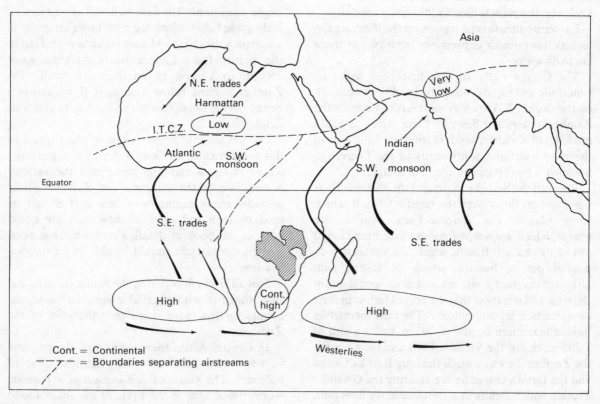

Fig. 9   Conditions over Africa in July

Climate and its causes

The globe in Fig. 8 is made up of water only so that there are no marked temperature differences. Imagine a map of Africa drawn on this globe, roughly between latitudes 35°N and 35°S. The two sets of trade winds blow over the continent from sub-tropical highs towards the Equatorial low pressure belt.

Because there is land and sea on our planet earth temperature differences occur. These result in the formation of (a) low pressure cells over hot areas and (b) high pressure cells over cool areas.

Conditions over Africa in July

It is winter in the southern hemisphere which means that there is a high pressure cell over South Africa. This cell is part of the sub-tropical high pressure belt.

Over north Africa pressure is low and it becomes very low over Pakistan where temperatures are high in summer.

The dashed line in Fig. 9 is marked ITCZ which means Inter-tropical convergence zone. This is a zone where air-streams approach one another, the warmer rising above the cooler and causing rain to fall if the air is moist enough. The ITCZ merges, breaks down and reforms.

Air-streams or winds which converge on the ITCZ in the southern hemisphere in winter are as follows.
1 South-east trades from the sub-tropical high pressure belt which become the south-west monsoon on crossing the equator. *Monsoon* means season and a monsoon is a seasonal wind which blows for some months over a large area.
2 North-east trades including the *Harmattan*. This wind blows from the Sahara over West Africa. It is a very dry wind which brings relief to the people of the humid parts of West Africa.

Of these air-streams only the south-east trades blow over Central Africa. These winds are dry except for a moderately moist lower layer. They bring light rain to the mountains in the east.

Conditions over Africa in January

Since it is summer in the southern hemisphere, a low pressure cell develops over southern Africa. The

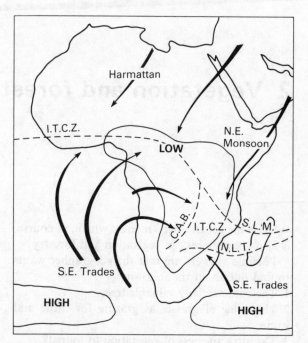

C.A.B. = Congo Air Boundary
N.L.T. = Northern limit of trade winds
S.L.M. = Southern limit of monsoon

Fig. 10   Conditions over Africa in January

sub-tropical high pressure belt is therefore interrupted and moreover, it has moved southwards. Over North Africa pressure is high and over Asia it is very high.

The winds blowing towards the ITCZ over southern Africa are as follows.
1 South-east trades of the Indian Ocean.
2 North-east monsoon which, you may remember, is a seasonal wind.
3 Recurved south-east trades of the Atlantic Ocean. These winds are known as the Congo Airstream, the source of most rainfall of Central Africa.

Within the ITCZ, convergence rainfall occurs when two air-streams meet. More air will be entering the zone than it can hold. The extra air escapes by rising. As the air rises, it cools, and, if it is moist it will become saturated. Clouds will form and eventually the tiny cloud droplets grow into raindrops. When the raindrops are so big and heavy that the upcurrents caused by the convergence can no longer support them in the air, they fall as rain. Convergence rainfall is more widespread over Central Africa than convectional rainfall but less intense.

9

2 Vegetation and forestry

What is the geographer's interest which, of course, is also your interest, in vegetation and forestry?

Possible answers are that the geographer wants to find out about the following.

1 The commercially valuable trees.

2 The value of grasses as grazing for cattle and game.

3 The attractiveness of vegetation to tourists.

4 The influence of climate, aspect, soils and relief on vegetation.

5 The facts about man's interference with vegetation.

6 Distribution of vegetation. This is a long and varied answer and it will help you as you go through this chapter to note examples of any of these aims of a geographer.

Look at your school atlas and you will see on the vegetation map that Central Africa is shown as *savanna*. A rail journey from Lusaka to Plumtree would reveal just what a tremendous variation there is within this one vegetational zone. Indeed, we can recognise six types of vegetation whose distribution is shown in Fig. 11. This map looks complicated at first sight, but it is easy to remember if you know a few relationships. Some of these are illustrated below.

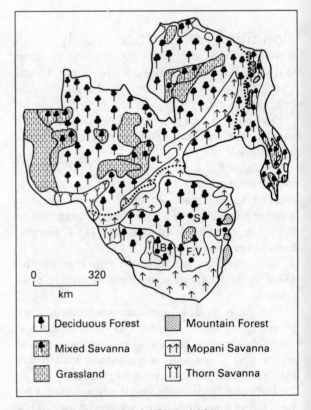

Fig. 11 The vegetation of Central Africa

Deciduous Forest **Mountain Forest**
Mixed Savanna **Mopani Savanna**
Grassland **Thorn Savanna**

The climate of Central Africa favours forest, woodland or bush, but not grass. Yet there is much grass. This is a result of three other major factors which influence vegetation. They are soil drainage, fire and man.

In *dambos*, or depressions that are waterlogged for part of the year, the water table is too close to the surface to permit trees to grow. For this reason we frequently find grass along river courses.

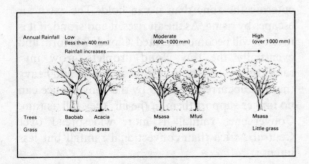

Riverine forests grow where the drainage is good. Fires caused by lightning are not uncommon in Central Africa, even during the rainy season. It was reported, for instance, that on 19 January 1969 in a good rainy season, two fires broke out at Inyanga within five minutes of one another, burning out some 20 ha each before they were extinguished.

However, fire used by man is much more effective in changing the vegetation. From Stone Age times to the present, man has used fire as an aid to hunting and to clearing the land for cultivation and grazing. This has led to big changes in vegetation. Msasa woodlands, which cover so much of Central Africa, seem to be the result of fire, cultivation and grazing combined.

We tend to assume that the vegetation of the veld has remained the same for generations. Evidence like the above disturbs our beliefs especially when we see it with our own eyes. Bush encroachment is one sight we will probably see. It is caused mainly by the increasing number of animals eating the grass. Too many animals mean less and less grass. In turn, this means that burning of the grass before the rains is less effective in producing rich young shoots. Bushes invade the poor grass areas and the pattern of vegetation is changed; in consequence the pattern of man's activities is also changed.

Types of vegetation
Deciduous woodland
Deciduous trees are those which shed their leaves once each year in order to withstand the drought of the winter. They include the *msasa*, the *mukuti* of Zambia and the *mchenga* of Malaŵi.

These woodlands cover more than half of Central Africa and give the very beautiful spring colours of red and russet, so characteristic of our landscape. Perennial herbs add their colour just prior to the rains and the perennial grasses reach their full green during the summer rains.

The *msasa*, dominant in Zimbabwe and common in Malaŵi and Zambia, needs a well-drained soil. It has a very long tap root and it can grow to over 18 m in height in deep soil where rainfall is high. It is fire-resistant and propagates itself by seeds and root-suckers. Commercially, the wood is of limited value. The grasses associated with the msasa woodlands make good grazing.

Deciduous woodlands occupy the thin, poor soils of the plateaus and escarpments of Malaŵi up to an altitude of about 1 900 m. The trees are small on such soils and the woodland is open. In the southern and central regions these woodlands occur above 600 m, but north of Nkhota Kota where annual rainfall is higher (above 2 000 mm) they are to be found on the lake shore.

Msasa are seldom found in Zimbabwe below an altitude of 750 m, a height which seems to be a climatic minimum. They grow on the slopes of the Chimanimani and are now returning to the plateau grasslands.

In Zambia, deciduous woodlands occupy the plateaus and escarpments. The woodland of the escarpments is not easily accessible and has probably not been changed by man.

The *msasa* is a common tree which reaches its greatest height in the wetter north.

Mopani savanna
Mopani is a Bantu word for butterfly, which describes the shape of the leaves, which turn their edges to the sun, thus giving little shade at the hottest time of the day. The *mopani* is deciduous and fire-resistant, and cannot tolerate frost. It is characteristic of areas of high temperature and low rainfall, and is associated with the baobab.

Although *mopani* grows in soils that are waterlogged for part of the year, it does best in well-drained soils and may reach a height of 18 m. Although the *mopani* is associated with hot, dry areas, it will grow where the annual rainfall is

Mopani bush

between 500 and 650 mm, but under these conditions it occurs only in sodium rich soils. On such soils, which may be derived from minerals in some granites, the *mopani* is a short tree.

The value of the *mopani* tree lies in its protein-rich leaves, which are eaten by cattle, goats and game when grass is scarce.

Using Fig. 11, describe the distribution of the *mopani* in Central Africa.

Mixed savanna

As the name suggests, no one type of tree is dominant, except over small areas. Grass may be the main type of vegetation in one area; in another, deciduous trees, while in a third, evergreens may flourish.

In Malaŵi on the plateaus where there are fertile soils unused by farmers, a variety of trees grow. The largest such area forms a crescent to the north of Lilongwe. Another consists of patches to the north of Blantyre. One tree that is notable for furniture-making is the *Mukwa* (*Kiaat* of South Africa).

Chipya is the name given to mixed savanna in Zambia. Teak, one of the few commercially important trees, occurs in the Western Province. Of lesser significance are the stands of *Mukwa* on the borders of Lake Bangweulu and in the lower Luapula vally.

The mixed savanna of Zimbabwe consists of teak (umgusi) forests in Matabeleland, which provides material for railway sleepers and floor blocks.

Thorn savanna

Trees in this landscape are umbrella-shaped or flat-topped to reduce the amount of evaporation from the ground beneath them. They are thorny and often very gnarled. Large areas of grass make this country suitable for extensive ranching, although the low, unreliable rainfall demands that the rancher makes provision for watering points.

Mountain forests

These are of very limited extent.

In Malaŵi they grow at altitudes of between 1 500 and 2 100 m on the higher slopes of Mulanje, Thyolo, Zomba, Viphya and Nyika plateaus. The stands consist of several species; the *Mulanje* cedar is one of these and has given rise to a forestry industry on the lower slopes of Mount Mulanje.

In Zimbabwe the only forest of this kind is the Chirinda Forest at Mount Selinda.

Grasslands

These are the result of either poorly-drained soils or burning of the earlier tree cover. They are not a response to seasonal rainfall.

Large areas of Zambia are under grass. They include the many *dambos* of the Zaire-Zambezi watershed, the Lake Bangweulu area and the floodplains of the Zambezi in the Western Province.

The grasslands of the Nyika Plateau are the most extensive of Malaŵi, although the Viphya and other plateaus have large areas under grass. At much lower levels, as along the lower Shire River and on the borders of Lake Chilwa, swamp vegetation occurs. This includes reeds and a variety of water-loving plants and grass.

Zimbabwe too has both plateau grasslands on the Eastern Border Highlands and the grasslands of the *vlei* or *dambo* and the river floodplains.

Natural vegetation and us

Up to now in this chapter we have dealt with vegetation not planted by man. This kind of vegetation is just as important to our survival as that which is planted by man such as crops and grasses. The table sets out some of the ways in which natural vegetation helps us:—

Natural vegetation

protects our **soil** (see page 154).
protects our **water resources**
provides grazing for our **livestock** and **game**
provides wood for **fuel**
provides grass for **thatching**
provides timber for **industry.**

Things to do
1 Find out the names of the trees that grow near your home or school. List the indigenous and exotic trees.
2 Examine some trees in an area which is regularly burned and compare them with trees in an unburnt area.
3 Describe some of the factors that influence the distribution of vegetation in your country.
4 Sketch some of the trees which grow near your school.

3 Agriculture

Factors which influence farming

Imagine you are a farmer and you are interested in growing cotton. What facts would you want to find out about the crop? Jot them down on a piece of paper as they occur to you.

As a potential grower you would be classed as a commercial farmer. Your choice of cotton or any other crop you might choose would be strongly influenced by economic trends and factors, e.g. size of market, present price, costs of fertilisers and pesticides, labour costs etc. The physical obstacles can usually be overcome by artificial means as in the cases of drought by irrigation; soil deficiencies by fertilisation and crop pests by spraying with the appropriate pesticide. Naturally, these remedies are expensive and a commercial farmer must keep a constant check on his profit and loss account.

Now let us look at some of the points which you may have jotted down about cotton.

Rainfall and cents

The crucial factor in determining crop yields in any season is rainfall. Poor seasons are so frequently the result of drought. Unreliability of rainfall, together with high rates of evaporation have been dealt with elsewhere and, indeed, form one of the themes of this book. Farmers' incomes and, in turn, incomes of those who deal with farmers are affected by seasonal crop production and we may say that *'rainfall and cents'* are related.

While droughts cause crop failure, too much rain is also a menace, encouraging weed growth and preventing crop lands from being cleaned and cultivated. Rain at harvest time will damage cotton, for instance.

Heavy rains in the tropics are linked with high intensity and it is just this which sets off the cycle of erosion where the land is not covered with vegetation.

Rain drops falling on bare soil. Each drop moves particles of the soil.

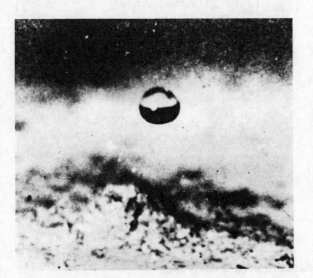

Temperature

Temperatures during the rainy season are high enough to permit the growth of most crops. Winter frosts, on the other hand, can cause serious crop damage as on tea estates and in market gardens.

Relief

It is through drainage, waterlogging and erosion that relief influences farming in Central Africa.

Read the preceding sentence again and think of examples or instances which illustrate the three relationships. Some answers are given in the next paragraph.

Irrigation clearly needs flat or gently sloping land if costs of pumping the water from one level to the next are to be avoided. The slope of the land is also important for non-irrigated crops too. Tea and coffee, for instance, need a heavy rainfall, but cannot stand waterlogging of their roots. Thus, in Malaŵi, tea grows on the southern slopes of Mulanje Plateau and in Zambia coffee also grows on hill slopes.

Depressions are usually waterlogged and are frequently used as winter grazing grounds in all three countries. Escarpments and steep hill slopes are closely associated with soil erosion, except where they are covered by vegetation as are the Zambezi escarpments.

Soils

The soils of Central Africa have weathered from many different kinds of rock. In any one district it may be possible to observe colours of soil, ranging from black through various shades of brown, orange and red, to grey and almost white. The consistency varies from very heavy clays to wind-blown sand.

Different soil types have a definite effect upon the pattern of farming. Maize and cotton, for example, prefer clays since these have a high inherent fertility and can hold moisture for longer periods than can sand. Nevertheless, sandy soils are well suited to Virginia tobacco, which would develop thick, dark, juicy leaves, if planted in clay. Furthermore, sandy soils are well drained and well aerated. Heavy fertilisation and perhaps irrigation explain why high yields of maize and cotton are obtained from sands.

The acidity/alkalinity of the soil is also important,

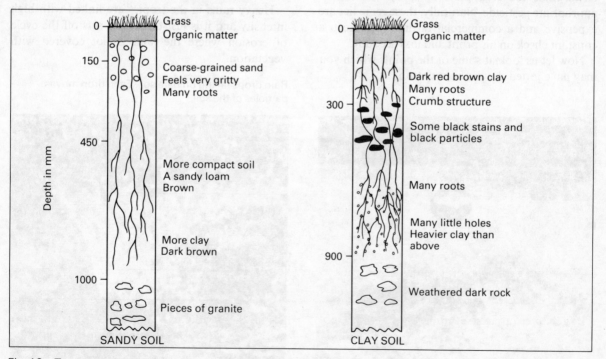

Fig. 12   Two examples of information that can be gathered from a study of soil profiles.

14

Soil erosion in the Ngezi area

since some crops prefer a more acid soil than others. Generally, tropical soils tend to be slightly acid, highly oxidised (due to high temperatures and much moisture), and fairly badly leached. Hence the farmer must frequently face a large bill for artificial fertilisers and manures in order to maintain good yields.

Cotton, incidentally, does not give a good soil cover and the soil is therefore more likely to erode.

Irrigation

Details of schemes like the Sabi-Lundi, Kafue Flats and the Nchalo Sugar Estate will be found in later sections of this book, but much remains to be done to utilise to the full the water resources of Central Africa. Irrigation can permit the use of land for cropping or stocking the whole year. However, high evaporation rates make small dams on individual farms wasteful. A few large dams permit best use of the water.

Knowledge and capital

In Central Africa most farmers are subsistence cultivators. They are content to produce enough food for their own needs and they are ignorant of commercial crops and livestock production, as well as being poverty-stricken. The subsistence cultivator is hidebound by tribal custom which conflicts sharply with farming for profit; he lives almost entirely in another world—the world of the 'have-nots'—the world which is as yet undeveloped. To alter this world for the mutual benefit of the cultivator and the state is the greatest economic challenge in Central Africa today.

The chapter on agriculture in the Zambian section gives some detail of the shifting cultivator and the Malaŵi section indicates how some of the problems of subsistence farming are being solved.

Transport to markets

Try to answer the following questions:
1 Why are market gardening and dairying carried on near to urban centres?
2 Why is it expensive to export goods to overseas markets?
3 State one reason for the concentration of commercial farming along the railway belt of Zambia.

It is obvious that communications will have to be improved in all three countries if subsistence farming is to be eliminated and the farmer persuaded that he must produce for the market.

Things to do
1 List the problems facing the subsistence cultivator under the headings methods of cultivation and attitudes.
2 Having considered the problems in question 1, can you suggest any solutions?
3 Soil conservation is vital to our survival. Discuss in class ways of conserving the soil.

Stock raising
Beef cattle

The breeds are reared in different parts of Central Africa depending mainly on the temperature. The following table provides a general guide:

Table 2 Breeds of cattle related to altitude and temperature

Altitude	Temperatures	Breeds of cattle
Above 1200 m	Less than 19°C	Pedigree Afrikander, Sussex, Aberdeen-Angus
1100–600 m	19°C–21°C	Afrikander-Hereford cross-breed
Below 600 m	Above 21°C	Indigenous breeds like Tuli, Mashona, Ngoni

Factors governing intensity of cattle rearing
1 Rainfall

This is adequate over most of Zambia and Malaŵi, but in the south and south-east of Zimbabwe rainfall is low and unreliable, permitting only the most extensive type of ranching. Large areas may be badly drought-stricken in some years, resulting in

15

Cattle suffering as the result of drought in Matabeleland. These animals should be transported to better watered areas but what are the long term solutions to cattle rearing in areas subject to droughts?

heavy losses of stock and necessitating drastic reduction of herds. Can you suggest another way of overcoming drought?

2 Temperature

Can you name the hottest parts of Central Africa? The table on p. 15 showing altitudes and temperatures should help you to name the areas of the lowveld, namely the valleys of the Shire, Luangwa, Zambezi and Sabi-Limpopo rivers. Here temperatures are too high for the successful rearing of exotic breeds, while native breeds are grazed.

3 Vegetation

Since much of the vegetation of Central Africa is grassland or open woodland, cattle rearing is favoured. But, as you will probably know, man has destroyed some of the natural vegetation by burning, over-grazing, or by the indiscriminate felling of trees for fuel and the vegetation which appears subsequently is bush.

Thinned out bush at Chegutu. Shade is provided for cattle

How can the farmer control the bush?

He can use one or more of the following measures:

1 Maintain the grass in good condition.
2 Burn existing bush, stumping or felling trees.
3 Use arboricides (poisonous sprays), which are expensive.
4 Use mechanical methods of clearing which at present are uneconomic.

Methods

Mechanized equipment
(Bulldozing-chaining-
root ploughing-weedbreaking)

Poisoning
(Not effective on some species)

Felling   Stumping   Ring-barking

Methods of dealing with bush encroachment

Burning is widespread and research workers recommend that it be done at long intervals, that is, every five years. While this figure is likely to vary from one area to another within Central Africa there is no doubt that except where the grass gives a thick cover for fierce burning, annual firing is a bad practice.

At this point it would be best to clear up what some of you believe to be correct in grass management. There is the idea that annual burning in the winter promotes the growth of fresh new grass about September, thus providing feed for when there is a shortage. Officials and farmers alike agree that this practice often does more harm than good. In many instances the delicate natural structure of the top layers of soil is destroyed. Burning can also promote soil erosion.

Disease

Of the many diseases which affect cattle, the most serious is trypanosomiasis or nagana. It is usually fatal and is transmitted by the tsetse fly.

The areas infested by the tsetse fly are indicated in Fig. 13, and you should try to estimate what percentage of the land of Zambia and Malaŵi is affected. In Zimbabwe the figure is approximately 14%. These figures have a double significance: in the first place the tsetse belts generally mean that grazing is lost to the nation and secondly, that to clear these belts is costly. In Zimbabwe in 1969 the cost of clearing part of the Gokwe, Gatooma and Lomagundi districts was of the order of $19 per 100 ha.

Cattle are prone to many other diseases such as East Coast fever and liver-fluke. Tick-borne diseases are prevalent all through the year and it is for this reason that cattle are dipped.

An engorged Tsetse fly

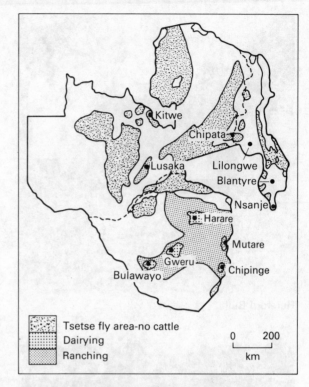

Fig. 13   Areas infected by tsetse flies

Nearness to markets

If you think of cattle travelling for long distances you will probably conclude that the beasts are likely to lose mass, which means less money for the farmer. Few farmers today either lack their own transport or are far from a public transport system. However, in the case study of Chisamba Ranch you can read about the trekking of cattle for a distance of 60 km to a rail siding.

Beef production

Sizes of national herds:

Malaŵi	820 000	(other figures not available)
Zimbabwe	2 400 000	(plus over 2 800 000 in communal lands)
Zambia	300 000	(plus over 2 000 000 in communal lands)

Can you suggest why Malaŵi and Zambia have such small herds compared with Zimbabwe?

Using Fig. 13, try to describe the distribution of beef cattle in the three countries. This map gives no idea of the numbers of cattle in any area and

17

Hereford Bull

Afrikander Bull

Zebu Bull

Aberdeen-Angus

Tuli Cow

Brahman Bull

you may be surprised to learn that in the wetter areas of Zimbabwe the density of cattle is about one animal to 1·6 ha, while in the drier areas the figure varies from one animal to 4 ha to one animal to 10 ha.

Beef exports have increased steadily over the past decade and rapidly during the last two or three years. Local demand frequently exceeds the available supply and Zambia and Malawi sometimes import meat. Zimbabwe is noted for producing high-quality beef and prior to 1965, exported quantities to Europe.

The potential and the problem

Vast areas of Central Africa have potential as ranching regions, but first three major steps must be taken. They concern disease, distance to markets and attitudes. Can you think of them?

The Western Province, for instance, is isolated and disease is an even greater limiting factor in Zambia.

In Zimbabwe droughts are a problem, particularly in Matabeleland, but the government has given, and is continuing to render, assistance in dam construction.

To understand the depth of the problem of the attitude of the 'traditional' African to his cattle, read about this and the associated problem of over-grazing on page 165 in the Zambian section of the book.

Dairying

An interesting pattern is revealed in Fig. 14. Clearly, there is a decrease in the number of dairy farms as we move beyond 48 km from Bulawayo. The number of dairy units between 16 and 32 km exceeds the number inside the 16 km ring where land costs more and tends to be used for market gardening or for large residential plots.

Distance is the main factor influencing the distribution and this is closely associated with transport, for a poor road system will limit the

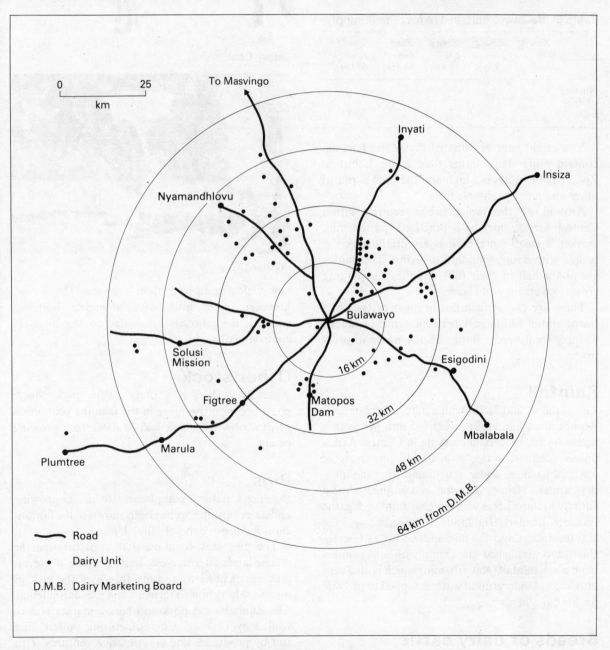

Fig. 14   Distribution of dairy farms in relation to Bulawayo

distance of dairy farms from a town. Where there is a good road, milk is carried considerable distances, as, for instance, from Harare to Kadoma. Such a journey – over 143 km – is necessary since there is no bottling plant in Kadoma.

You should copy into your notebook and then complete the table outlined below. It emphasises the influence of this factor of distance from markets.

Table 3 Bulawayo milkshed (Area of milk supply)

	Zone 1 (0–16 km)	Zone 2 (16–32 km)	Zone 3 (32–48 km)	Zone 4 (48–64 km)	Zone 5 (over 64 km)
Number of dairy units					

You might have anticipated that Zone 1 would contain more dairy farms than Zone 2, but in Zone 1 land values are high and the land is put to other and more profitable uses.

Around all the larger urban centres within Central Africa, dairying is practised but the milk market is small since milk is essentially used by people with a high standard of living. The dairies use about half of their milk supplies for making cream, ice-cream and cheese.

There are cheese factories in most of the chief towns and in Chipinge, where enough is produced to meet local needs. Butter also is made in most towns.

Rainfall

This is the second factor which influences dairying. An optimum figure of at least 635 mm per year is necessary for successful dairying in Central Africa unless adequate water is available for crops of artificial pastures under irrigation during the long, dry winter. Hence, dairying is confined almost entirely to those areas with a higher rainfall, e.g. the Eastern Border Highlands of Zimbabwe, the Harare district and the midlands as far as Gweru. Bulawayo's milkshed (area supplying milk) suffers from a low rainfall (460–610 mm) which is also very unreliable. Underground water is tapped to provide for the dairy herds.

Breeds of dairy cattle

The Friesland is the most popular breed since the

Jersey Cow

Friesland Cow

cow yields more milk than a Jersey. The Jersey, however, gives milk with a higher butterfat content. Both breeds are suited to the highveld environment.

Other stock

Apart from beef and dairy cattle, pigs, sheep, goats and poultry figure in the farming economies of Zimbabwe, Zambia and Malawi, to a growing extent.

Pigs

Pigs are a natural complement to maize growing and dairy farming, as has been shown in the famous *corn-and-hogs* belt of the United States.

The pigs may be allowed to root through the mealie-lands after harvest. In Zimbabwe, however, pigs are penned as rooting increases the risk of disease. Many 'mixed farmers' run pigs as a sideline. The Zimbabwean pork and bacon market is controlled by *Colcom*, a manufacturing undertaking run by producers and co-operative ventures. This organisation generally guarantees to buy all pigs offered, exporting any surplus which remains after the home market is satisfied. The Pig Industry Board was established in 1937 to assist this branch of agriculture, but as profit margins are not high and as there is a limited internal market, the pig-rearing industry is unlikely to expand greatly in the near future. The total pig population for the whole of the country numbered 132000 in 1980, a big drop in numbers from 1977 (226000).

Sheep

Sheep-rearing is less important in Malaŵi and Zambia. In Zimbabwe, it was until recently limited to the short-grassed Eastern Border Highlands, but with emphasis on diversification, an increase has occurred reaching a total of about 750 000 head in 1976. Over much of the country the following factors hinder the rearing of sheep:

1 High summer rainfall, which, combined with poor management, encourage foot-rot, internal parasites and other diseases.

2 Tall grass which is unsuitable for grazing. Some grasses have sharp seeds which penetrate and cause abscesses on the sheep's skin.

3 Limited market for mutton since few Africans eat it. Moreover the quality is so poor that European demand is often met by imports.

Goats in a dry bush area

Goats

Goats are browsers, that is, they can live by eating branches and leaves. They are, therefore, of some value in bush control. Also they are a source of meat in communal areas where, however, they have denuded large areas of all vegetation. Their numbers have doubled over the past ten years.

Things to do

1 Try to arrange a visit to a farm which carries some beef or dairy cattle. Find out all you can about the rearing of cattle from the farmer.

2 Look up the word *silage* in your dictionary. What is used to make silage for winter feeding of the cattle in your home area?

3 If you live in a small town, try to collect the facts for a diagram like Fig. 14.

4 Discuss in class why the farmer in Africa places so much importance on his cattle.

5 List all the products that we get from cattle. A visit to an abattoir will help.

6 Examine this picture of erosion. Use it as a basis for an essay on soil erosion and soil conservation.

Dorper rams used for cross-breeding with indigenous ewes

A flock of Corriedales in Zimbabwe

Erosion, Ntabazinduna

21

4 Industry

Factors influencing the location of manufacturing industry

In this heading, the word 'location' is used to indicate the area and not the actual site of an industry, as for example, Harare will be referred to rather than to that city's industrial sites. The words 'manufacturing industry' also require some explanation. How would you define this kind of industry? If you are uncertain after thinking about the question look at this example of division of industry.

Table 4 Types of industry

Name of type of industry	Examples	Other name of type of industry
Primary	Farming, mining, fishing, forestry	Extractive industries
Secondary	Processing of grain crops, minerals, timber and fish	Manufacturing industries
Tertiary	Teaching, practising medicine or law, banking, housekeeping	Service industries

This table clarifies the position of manufacturing industry in relation to other kinds of industry. Such industry, in fact, changes raw materials, thereby adding to their value. Sometimes, you will come across the terms *heavy* and *light industries* which are branches of manufacturing. *Heavy* refers to the large quantity of raw materials used, or to the size of the machinery, or to the amount of pollution caused. The best examples, perhaps, are copper smelting, iron and steel manufacture and the chemical industry. *Light* industries use less bulky raw materials, smaller machinery and are not associated with dirt or smoke.

A number of important factors must be considered by the industrialist before he decides upon the location of his new factory. They are:

Government policies
Raw materials
Labour availability
Power resources
Transport
Markets
Water supply

It will be a good thing to look at each of these factors in turn, but you will appreciate that they all operate at the same time and that the location of an industry is the result of the *interaction* of the factors rather than the result of only one of them. This does not mean, however, that one factor need not be dominant.

Government policies

So far as location is affected, governments are naturally keen to allow the operation of the laws of supply and demand with the minimum of interference. The Zimbabwean Government is encouraging the development of labour-intensive industries near the communal lands in order to raise the standard of living of those practising subsistence cultivation. The Malaŵi Government has moved the capital to Lilongwe and is encouraging the development of industries in that town.

Raw materials

Raw materials that are perishable or which lose much mass in processing attract manufacturing industry. Some instances of these are shown below:

100 t of logs gives
93 t of pulp
3 t of seed cotton gives
1 t of lint
7 t of cane gives
1 t of white sugar

It can be understood from this table why cotton ginneries are situated in the cotton growing areas and sawmills are located near the forests. Try to write down actual examples of sawmills, ginneries and sugar mills.

Perishable raw materials like milk and vegetables are used near the point of production, although transport plays an important part. Harare, for example, obtains milk from a wide area because of good roads. Bulawayo obtains milk from farms within 50 km of the Dairy Marketing Board dairy (see Fig. 14).

In Zambia most fish is smoked or dried since in the rainy season most roads are flooded or dangerous.

Tea must be processed very soon after it is plucked. This, together with a weight loss which occurs, accounts for the location of factories on the tea estates of Malaŵi and Zimbabwe.

Labour availability

There is a large force of semi-skilled and unskilled workers in Central Africa. Such labour is still a small part of production costs compared with labour costs in developed countries such as the United Kingdom. Earnings of workers in Zimbabwe and Zambia are roughly the same, but in Malaŵi they are only half of this sum.

Labour from overseas is imported in all three countries, but as local training facilities expand, technologists and technicians will become available.

Malaŵi still exports labour and some 14% of her young men seek work mainly in South Africa and partly in Zimbabwe. Money remitted by these workers to their relatives in Malaŵi earns foreign currency for the country.

Power resources

In the eighteenth and nineteenth centuries, industries in England and the continent of Europe were concentrated in the coalfields. This seems extraordinary to us in Central Africa where most industries are many kilometres from coal. It is indeed fortunate that the spread of the thermal power stations and the development of Kariba have led to great dispersion of industries in Zimbabwe and Zambia. In Malaŵi to a much smaller extent the thermal station at Blantyre and the Nkula Falls and Tedzani Falls hydro-electric stations have also ensured that industries are adequately served. However, the industrialist in Malaŵi is more limited in his choice of location than is his fellow industrialist in the other two countries.

In summary while electricity production and supply have contributed to the growth of industry in Central Africa they have in general had little influence on the location of industry.

Transport

The collection of raw materials at a factory, the distribution of the finished product and the movement of labour to and from the place of work usually depends on transport of some kind. Railway sidings have been provided by municipalities on some of their industrial sites, while other sites are served by roads only. However, it is impossible to be sure just how important this factor is in the location of an industry. Railways have attracted more industries than roads, if judged by the setting up of cotton ginneries and bulk grain storage depots in Zimbabwe and the general growth of industry on the line of rail in all three countries.

Markets

Access to markets is the main factor influencing industrial location in Central Africa. Newspapers, soft drinks, beer and flour are all produced in the larger towns of the three countries.

Assembly industries are likely to be located at the market, largely because freight rates are usually higher for the finished product than for the raw materials. Thus, components for refrigerators and cookers and motor vehicles will be located at the market for assembly. Lusaka, Blantyre and several Zimbabwean cities have domestic appliance assembly plants. The assembly of cars and trucks is carried on in Lusaka, Ndola, Mutare and Harare, where market attraction exerts the greatest influence. Little skilled labour is required on the assembly line and, as in the USA where assembly plants were set up in Texas and California – away from the old-established Detroit area – the market location has proved economic. In Zimbabwe, Ford Motor Company opened an assembly plant in Harare, and the British Motor Corporation (now British Leyland) set up their plant at Mutare in the early 1960s. The latter city is nearer to Beira than Harare, so that the import of the assembly kits would cost British Leyland less than it would Ford. After assembly, British Leyland has the cars driven to other cities in Zimbabwe to save rail costs.

Ford Motors probably anticipated that Harare offered a larger market, that it was more centrally situated for distribution and that it offered the best opportunity for expansion of the motor-engineering industry. Both Ford and British Leyland left Zimbabwe after the declaration of UDI in 1965. Their factories continue to be used for the assembly of cars and trucks of various makes.

In Zambia, as the result of a government decision, the first assembly plant for cars was located at Livingstone to appease a municipality that complained of industrial neglect due to its remote location.

Another industry which is intimately linked with its market is the newspaper industry.

Things to do
1 Suggest reasons why Harare is the main manufacturing centre in Central Africa.
2 Discuss the influence of markets on the location of industries in Zambia and Zimbabwe.
3 List the factors which are likely to lead to an expansion of industrial activity in Malaŵi.
4 a) If you were a manufacturer of bicycles suggest with reasons where you would set up a factory in Zimbabwe.
b) Suppose you were asked to establish a cotton ginnery and spinning mill in Zambia, suggest with reasons your choice of location.

Part Two
Malaŵi

5 Relief

Which is the most dissected of the three countries in Central Africa?

Malaŵi's major relief features are simple, consisting of (1) the rift valley occupied by Lake Malaŵi and the Shire River, (2) the middleveld, and (3) the highveld. Only the rift valley is continuous and it is the divided nature of the other two relief regions that gives the country a scenic beauty which is enhanced by the lake. One geographer who wrote a book on Nyasaland entitled it, *The Land of the Lake*. Copy Fig. 15 into your notebook and as you read the following description of the three areas write down the main points beside the map.

1 Rift valley

Lake Malaŵi is the third largest freshwater lake on the African continent. It is 580 km long, averages 40 to 100 km in width, and has a depth of 704 m at the deepest point which is off Usisya Bay, near Ruarwe. This depth is equivalent to 232 m below sea level.

The coasts of the lake vary from narrow strips of land, swampy in parts, to wider areas which rise by a series of escarpments to the middleveld. All of this land was once under the waters of the lake. Elsewhere, the coast rises steeply, as in the northeast to the Livingstone Mountains and in the west where the Ruarwe scarp rises 1 520 m above the lake. Both of these scarps represent faults which are the borders of the rift valley. Dissection of the scarps has led to some spectacular gorges such as that cut by the Luweya River for some 40 km through the eastern part of the Viphya Plateau.

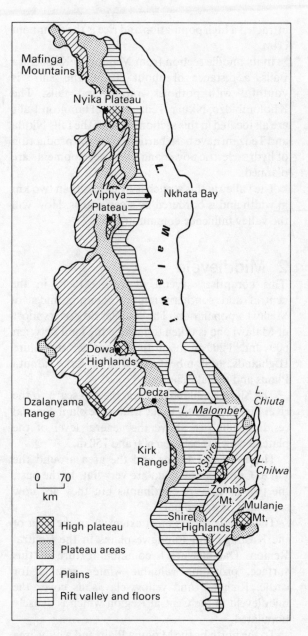

Fig. 15   Malaŵi relief units

The outlet of the lake, the Shire River, is some 480 km long. Its course is very varied. From its source it meanders into Lake Malombe, a shallow lake. From here to Liwonde, the Shire has a wide floodplain through which it meanders and forms ox-bow lakes. The river falls about 8 cm per two km in this section. The fertile alluvial soil has

25

attracted a high population and rice is the dominant crop.

In its middle section from Matope to Kapachira Falls, a distance of about 80 km, the Shire is youthful with potholes, rapids and falls. The Kholombidzo, Nkula, Tedzani and Hamilton Falls are all located in this section. Two of the falls Nkula and Tedzani have been harnessed for the production of hydro-electric power and other developments are planned.

The valley in this stretch is often less than two km in width and is bordered by steep scarps. How will the valley influence communications?

2 Middleveld

This comprises several plateaus which, in the central and southern regions, contain most of Malaŵi's population. The middleveld covers most of Malaŵi and is taken to include the land between 600 and 1 200 m in altitude, that is, the Shire Highlands, Malombe–Lake Chilwa–Lake Chiuta Plains and the lake shores.

The Shire Highlands present a steep scarp to the river but slope gently to the Malombe plain. Several residual hills rise above the general level of the plateau which is between 600 and 750 m.

The Malombe Plains and the area around the Lakes Chilwa and Chiuta are very flat. In the past, the two lakes were continuous but they are now separated by a sand bar.

The middle veld is most extensive in the area of the Kasungu and Lilongwe plains in the Central Region. Dambos are a common feature of this surface, providing valuable winter grazing for cattle. Rich red and yellow clay soils cover the middleveld in the Central Region which is densely populated.

To the north lie the Mzimba Plain and a hilly area to the west of Karonga. In the latter, the North Rumphi River has eroded a number of canyons in rocks of the Karroo system. Do you know the difference between a canyon and a gorge?

3 Highveld

It is made up of several widely separated areas at altitudes of from 1 200 to 3 000 m. Fig. 15 shows the location of these areas.

The Mulanje Massif, the highest and the most impressive, as seen from the aircraft on approaching Chileka airport, is a series of broad steps separated by steep slopes. It is made up of syenite, a resistant igneous rock. Above the plateau at 2 734 m rise several peaks, the highest of which is Sapitwa at 3 000 m. This is the highest point in Central Africa.

Another mass of syenite underlies the Zomba Mountain which rises to 2 087 m at the northern end of the Shire Highlands. On its western side, the mountain drops 1 220 m to the rift valley floor and to the north and west are other steep scarps.

In the dialect of northern Malaŵi, nyika means 'from whence the water comes'. Because of its height, about 1 980 m, and its size – it is the largest high plateau in Central Africa – the rainfall is heavy. Its steep scarps present a severe obstacle to road links with Karonga. The highest peak on the plateau is Nganda, at 2 698 m.

The Viphya Highlands are smaller and much more dissected than the Nyika Plateau. On the east, the Viphya plunge into the lake over the Ruarwe scarp which is 1 524 m high.

Other areas of highveld are the Mafinga Mountains (2 164 m in height), the Dedza-Kirk Range, Dzalanyama Range and the Dowa Highlands.

Things to do
1 Write any new terms which you have met in this chapter. Opposite each write its meaning.
2 Using an outline map of Malaŵi with another pupil, question each other on the names and location of the relief features.
3 Write what you think are the difficulties of developing Malaŵi's resources. Think particularly about the part played by relief.

Climate and hydrology

The general causes of climate have already been discussed in the general Central Africa section. In this chapter, the climate of Malaŵi will be considered briefly.

According to a general classification of world climates, Malaŵi falls within the tropical continental climate with dry winters. Some geographers call this tropical savanna climate. This climate has one main wet season in summer when Malaŵi comes under the influence of the southward

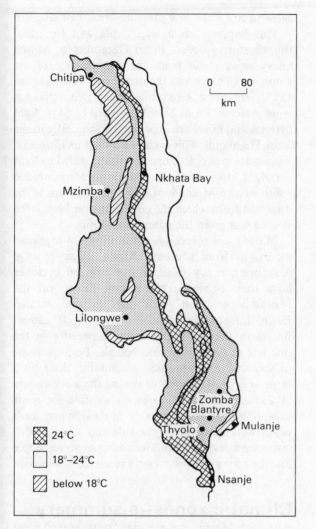

Fig. 16   Malaŵi average annual temperature

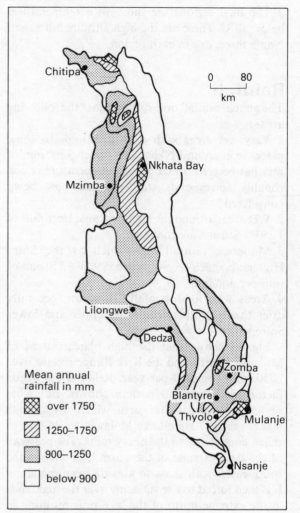

Fig. 17   Malaŵi rainfall

movement of the ITCZ and is mainly dry during the rest of the year.

Study Figs. 16 and 17 showing average annual temperatures and mean annual rainfall for Malaŵi. Compare these maps with the map on pages 8 and 9, showing prevailing winds over Africa in January and July respectively. Which winds affect Malaŵi? Which of these two places is the warmer, Mulanje or Lilongwe? Can you give the reason for the difference in temperature? Where would you like to spend your holiday in September–October?

Look at Fig. 17 again. Name three areas that receive over 1 750 mm of rain per year and three areas with under 900 mm.

Regional temperature

Look at the annual temperature map and study it carefully. This map (Fig. 16) reveals three temperature regions with varying temperature ranges. These are:

1 Regions with mean annual temperatures exceeding 24°C are generally hot. Can you name these areas?

2 The next region consists of those areas occupying most of the country–the medium plateau areas and plains fall into this category. Examples include the Shire Highlands, the Lilongwe and Kasungu Plains and the Limpasa and Mzimba Plains with temperatures between 18–24°C.

3 The final regions are those with temperatures below 18°C. These are the high altitude hill zones. Name three, one in each region.

Rainfall

The annual rainfall map distinguishes the following areas:

1 Very wet areas with over 1 750 mm. In some places, e.g. around Nkhata Bay over 3 300 mm of rain has been recorded. Which temperature region roughly corresponds with the one now being considered?

2 Wet areas around the high plateaus. Here falls of 1 250–1 750 mm are common.

3 Moderate rainfall areas such as the Shire Highlands which receive between 900–1 250 mm of rain per annum.

4 Areas with light rainfall. These are generally drier than (3) and include the upper and lower Shire valley.

Fig. 17 shows that the high plateau areas of Mulanje, Zomba and the Kirk Range receive over 1 750 mm of rainfall per year. Relief is the major factor in the rainfall pattern shown. But what about the Nkhata Bay area which also shows higher rainfall? Here Lake Malaŵi, in addition to relief, contributes to the heavy rains. The presence of the large expanse of the warm lake enables the south-easterly air mass to absorb more moisture. It is then forced to rise suddenly over the highlands in the extreme north of the lake thus resulting in abundant precipitation. Falls of over 2 500 mm have been recorded.

Can you explain why the Shire Lowlands receive less rain than the Nkhata Bay region?

Rainfall sources in Malaŵi

At the beginning of this chapter, we noted that Malaŵi has one main wet season lasting from about October to March or April. The first rains in October/November are convectional thunderstorms. What causes these rains? A study of the pressure and wind systems over southern Africa will help us to answer this question. At this time the sun is overhead in Malaŵi during its apparent southward migration to the Tropic of Capricorn. As the heating of the surface increases, low pressures are developed and the southerly winds blow in to fill the low pressure areas of rising air.

This happens on a large scale and torrential thunderstorms occur. From December to March heavy rains result from the convergence of the south-east Trades and the north-east Trades in the ITCZ, the zone separating these two opposing wind systems. From March to April or May, light drizzles and mists are experienced especially in the Shire Highlands. This is known locally as *Chiperoni* – an invasion of cold moist air accompanied by light drizzle. Chiperoni is a mountain in Mozambique south east of Mulanje Massif and since this is the direction from which the cold moist air blows, the drizzle was given the name Chiperoni.

Malaŵi also receives rainfall from cyclonic incursions from southern Africa. Their passage may bring heavy rains. These tropical cyclones have their origin in the Indian Ocean off the Mozambique coast. One such cyclone, named Edith, hit southern Malaŵi in 1956. It caused floods in the Shire Lowlands, especially in the districts of Chikwawa and Nsanje. Perhaps some of you will remember that a similar cyclone hit a large area of Mozambique during the week ending 30 January 1971. This was responsible for some exceptionally heavy rains in Malaŵi when most roads were rendered impassable and some garden crops were destroyed. In Mozambique, some people lost their lives and others were rendered homeless.

Climatic zones – a summary

Although Malaŵi has one main rainy season from November to April, there are diversities of climate over the country. Broadly, four climate zones dependent largely on altitude, may be recognised. Figs. 16 and 17 combined reveal:

1 Hot, dry areas. The Salima and central Karonga lakeshores fall within this zone.

2 Hot, wet areas confined to the northern region lakeshore in the vicinity of Nkhata Bay.

3 Warm wet areas which are the northern and central region plateaus and the Shire Highlands.

4 Cool, very wet areas – the high altitude hill zones of Nyika, Viphya, Dedza and Mulanje.

Hydrology

Have you ever thought how important water is to man? To geographers, the study of water resources is of vital importance because it is upon this that agricultural and industrial developments depend. The mean annual rainfall of Malaŵi is about 1150 mm. Of this amount, about 80% (900 mm) is lost through evapotranspiration. Compare this with Zimbabwe, page 76. This sounds frightening but we should remember that crops transpire and that some of the 900 mm is used by plants. Run-off and seepage into the ground accounts for the remaining 20% of the rainfall.

Fortunately for Malaŵi, some of the run-off water is carried by the numerous streams into Lake Malaŵi, the country's natural reservoir. In periods of good rainfall, the lake has always provided a surplus amount of water available for storage or flow down the Shire River, the outlet of Lake Malaŵi. But there are times when the lake's level has receded (nearly 6 m in the past five decades). Intensive studies of fluctuations in Lake Malaŵi levels have been conducted by several hydrologists. There has been no general agreement as to the causes of these fluctuations. All that can be stated is that there may be a close relationship between rainfall, run-off, evaporation and outflow from the lake. It has been estimated that the average annual lake evaporation is as much as 1800 mm. In dry years this evaporation may help to reduce the level of the lake. If this happened, the Shire would cease to flow. Fortunately, the level of the lake has been rising since 1948, giving surplus water.

Lake Chilwa is another lake in Malaŵi which causes concern. It occupies a shallow basin and has no outlet. When evaporation exceeds rainfall in the catchment, the lake becomes shallow. In 1968 the lake actually dried up.

From the foregoing account, it is clear that conservation of the lake catchment is of the utmost importance. The total catchment area of Lake Malaŵi is 96 218 km² of which 29 604 km² is water (mostly Lake Malaŵi) and 67 314 km² is land. Part of the Lake and some of the land area is in Tanzania and Mozambique.

Things to do
1 Study the table below and do the exercise that follows:

Table 5 Altitude and temperature

Station	Lat.	Long.	Alt.	Mean Temperature (°C)	
			metres	Jan.	July
Nsanje	16° 58′S	35° 17′E	210	27·2	25·0
Chitipa	9° 42′S	33° 14′E	1402	21	17

Temperature increases as latitude decreases. The table above contradicts this statement. Can you explain why Chitipa is not hotter than Nsanje?
2 Table 6 gives the monthly temperature and rainfall figures for Blantyre and Mangochi. Using the Blantyre figures, draw a rainfall column diagram. What are the advantages of showing the information in this way?
3 Give an account of the rainfall distribution of Malaŵi.

Table 6 Climatic data for two stations

	Jan	Feb	Mar	Apr	May	Jun	Jul	Aug	Sep	Oct	Nov	Dec
Blantyre												
Temperature (°C)	28	28	28	27	26	24	24	26	29	32	31	29
Rainfall (mm)	210	180	120	40	10	0	0	0	0	20	80	170
Mangochi												
Temperature (°C)	26	25	26	25	23	21	20	22	24	27	28	28
Rainfall (mm)	203	177	101	50	152	12	—	2	3	50	25	152

6 Vegetation and forestry (Malaŵi)

About one-quarter of Malaŵi is forested. The forest falls under two categories, namely, exotic (trees introduced from foreign lands) and indigenous (trees native to Malaŵi). The former yields forest produce under controlled management and is commercially valuable. The latter protects the main water catchment areas of the country and consists of trees that are commercially less valuable. Try to name some exotic and indigenous trees found in Malaŵi. An example has been given:

Table 7 Example of exotic and indigenous trees

Exotic	Indigenous
Blue gums (eucalypts)	Tsamba

Extensive exotic forests are found in the afforestation areas of Mulanje, Blantyre, Zomba, Dedza/Chongoni, Dzonzi–Viphya Plateau. Fig. 18 is a very generalized map showing the natural vegetation in Malaŵi. Study this carefully and describe the distribution of exotic and indigenous forest. Compare this map with the Mean Annual Rainfall Map (Fig. 17). Write down any relationships.

Indigenous forest

Despite the lack of good timber-producing forest on a large scale, there are, in Malaŵi, a number of very good indigenous timber trees. Look at the list you made earlier.

Let us examine the biggest area of major importance, namely the Mulanje Forest. Here, Mulanje cedar has been worked for the past 70 years providing softwood for various purposes.

The cedar forests occur at altitudes ranging

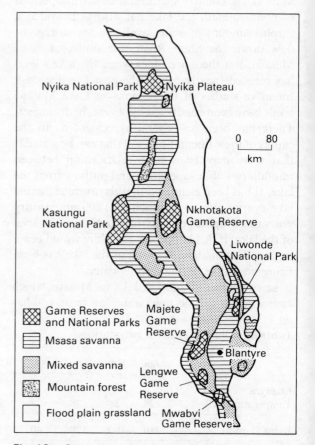

Fig. 18   Game reserves and vegetation

between 1 500 and 2 100 m. What are the difficulties of exploiting these forests? Until 1950, all the timber was pitsawn and head-loaded down the mountain by carriers. In 1950, a sawmill was established on Chambe Plateau and a year later a cableway was installed to carry sawn timber to the foot of the mountain. Can you suggest the outcome of this mechanisation? Yes, the work was speeded up and more timber was produced. Production of more timber meant fast depletion of the indigenous cedar. There was a need therefore to restore the deforested areas.

Exotic plantations

The deforested areas have since been planted with Pinus patula, a fast-growing species of white pine which is ready for use as sawn timber in 25–30 years. Apart from this species, there are a number of other exotic trees in Malaŵi. Why have these been grown? Think of the various uses of trees. Not only are trees grown to meet a country's timber and fuel requirements, they are also useful from the conservation point of view – prevention of erosion, flooding, drying out of the ground and protection of water supplies.

Government afforestation schemes

It is said that the first exotic softwoods were introduced into Malaŵi in 1927, on the Zomba Plateau. The Mexican patula pine was found suitable for the high altitude summer rainfall climate of Malaŵi. Study the rainfall map and locate areas similar to Zomba Plateau.

By 1960, 72 500 ha of conifer plantations had been established in the Southern, Central and Northern region high altitude hill zones. Planting has continued and with an annual planting programme of 30 000 ha, the scheme envisages a plantation area of 175 000 ha by the last decade of this century. Softwoods grow more quickly in Malaŵi than in Canada because of more equable temperatures.

Viphya pulpwood scheme

Study Fig. 19 showing the areas involved in the Viphya Pulpwood Scheme. Name the important areas. A total of 35 000 ha had been planted on the Viphya Plateau by 1967. This had increased to 41 750 ha during the 1967/68 season and to 221 000 ha in 1969/70. By 1980/81 there were about 280 000 ha of planted forest on Viphya.

This colossal expansion aims at pulpwood production, timber and wood for various purposes.

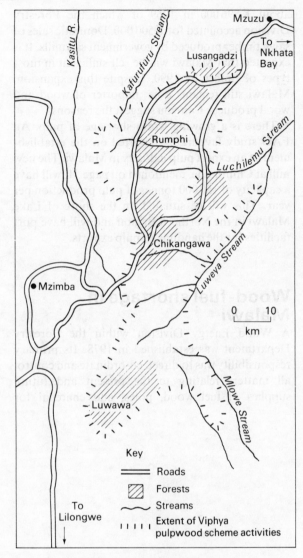

Fig. 19   Viphya pulpwood scheme

The installation of a new band sawmill at Mazamba near Chikangawa with a sawnwood/sawlog conversion of 50 per cent will have a capacity of 28 000 m³ per annum. The pulpmill will be located at Chintheche. Think of the advantages of Chintheche over Mzuzu for the location of the pulpmill.

The expansion of the forest industry has done two important things:

1 It has provided employment for many people– over 3 000–and

2 It has earned more revenue for the Department of Forestry. The total earnings of the Department of Forestry and Game rose from K 516 000 in 1968 to

about K596 000 in 1969 of which the Forestry Division accounted for K500 000. Domestic sales of sawn timber produced by government sawmills. It is expected that Malaŵi will be self sufficient in most types of timber by 1990. Despite this expansion, Malaŵi still remains a net importer of wood and wood products. Can you suggest the reasons?

There is a growing world shortage of pulp. An FAO study favourably reported on the establishment of an export pulp industry in Malaŵi. The new mill at Chintheche, mentioned on page 31, will have a capacity of 150 000 tonnes of pulp production per year. This will be situated on the shore of Lake Malaŵi in the Northern Region and will have port facilities for the handling of pulp exports.

Wood-fuel shortage in Malaŵi

A Wood Energy Division within the Forestry Department was established in 1978. Its primary responsibility was to direct, co-ordinate and control all matters relating to the present and future supplies of fuel wood, poles, and charcoal for domestic, institutional and industrial uses. See page 155.

Realizing that the natural forest resource is fast being depleted, the Malaŵi Government has been encouraging all people to plant more trees. Every year schools, colleges and the University together with the public take part in tree planting on the National Tree Planting Day which falls on the 21st January.

Eucalypts, gmelina and cassia are preferred for fuel. Over 12 900 ha of fuelwood and pole plantations are to be established under the Wood Energy Project which attracted a World Bank loan of K13.6 million during a five-year period 1979/80 to 1984/85.

Things to do
1 Name as many indigenous trees that you can think of and opposite each write one use.
2 Discuss the feasibility of the establishment of a pulp and paper industry in Malaŵi.
3 Why do you think a large area of natural forest is disappearing fast in Malaŵi? What are the consequences and what solutions can you suggest to stop reckless forest destruction?

7 Agriculture (Malaŵi)

Over 3 million ha of Malaŵi's surface area are under cultivation. Maize and subsistence crops such as millet, sorghum, beans and cassava; tree crops of tung, tea and coffee; and tobacco and cotton were the most important crops.

Look at Fig. 20. Which crops would you say are major cash crops in Malaŵi? Let us consider some of these crops briefly.

Maize

Most Malaŵians would not think that maize was a cash crop because it is mainly grown for local use. What name is given to such a crop? But although maize is a staple food of almost every Malaŵian family, it is now one of the crops earning some revenue for the country. Surplus maize has, with the development of export crops on a regular basis, been exported to neighbouring states like Zambia in the past.

Growing conditions

A subtropical summer rainfall crop, maize requires hot, humid conditions during the growing season lasting between 130–180 days. It prefers medium altitudes within the range of 600–1 200 m above sea-level.

Try to name the areas in Malaŵi which fall within these medium altitudes.

Most large-scale farmers in Central Africa grow hybrid varieties which mature in the longer time. A short maturing period is important·since the main rainy season generally extends over only about 3½ months. The minimum rainfall requirements under the high evaporation conditions of this

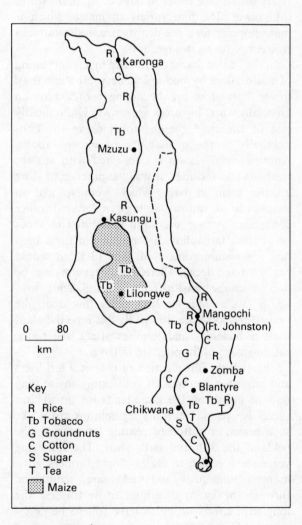

Fig. 20   Malaŵi crops

Key
R Rice
Tb Tobacco
G Groundnuts
C Cotton
S Sugar
T Tea
▨ Maize

climate are 500 mm per year, but maize does best in areas with 630 to 1 000 mm per year.

33

Yields

Yields vary considerably depending on the care exercised during land preparation and on soil fertility but where land is fertile yields of up to 75 bags per ha have been recorded. In Malaŵi the average is 20 to 25 bags per ha. This gives an average of between 2 and 2·5 t per ha. In the USA, yields of up to 7·5 t per ha are common. How can Malaŵi achieve such high yields?

Harvesting is done during April and July when the moisture content of the grain is between 10 to 12%. At this stage, the grain is quite dry and ready for storage either in bags or in maize stores (nkhokwe/. The flint variety of maize, which is more popular than the dent maize, resists attacks by weevils during storage.

In the United States of America much harvesting of maize is done by mechanical means. In Zimbabwe maize harvesters are becoming more common especially where big areas are grown. Undoubtedly one of the chief reasons for picking the cobs manually is the availability of cheap labour. Another main reason is connected with storage methods and facilities. It was the practice to store all the grain in bags, which were stacked in thousands at railway sidings, mills and other convenient storage sites, and sometimes in sheds or beneath tarpaulins. If the maize in these bags had a moisture content of over 12·5% it would easily rot and decay. Therefore harvesting must be done when the moisture content is sufficiently low, i.e. as late as May or July, depending upon the variety and local conditions. By this time the plant itself is bone-dry and termites attack the roots, causing many of the plants to fall over.

Through the introduction of chemical fertilisers and improved methods of cultivation, maize may now be grown on the same lands for up to four successive years. Generally leguminous crops like soya beans, or cotton or pasture leys occupy the fields in the fifth and sixth years. The following years see a return to maize. Some farmers grow maize continuously and yields are maintained through heavy applications of fertilisers, the long-term effects of which have still to be determined in Central Africa.

Uses

The maize grown on large farms is used for human consumption in the form of mealie-meal, breakfast cereals, etc. It is also cultivated as grain-feed for cattle, pigs and poultry. For ensilage, the maize is cut green to ferment in silos and in pits. Cattle are usually an important subsidiary on maize farms.

The Lilongwe Plain is the main maize growing area in Malaŵi. Elsewhere production is mainly for local use with little surplus for sale. Of late, maize production has been on the increase throughout Malaŵi. In 1966, the Agricultural Development and Marketing Corporation (the then Farmers Marketing Board) purchased 21 700 t of maize. This had increased to 89 800 t in 1967 but in 1969, only 52 300 t were bought. This drop was the result of poor rainfall in the previous growing season. In 1978, Admarc purchased 120·3 thousand metric tonnes of maize but only 918 thousand tonnes in the 1980/81 season. This was a result of a prolonged drought which hit mostly some parts of southern Malaŵi.

Tobacco

Tobacco was being grown in this country and exported to the coast before the arrival of the European. With his arrival, more attention was given to the crop as a money-earner together with coffee, tung and tea.

Growing conditions

The quality and flavour of tobacco is dependent upon the climatic environment, the soil, the type, variety and processing of the leaf. For optimum growth the plant needs a relatively constant temperature and water supply, a humid atmosphere and freedom from drought or periods of heavy rainfall, high winds or hail. Soils should not be too acid or contain chlorides, the drainage needs to be good, and it is necessary to maintain a high level of mineral nutrients through the application of fertilisers, especially potassium.

In Central Africa the summer rainfall, together with high humidity and high temperatures, provide an almost ideal climatic environment. The range of mean temperatures in the growing season (October to March) is small, being about 1·6°C on mean monthly figures in the Salisbury district, while the relative humidity during December to March does not drop below 60% as a rule. The well-drained sandveld soils are preferred by Virginia tobacco farmers to red soils. Tobacco likes a well-aerated soil too, and the close-particle structure of the redder clays cannot provide this. Long periods of drought are rare during the summer but heavy storms, long cloudy periods (especially in February) and hail do constitute natural hazards which the tobacco farmer has to face, so that crop-insurance is common.

By way of summary, it may be stated that many parts of Central Africa provide the correct climatic requirements for tobacco, that is, at least 635 mm of summer rain, an average temperature of about 21°C during the growing season, and plenty of sunshine, while the sandier soils have proved themselves very suitable for the crop.

Cultivation procedures

The seed-beds are prepared about September by burning and/or fumigating with gas, to kill all pests and diseases. The soil is cultivated to a fine tilth, and specially grown and selected seed is planted by watering-in, as it is very fine. The beds are carefully tended until the young seedlings are about 23 cm high and ready for planting out. The seedlings are planted 60 cm apart in the lands (in rows 90 cm apart for Virginia and in rows 60 cm apart for Turkish and Burley) about 25 October. They are given sufficient water to last until the early rains of November and December. The trend today is to dry-plant as early as possible (but not usually before 20 October) since the early crop grows fastest in the hot weather of October and November, producing good leaves, and avoiding to a large extent the possibility of blight and other diseases which come sometimes with the wet season. Picking starts as early as December and continues as late as April, when of course only wet-planted tobacco is being picked. During this long period, the bottom leaves are picked off as often as once or twice a week, the leaves being taken immediately to the curing barn, which must be situated on the farm.

Curing procedures

FLUE-CURING. Most Virginia tobacco (used chiefly

Virginia tobacco near Kasungu ready for curing

for cigarettes) is flue-cured. That is, the leaves are hung in barns for six to eight days, depending upon the moisture content of the tobacco, and subjected to temperatures up to 59°C. Heated air seals in the flavour and aroma of the leaves, and imparts the rich golden colour. The humidity in the barn is also carefully controlled to produce at the end as far as possible the right mass and colour of leaf, upon which will largely depend the market price obtained for the crop. Expert African graders usually grade the crop at once, and it is baled for despatch to the auction floors.

SUN-CURING OR AIR-CURING. This method of curing is usually adopted by African growers, mostly for the Oriental and Burley types. The tobacco is hung in grass-roofed sheds for a long period, withering slowly to a dark-brown colour.

Virginia and Burley tobacco have long broad leaves and cure to a golden and dark brown respectively. Oriental types are smaller with narrow leaves about 23 cm long which cure to a dark brown. Burley is tasteless and is used in blended cigarettes.

FIRE-CURING. This method is usually used for curing tobacco for use by pipe smokers. A central fire is made of a particular kind of wood which then gives off an aroma which the tobacco absorbs.

Curing of the different varieties of tobacco (Virginia, Burley and Oriental) varies from place to place. In Malaŵi Virginia tobacco is fire-cured. Can you suggest the reason?

Visit a curing shed, where you should try to find out what type of tobacco is being cured and the method used. If possible, visit a flue-curing plant and note the process involved. Why do most African farmers prefer sun/air curing to the flue-curing? Almost the entire crop in Malawi is produced in the Southern and Central regions by Africans on small holdings (Fig. 20). The major areas are Mulanje, Zomba, Lilongwe and Kasungu.

Production and trade

The greater part of Malaŵi's total tobacco crop is produced by small farmers.

Malaŵi is the world's second largest producer of fire-cured tobacco. In 1970, some 11·4 million kg were grown and marketed by about fifty thousand farmers whose efforts were encouraged and co-ordinated by the Agricultural Development and Marketing Corporation. In 1976, tobacco was the most important export crop earning some K65·2 million. The table below shows tobacco production in comparison with the main crops.

Table 8 Marketed production of main crops: 1976–1980

	1976	1977	1978	1979	1980
Tea (million kg)	28·2	31·6	31·7	32·6	29·9
Tobacco (million kg)	36·6	39·4	51·1	54·1	53·7
Seed Cotton (000 t)	19·6	25·0	24·2	22·4	23·1
Maize (000 t)	71·6	99·0	120·3	82·2	91·8

Almost all tobacco grown in Malaŵi is sold on the Limbe Auction Floors. Britain is the main buyer of Malaŵi's tobacco, but some is locally manufactured into various types of cigarettes by the main tobacco factories at Ginnery Corner and Limbe.

Tea

Historically, Malaŵi is the oldest tea-growing country on the African continent. Tea seed was first introduced to this country in 1878 at the Blantyre Mission from the Royal Botanical Garden, Edinburgh. This was unsuccessful, but later in 1888, a successful attempt was made at Livingstonia Mission by the then Free Church of Scotland. The plants were sent to Mulanje high rainfall area. There they were planted at Thornwood and Lauderdale estates, the pioneer tea estates that have flourished ever since. Later on, tea was introduced in Thyolo (formerly known as Cholo). The first tea plants suffered from disease, lack of water supplies and inadequate transport facilities.

Tea has become one of Malaŵi's main export crops, providing over 20 per cent of the export revenue, and employing over 38 000 people. Study the statistics in Table 8. What do the figures show about tea production? Suggest reasons for this trend.

Growing areas

In Malaŵi, some areas possess very good conditions for tea-growing, but only a few have a high enough rainfall. Look at a good atlas map which shows the relief of Malaŵi. Study it carefully and locate the high plateau areas of Mulanje, Thyolo and Nkhata Bay. These are the main tea-growing areas.

The chief requirements of tea may be listed as:

HIGH RAINFALL. 1 150 mm to 1 500 mm per annum is the optimum rainfall. Tea cannot grow successfully where there is less than 1 000 mm per annum unless year-round irrigation facilities exist.

HIGH TEMPERATURES. The mean annual temperature in tea-growing areas should be about 21°C (that is higher than that of Lusaka or Bulawayo) with little or no chance of frost.

WELL-DRAINED SOIL. Loams, with good drainage, usually on gentle slopes, are essential for tea, which cannot stand water-logging at its roots. The soils should be acid (pH of about 4·5).

ABUNDANT LABOUR. A large labour force is required during the tea plucking period since each tea bush is plucked approximately every seven days. As yet no mechanical method of tea plucking has proved satisfactory. Traditionally, it was thought that adequate shade induces the growth of tea leaves and prevents scorching as well as providing shelter for the pickers. Recent research has proved this wrong. Where shade trees have been cleared, yields have increased and so most tea estates are now cutting down all the old shade trees.

Makwasa Tea Estate

Study Fig. 21. In which district is this tea estate? How far is the estate from Luchenza Railway Station?

Makwasa Tea Estate (Fig. 22) is part of Thyolo Highlands Tea Estates Limited, and was developed from virgin bush starting in 1924 when 15·7 ha were planted. By 1963 the estate had a total of 224 ha of tea, and this has steadily increased to 563 ha in 1982. In addition to tea, Makwasa Estate has 317 ha of bluegum, which are required to provide fuel for the tea factory.

The estate labour force

Makwasa Estate employs approximately 2 000 people plucking and weeding tea during the peak

Tea Plucking on the slopes of Mulanje. Note the difference between this photograph and the photograph on page 100, e.g. slope of land, trees, height of plucking table, etc.

37

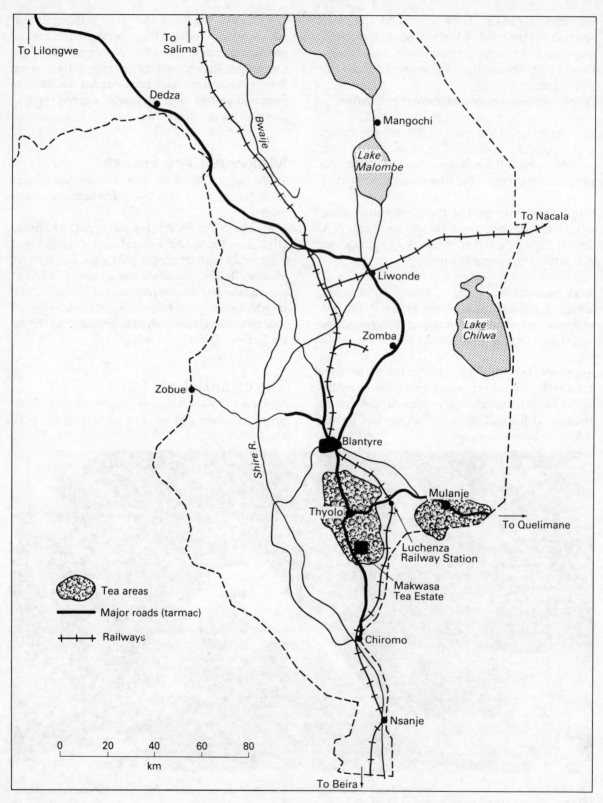

Fig. 21   Main tea growing areas in the southern region

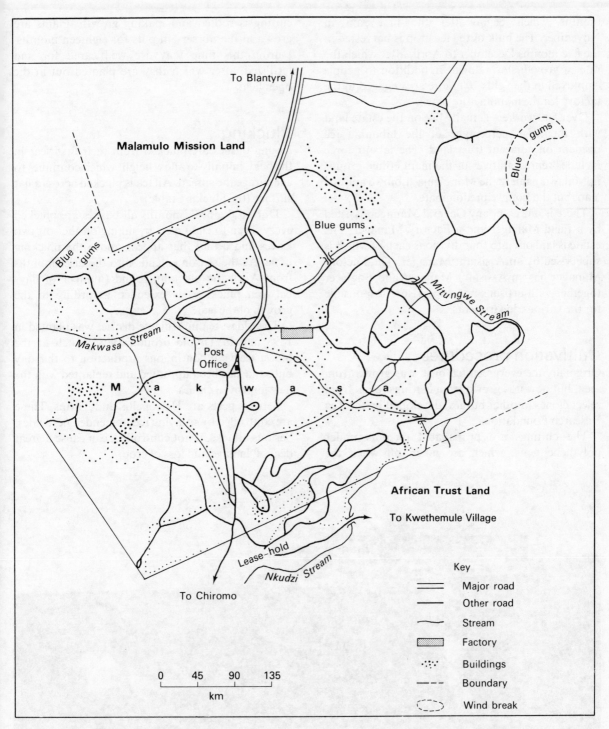

Fig. 22   Makwasa Estate land use map

months which begin after the first rain in November. The bulk of the tea crop is harvested in the five months December to April, after which the rate of growth slows down. In addition to people employed in the fields 200 more are engaged in the factory for the manufacture of tea.

Over 500 workers actually live on the estate land with the large percentage of the labour force resident on adjacent trust land. The labour force includes representatives of the main ethnic groups in Malaŵi, namely the Mang'anja, Lomwe and the Yao, but the Lomwe predominate.

There is one company General Manager assisted by a Field Manager and a Factory Manager. The estate is laid out into four divisions each of which is supervised by an Assistant Manager. The Factory Manager has an Assistant Manager and Engineer together with artisans and supervisors responsible for the various departments.

Cultivation procedures

Originally the evergreen tea bush was grown from seed, but now it is grown from cuttings taken from select clones (mother bushes) developed by the Tea Research Foundation.

The cuttings are propagated in pots under polythene tents, which are taken off when the cutting is rooted and making growth. Plants are grown in the nursery in pots for eighteen months. During this time they are well cared for and fertilized, after which they are planted out in the open field.

Plucking

Young bushes are plucked from their first year in the field, initially to allow height which continues to encourage the spread. All tea is plucked across a flat surface (the plucking table).

During the peak months all bushes are plucked every seven to eight days by taking off the soft two leaves and a bud that appear above the plucking table. As the season extends into the drier months from April the plucking round (number of days between plucking) is extended according to the growth of the leaf.

The oldest tea in Mulanje district was planted in 1893 and in Thyolo around 1908. Much of the oldest tea is in continuous production to this day but some has been uprooted and replanted with the new improved clones.

Serious pests are Heleopeltis and Thrips. These are controlled by spraying recommended pesticides. Serious attacks, if not controlled, can cause a great deal of damage and loss of crop.

Makwasa tea factory. Describe the position of this factory on the estate as shown in Fig. 22

Arrival of tea leaf from farms. This factory processes tea from several farms

Processing (Manufacture)

Tea must be processed as soon as it is plucked. The various stages are:

WITHERING. The fresh leaf is put into troughs through which air is blown to reduce the moisture content of the leaf by about 30 per cent.

CUTTING. In Makwasa factory the leaf is then fired into a Lawrie Tea Processor, which is like a maize mill. This reduces the withered leaf into small particles.

FERMENTING. The cut leaf is then fed onto a fermenting machine which turns the leaf while keeping it cool. The colour changes from green to copper. The process takes about 60 minutes.

FIRING. After fermentation the tea is fired. There are several different types of tea driers; all subject the tea to immediate heat to stop fermentation and reduce the moisture content of the leaf to 3·5%.

SORTING. After firing, the tea is sorted over machines with different mesh sizes. This produces the different grades (particle size) of the black tea. Each grade is kept in a large bin until sufficient quantity has accumulated to pack.

PACKING. Packing is done into plywood chests which are lined with tissue paper and aluminium foil to prevent taint or moisture spoiling the tea. Chests are then sent in containers to overseas auction, or buyers. Some grades are sold locally at the Limbe Auction Floors.

General

Makwasa factory manufactured over 2 000 000 kg of made tea in the 1980/81 season. Depending on rainfall and other climatic factors the crop is steadily increasing due to young tea coming into production and improved standards of field management.

Spreading tea in the withering room of the Makwasa factory

The Smallholder Tea Authority

In 1964, the tea industry, monopolised by expatriates, opened its doors to Malaŵian farmers who were encouraged to grow the crop by the Malaŵi Government. The Malaŵi Smallholder Tea Authority, which cares for Malaŵian tea farmers' interests was formed and registered in 1967. Since then Malaŵians have made great strides in tea growing in both Thyolo and Mulanje districts where 4 500 Malaŵians grow tea on 2 644 ha of land. Originally, Kawalazi in Nkhata Bay district was among the smallholder tea growing areas, but this was discontinued and the authority concentrates its attention in the Thyolo and Mulanje districts.

By June 1980 Mulanje Smallholders produced 4 189 268 kg of green leaf while Thyolo produced 1 038 577 kg of green leaf. Smallholder tea is processed in Mulanje where the Malaŵi Tea Factory Company Limited (MATECO) was formed in 1975 to process tea leaf from smallholders. Smallholder tea has consistently commanded top prices from Malaŵi tea on the world market. In 1981, the smallholder tea factory handled 5·5 million kg of green leaf, which when processed gave 1·23 million kg of made tea.

By 1983/84, up to 2 million kg of made tea is expected to be produced. To meet the growing volume of smallholder tea, the company acquired 8 ha of land from the Ruo Tea Estates for a second tea factory at Njola opposite the Admarc Canning Factory in Mulanje.

Cotton

Cotton is grown in Central Africa mainly to supply local demand for middle and low grades. Higher grades are imported from Egypt and the USA.

The cotton boll is the seed case of the plant. The fluffy boll which becomes the thread and then the cloth, contains the seeds as well. These must first be removed by a process called ginning. The bolls are picked by hand (again comparatively cheap labour makes this possible as is the case of tea) although mechanical means of harvesting have been employed in other countries. Machines do, however, carry out most of the processing, which includes washing to remove the natural oils which would make dyeing difficult, combing, teasing, carding, spinning and finally weaving. The cloth is mostly used for clothes for the African market in neighbouring countries.

Cotton has been cultivated in this country for many years. In 1860, it was recorded that 'Thonje kaja', that is native cotton, was cultivated by people of the Lower Shire Valley and Lake Nyasa. It was not until 1910 that an Egyptian type of cotton was introduced, to be followed later by upland cotton varieties.

Cotton requires temperatures of over 24°C during the growing season. Except where irrigation is practised, adequate rainfall of about 600mm per annum is required.

In Malaŵi, over 80% of this crop is cultivated in the hot, drier areas of the rift valley especially in the lower Shire Valley where the fertile, waxy (Makande) soils are very suitable. The lakeshore plains are also important growing areas. Showers may spoil the lint if they fall during the picking season. As picking is annual, an abundance of labour is required for successful cotton production. THE CHIKWAWA COTTON DEVELOPMENT SCHEME was inaugurated in 1968–69. The scheme initially started with 52 000 ha in the Lower Shire Valley, the most productive cotton growing area in Malaŵi. The scheme, financed by the International Development Association (IDA), aims at (1) increasing cotton production (2) the development of public facilities such as roads, water supplies and marketing and (3) encouraging resettlement in the hitherto empty areas. It is estimated that 2 000 families will be settled here and that in five years over 8 000 ha of arable land will be surveyed and planned for controlled settlement. The scheme is based at Mgabu (see Fig. 23) where the project manager is housed together with extension officers and trainees.

Groundnuts

This crop has been grown for many years as a subsistence crop, but recently other farmers have shown considerable interest. The general policy in all three countries is to expand production, for the ration trade (wages often include rations), for export, and, in Zimbabwe especially, for the oil-expressing and stock-feed industries. The crop offers a good alternative to maize production, being leguminous, and is being encouraged, especially in Malaŵi, on this basis.

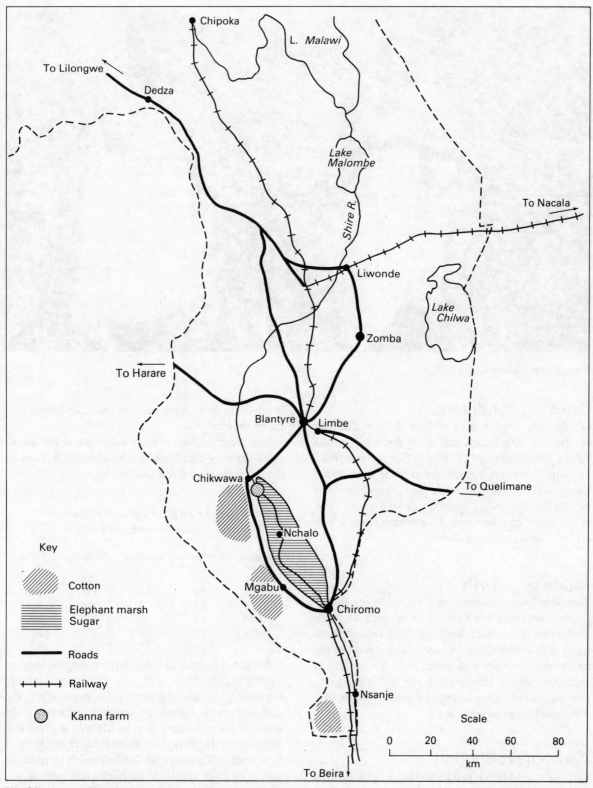

Key

(cotton hatch)	Cotton
(horizontal lines)	Elephant marsh Sugar
▬▬▬	Roads
┼┼┼┼	Railway
◉	Kanna farm

Fig. 23 Lower Shire Valley cotton and sugar development

A crop in the lower Shire

Growing conditions

Groundnuts require a rainfall of at least 635 mm per annum. This means that many parts of Central Africa are suitable as far as rainfall is concerned. Growing temperatures should average over 15°C. Sandy soils are best because the groundnuts can be lifted more easily. Being a nitrogen-fixing crop groundnuts can be sown in rotation with other crops to advantage (see above).

Mode of growth

The nuts (peanuts) are found on the roots of the plants, contained in a husk which is useful as cattle feed when dried. Each husk contains two or three nuts. These nuts have a very high food value, containing protein and much oil. The latter is extracted for use in vegetable oils and margarine. Peanut butter, salted and roasted peanuts are more easily appreciated uses.

Areas of production

Until 1962 Malaŵi produced more groundnuts than either Zimbabwe or Zambia, but since then production has slowed down and Zimbabwe has taken the lead.

The bulk of Malaŵi's production is by small-scale farmers chiefly from the Central Region in the Lilongwe and Kasungu district.

Table 9 Marketed groundnut production (thousand tonnes unshelled)

Season	Zimbabwe	Zambia	Malaŵi	Total
1977	47	16	225	288
1978	13	12	135	160
1979	17	3	296	316
1980	13	4	383	400
1981	17	3	237	257

Seasonal fluctuations are large owing to varying weather conditions. Exports vary considerably according to the surplus remaining after the domestic needs have been supplied. In some years most of the marketed crop in Malaŵi is exported, whereas only half the marketed crop that is produced in Zambia and Zimbabwe is exported. In addition, over a million litres of expressed oil are exported each year.

Mr Phiri's farm in the lower Shire

Things to do

1 a) What are the uses of maize in Malaŵi? Think of the uses of the green maize stalk, the cob and the grain both at home and in industry

b) How can Malaŵi become self-sufficient in maize production?

2 a) What crop is shown in the photograph above?

b) Where do you think this photo was taken? Is this a rain-fed farm or an irrigated one? Give one reason for your answer.

3 Study the photograph on page 44.

a) What crop is being harvested?

b) What is the difference between the method of harvesting this crop and tea?

4 Discuss the importance of the Lower Shire Valley Scheme in the economic development of Malaŵi.

Chikumbi case study

Only a third of Malaŵi's land area is considered suitable for arable agriculture, about a sixth for tree crops and the rest is classified as rough grazing land, woodland, swamp, hillsides and steep escarpment. Over 10% of Malaŵi's total land area is tilled. This means that certain areas are obviously more suited to the production of food crops than others. It is important to see the reasons for the distribution of agriculture because this, in turn, affects settlement. In this way relief indirectly determines the distribution of population.

Compare the relief and crop maps of Malaŵi and try to name the areas where most of the good agri-cultural land is found? Which region of Malaŵi consists of the least agriculturally developed land? Although only a tenth of the total surface area of Malaŵi is currently under the plough, efforts are being made to increase this by use of agricultural extension workers. Marginal land is being made productive by careful soil management and use of manure and fertilisers.

A little over 90% of the total population of Malaŵi is engaged in farming. The majority of the people are subsistence farmers but since the economy of Malaŵi is basically agrarian, the government is attempting to encourage most farmers to adopt modern methods of agriculture and thus be able to produce more crops for home consumption and for the market as well. All over Malaŵi, there are progressive farmers who are following modern methods of agriculture. These progressive farmers, during the last decade, were called 'Master Farmers'. The Master Farmers Scheme was designed to help African farmers to consolidate their plots into an economic unit and to plan their farms. In 1969, the name Achikumbi replaced the colonial name, 'Master Farmer'. Achikumbi are farmers who make a business of farming and who keep their land in better condition than they found it. Since 1966 when farm planning started, Achikumbi were selected by agricultural field staff officers using the following criteria:

1 The farm should be carefully planned and the farmer should be working within the framework of the plan.

2 The soil and water conservation measures recommended in the plan should have been carried out to a high standard.

3 The essential development of the farm should have been completed.

4 The farmer must be farming profitably and to a high standard on all the land under his control.

Apart from fulfilling these requirements, the Chikumbi (Chikumbi is the singular of Achikumbi) should be responsive to advice and willing to try out new ideas. Let us take a look at one Chikumbi who is among several progressive farmers in the southern region of Malaŵi. For our study, I have chosen Pastor James M. Malinki's estate called Mlombozi Estate, located in Fred Nteya's Village, Chief Makata, Blantyre District.

Population of Fred Nteya Village

Fred Nteya Village is a fairly large village which had 545 males and 616 females in 1977. Almost the entire population consists of subsistence farmers except for two progressive farmers who are Achikumbi. If all the villagers live on the land save a few who go to look for employment in towns, what does this state of affairs suggest about the productivity of the land?

Mlombozi Estate

Fig. 24 shows the location of Mr Malinki's estate. This estate lies some 32 km from Blantyre, north-east of Lunzu Trading Centre. The estate is 28·8 ha in size and it lies at an altitude of about 760 m in the undulating plains of Mlombozi River. Most of the estate is on gentle slopes. The soils vary between sandy loams to sandy clay loams underlain by deep red clays. Study Figs. 16 and 17. How much average rainfall does the estate get per annum? What is the average annual temperature at Mlombozi Estate?

Let us now examine the land area and its use. Look at Fig. 25. Notice the position of the broad-based terraces. What grows in each section of the terrace? Notice the position of the waterways (WW) in relation to the river. Why is the area very close to the river not cultivated? Which crop is cultivated the most, and which the least? Maize is the staple food crop in Malaŵi and at Mlombozi Estate as well.

Whereas in the gardens surrounding the estate maize is grown as a subsistence crop, Mr Malinki uses this crop as a cash crop, for feeding his cattle and chickens and for home consumption. The surrounding villagers come to buy his maize not only for making a kind of porridge (Nsimah-ugali) but also for brewing beer. It is on account of its multi-purpose uses that maize occupies such a unique position in the Mlombozi land-use pattern. Groundnuts occupied 1·60 ha in the 1968–69 season. This was only a sixth of the area covered by maize. The other crops (cassava, fruits and sweet potatoes) take up approximately 0·405 ha.

In 1969–70, the following were the areas under the main crops:

Table 10

Crop	Area (ha)	Yield
Maize	10	320 bags
Groundnuts	2	50 bags
Fruits	0·5	
Cassava		—

Mr Malinki, a Chikumbi or master farmer, in front of his house

Mr Malinki examining his crop

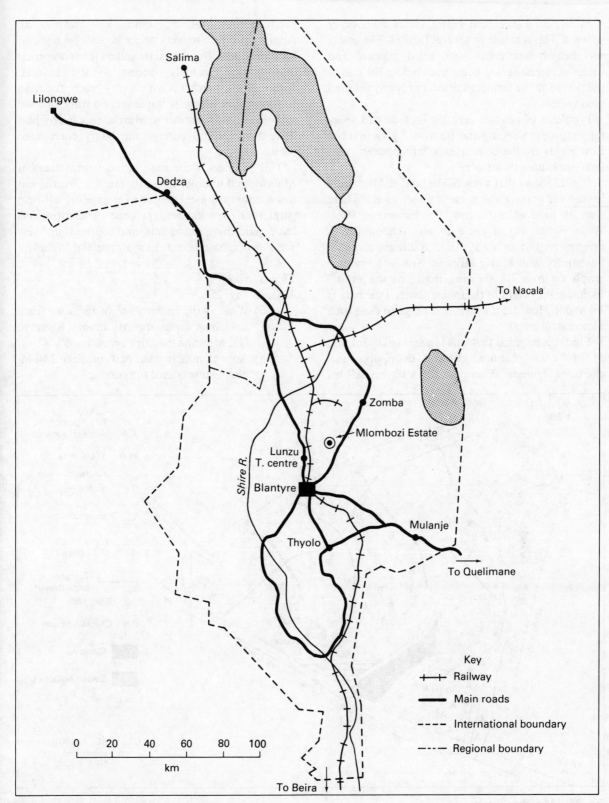

Fig. 24   Location of Mlombozi Estate

Mlombozi Estate had better yields than other villages. This was due to several factors. The estate was heavily manured using kraal manure and compost; weeding was completed before the end of the rains and the farmer planted a properly selected seed variety.

Problems of peasant farming include bad spacing, improper weeding and poor seed germination. Low yields are the consequence which means that fertiliser cannot be bought.

Fig. 25 shows that some of the land at Mlombozi is used for grazing and some is under forest. There were 10 head of cattle and 100 chickens in 1981. What is the use of these to an Achikumbi? A progressive farmer always tries to integrate animal husbandry with arable farming. Study the photograph on page 46 showing maize at the estate. Estimate the height of the maize plants if the man is 1·6 m tall. How did the farmer manage to raise such a successful crop?

Findings revealed that this farmer makes full use of his kraal manure, chicken droppings and chemical fertiliser. Where does this farmer sell his produce? At Matindi, some 5 km away is an Admarc produce market where he sells his agricultural products. But the estate suffers from one great disadvantage, namely, access to the market. Although the market is within easy reach, the road to Mlombozi Estate is impassable during the wet season. From December to March, only four-wheel drive vehicles can survive the badly corrugated road.

This problem is common in most rural areas of Malaŵi, and in order to combat it, the government has encouraged local people to engage on self-help rural road development projects. These projects have paid high dividends and opened up new areas–a common feature in most parts of Malaŵi.

Things to do
1 Study Fig. 25
   a) i) What is the importance of the wire fence stretching from the Mlombozi River to Old Mlombozi-Lunzu access road?
      ii) Approximately what percentage of Mlombozi Estate is used for grazing?

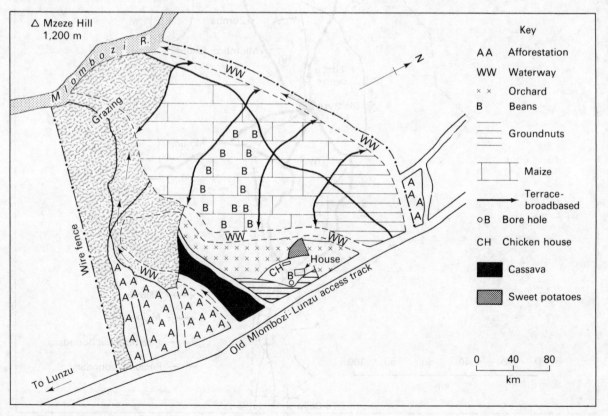

Fig. 25   Mlombozi Estate

48

b) What differences do you notice between Mr Malinki's farm and his methods of farming and either a commercial farmer in Malaŵi or an untrained subsistence farmer.

2 Look at the right-hand photograph on page 46.
a) What crop is this?
b) Write a short paragraph describing the conditions necessary for the successful cultivation of this crop.
c) What uses do people make of this crop?

3 What is stall-feeding? What is involved in this exercise?

4 Look carefully at the photograph below and answer the questions that follow.
a) What kind of fruit is shown in this photograph?
b) What do you understand by grafting? What use is it?

5 Discuss the importance of the Achikumbi Programme as initiated by the Extension Aids Department of the Ministry of Agriculture.

6 What is the value of tree planting and afforestation to a farmer, a village and a country?

Uprooting groundnuts

Cattle-rearing

We shall examine cattle-raising in Malaŵi under the following headings:
1 main breeds;
2 their distribution and the factors governing this;
3 future prospects for development.

Main breeds

Have you ever noticed herdsmen in your area feeding cattle or driving them to a dipping tank? Could you name the breeds of cattle? Try to recollect a scene of animals at a dipping tank. If you had been observant, you would have noticed that there are two main breeds:
(a) the hump-backed zebu (see photo p. 18 Central Africa Section) which is said to have been introduced to Africa by Semitic people nearly fifteen hundred years ago. This breed has acclimatised itself to African conditions so well that it is the main type found throughout east, central and southern Africa.
b) a horned variety mainly found among the Ngoni and hence called the Ngoni cattle. This is possibly a cross-breed. It is believed this type was also introduced by Semites about 500 years ago.

Commercially, these two breeds are of relatively low value. Can you suggest reasons for this?

Since they are generally not properly looked after, their meat is tough and poor and milk production is low. Socially, however, they play a

Fruit at Mlombozi Estate

49

very important role. Cattle mean wealth in most agricultural communities. The larger the herd owned by an individual the higher the prestige he commands in his community. Where in Malaŵi is this especially true? Among the central and northern region Ngoni and Tumbuka peoples cattle are of particular significance in marriage ceremonies. A man wishing to marry will be required to pay several head of cattle for his bride. What name is given to this marriage custom? If you do not know the answer to the above question, ask your father or history teacher for more information.

Those of you who live near Blantyre or Zomba or near some European farms might have noted the difference between the breeds kept there and the two discussed above.

These have recently been introduced into the country. They include the high milk-yielding Frieslands and the South African Afrikander beef breed. Few Malaŵians keep these as they entail high capital expenditure and great care. This last paragraph explains why these breeds are mostly confined to European estates.

Cattle distribution and factors governing it

Study Fig. 26 showing cattle distribution in Malaŵi. Which regions have most cattle? Can you give three reasons for the high cattle population density in these areas?

Study the following statistics carefully. The cattle population is estimated to have increased by 4 per cent during 1980, from a population of 789 529 in 1979 to 820 000. Of the 820 000 head of cattle 410 000 were in the Central Region, especially Dedza, Ncheu and Lilongwe. 310 000 in the Northern Region and 100 000 in the Southern Region. What factors account for the lower cattle density in the Southern Region?

There are three main reasons: (1) more people live in the Southern region than in the other two regions; (2) more land is cultivated than elsewhere in Malaŵi, and (3) a large percentage of the region is infested with tsetse fly (see Fig. 27). The tsetse fly causes trypanosomiasis or 'Nagana', a deadly disease if not properly handled. The Department of Veterinary Services has, however, taken steps to limit the spread of this fatal disease by use of drugs and tsetse fighting teams.

Successful cattle raising is limited by other diseases such as tick-borne fever and foot and mouth disease. How can a cattle farmer deal with tick-borne disease? The only effective remedy to combat this is to destroy the ticks on the animals by dipping them once a week or spraying them at intervals. Dipping tanks found all over the country aim at this objective. Invasions of foot and mouth disease (chigodola) were common a decade ago. These originated from Tanzania and were confined to the area along the Songwe River border with that country. The disease was brought under control by stringent supervision of cattle movements. Quarantine regulations also limited the spread of this insidious disease.

Most areas in Malaŵi are suited to cattle because of adequate rainfall, but there is a lack of pasture during the dry season. At this time, the grasslands and plains are scorched and

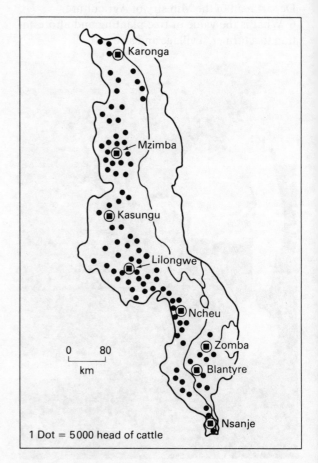

Fig. 26   Distribution of cattle

water is scarce. Few people can afford to stall-feed their animals. As a result of these problems, the animals become thin and, if they are slaughtered, the meat is tough and unpalatable.

The concentration of cattle in the Northern region has led to a shortage of meat in some years in the Southern region. Two reasons explain this, namely, inadequate transportation and a lack of cold storage facilities. With Danish aid, a cold storage plant has been built at Blantyre and another in Lilongwe is planned.

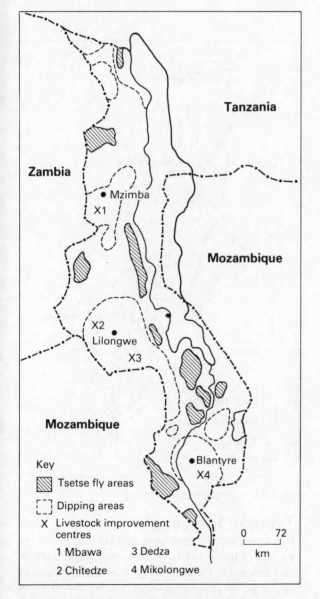

Fig. 27   Areas infected by tsetse flies in Malaŵi

Dairying

There is no large-scale dairying in Malaŵi and the government is trying to expand this aspect of the economy. A few European farmers have, however, successfully managed to maintain a satisfactory standard of dairying around the urban centres of Blantyre and Zomba. Why is dairying confined to these urban centres?

Prospects for development

According to the Department of Veterinary Services, Malaŵi's national herd increased by 3·5% in 1969 to an estimated 498 000 head. At the same time the increase in human numbers was 3·3% per annum! The increase in the national herd resulted from a comprehensive breeding policy being carried out at various livestock improvement centres. Find these in Fig. 27 and locate the centres in your atlas.

The table below illustrates the increased slaughterings by the Cold Storage Company.

Table 11   Cattle slaughterings 1976–1980

Year	Number of cattle
1976	61 000
1977	69 000
1978	7 000
1979	79 000
1980	82 000

What do these figures show?

Improvements in cattle raising can make a substantial contribution to the country's economy. There is great demand for quality beef and milk and this may be achieved by good housing, disease control, better feeding, and improved breeding and marketing.

Things to do

1 How can cattle feeding in Malaŵi in the dry months be improved?

2 Write down as many cattle products and their uses as you can think of.

3 Construct a pie-graph showing cattle slaughterings by the Cold Storage Company from 1976 to 1980.

4 Give an account of the distribution of cattle in Malaŵi, noting the factors which influence this distribution.

8   Fisheries (Malaŵi)

Some people think that fishing cannot be important in a landlocked state like Malaŵi. Do those of you who live in Malaŵi agree with this trend of thinking? Not at all. Have you seen big lorries with the sign FISH in your area? Where does the fish come from? Which are the main fishing areas in Malaŵi? When you have read through this chapter you will be able to answer some of the questions you are unable to answer now.

The rivers and lakes of Malaŵi abound in fish and many people along the lake shores supplement their subsistence agriculture with fishing. This is an important undertaking for two reasons:

1 Since most people in the country live on a protein-deficient diet based on starchy foods like maize and cassava, fish meets this deficiency.
2 The development of fisheries contributes substantially to the economy of the nation.

Fishing is also important, of course, as a sport which gives a number of people pleasure, satisfaction and recreation. Angling in Lake Malaŵi encourages tourism.

Fishing areas

Study Fig. 28 showing main fishing areas in Malaŵi. This map shows that the southern areas of Lake Malaŵi are heavily fished. Here are found in great abundance aquatic micro-organisms on which the fish feed. Other areas where fishing is done on a commercial scale include Lake Chilwa, Lake Malombe, Likoma Island, Nkhota Kota and Salima. The lower Shire River area is mainly important for subsistence fishing especially in the Elephant Marsh near Chiromo and Ndindi Marsh south of Nsanje.

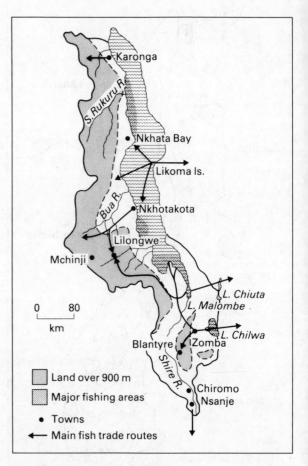

Fig. 28   Fishing areas and routes

Types of fish caught

Have you visited your local market and noted the variety of fish sold? Look at Figs. 29 and 30. Can you recognise these types of fish? Before reading on, write in your work-book four different types of fish you have seen being sold.

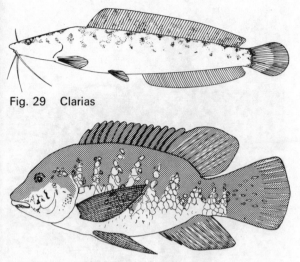

Fig. 29 Clarias

Fig. 30 Saro therodon (chambo)

It has been estimated that over 200 species of fish exist in Lakes Malaŵi and Chilwa but the main types are: Chambo or bream (Saro therodon spp), a rare species found nowhere else in the world, Nchila (Labio Mesops), Utaka (Haplochromis spp), 'Catfish' – Mlamba (Clarias, Bagras etc.) and Usipa (Eugraulicypris sardella).

Lake Malaŵi is generally deep except in the two southern ends and the main Chambo fishery is confined to these and the shallower lakes Malombe, Chiuta and Chilwa. The government established a small ice plant at Mangochi in order to encourage African fisherman and in 1957 the Cold Storage Company established a refrigeration plant in Limbe. This is capable of storing over 40 t of fish.

Fish-farming

In 1953, a small fish-farming demonstration was started at Nchenachena and training courses for prospective fish-farmers were started in 1956. By 1960, some 60 fish-ponds covering 7 ha were in use and more are planned. The Department of Game and Fisheries established a major unit for demonstrating fish-farming at Domasi near Zomba and prospects for fish-farming are great.

Fishing methods

Most African fisherman use the less efficient traditional methods of fishing such as the line, the long, narrow fishing baskets (Miono) and nets of various meshes made from some local trees that bear fibres such as 'bwazi' and Mlambe (baobab). Some use dug-out canoes (see photo) and employ nylon gill nets manufactured in Blantyre and Luchenza and various types of seine (see Figs.

Canoe making in Malaŵi. Trees used for dug-out canoes are becoming scarce.

Commercial fishing on Lake Malaŵi

74 and 75, Zambia Section).

Large-scale non-African fishing, concentrated on the south-east end of Lake Malaŵi, is strictly controlled. Why is fishing restricted and controlled? What would happen if fishing was left open to everyone at all seasons? In the area being considered, the main method of fishing is 'open water ring net', but gill-netting for Nchila and catfish plays a major part, especially in November and December when Saro therodon are breeding and ring netting is prohibited.

Transport and marketing

The map (Fig. 28) shows fish movement from main fishing areas. Until recently, the main feature of non-African fisheries was that transport and marketing of the fish was carried out by the fishing firms themselves. Now, the transportation of the bulk of the catch is undertaken by the Cold Storage Company in refrigerated vans to Blantyre where storage facilities are available. Vendors then buy fish at wholesale prices and they in turn sell it in the markets of the densely populated areas at retail prices.

Traditional method of fishing on Lake Malaŵi. Using a cane fish trap

Production

Commercial fish production has been on the increase. In 1948, less than 508 t of fish were produced. In 1958, over 4 000 t and in 1968 20 000 t were realised. In 1977 total landings reached 74 000 t and in 1980, 78 000 t valued at K10·90 million were produced. The Utaka type fish predominated the catches of the small-scale fishermen for the 1980 fishing season. Lake Chilwa registered the highest annual catch on record. Research and exploratory fishing continued on Lake Malaŵi waters.

Things to do
1 Using the information given in this chapter, calculate the percentage increase of fish caught between 1958 and 1977.
2 Visit a local market and try to identify the types of fish sold. Find out where they are caught and how.
3 Compare fishing on Lakes Kariba and Malaŵi.
4 Write an essay on subsistence fish production in Malaŵi.

9   Power (Malaŵi)

What are the various sources of power used in the world today? Can you name the commonest source of power that was used in Malaŵi about fifty years ago?

For some time in Malaŵi, imported coal has been used to generate electricity. From where do you think this coal was imported? Hwange in Zimbabwe and the Moatize Colliery near Tete in Mozambique have been the suppliers. The Middle East has also provided Malaŵi with fuel in the form of oil, and a few privately owned hydro-electric power plants have been in use in certain places in the country. Which countries make up the Middle East? How does the imported oil reach Malaŵi?

Malaŵi's hydro-electric power schemes

Which is Malaŵi's major hydro-electric power station? When did it come into being? Malaŵi's biggest river, the Shire, has a considerable power potential. The middle section of this river is broken by five main falls and cataracts. Look at Fig. 31 as you read this section and with the help of an atlas map of Malaŵi, note the positions of the main falls and cataracts referred to above. In this section of the Shire River, the Thyolo Highlands and the Kirk Ranges come close together like large pincers so that the river appears to wriggle its way southwards with difficulty. As it tumbles down, the river drops a total of about 420 m, giving an average slope of 5 m per km, thus making this section most suitable for development of water power. Engineers have estimated that the power potential of the middle Shire is equal to 600 MW, almost the same as the output of Kariba's south bank power station. So far two schemes, Nkula

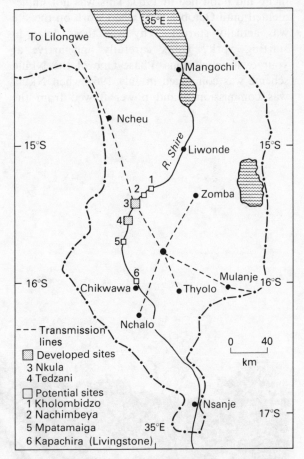

Fig. 31   Malaŵi's hydro electric power schemes

Falls (capacity 24 MW) and Tedzani Falls (capacity 20 MW) are in operation, the first being completed in 1966 and the second in 1973. A 66 kv transmission line between Nkula and Lilongwe was brought into operation in 1972 and a 3 MW diesel unit installed in the new capital. Likewise, a small amount of electricity is produced in the Northern Region by diesel plant.

Nkula Falls H.E.P. scheme

Study this photograph. What is the name of the tall tower in the right-hand corner of the photograph? What are those three big pipes called? What use are they? A hydro-electric power station was first proposed during the days of the Federation of Rhodesia and Nyasaland. A team of consultants surveyed the Shire with emphasis on the suitability of the Nkula site and its superiority over other sites in the middle Shire section. A report (the Jack Report) was finally submitted to the government and published in 1960. This was not implemented until October 1963 when work on the site was actually started. Why was there delay in starting work? Think carefully and arrive at your own conclusions. Phase One of the Nkula scheme was completed in July 1966 when Nkula was commissioned and power flowed from the site to Blantyre and most parts of the southern region for domestic and industrial purposes. Nkula, with three turbines, has a capacity of 24 MW, although initially installed capacity was 16 MW.

Why was Nkula selected rather than other suitable sites? Nkula overshadows other sites in three respects:

(1) it has the greatest natural head of water, (2) Nkula is close to Blantyre (48 km), the country's industrial and commercial hub, and (3) the flow of the Shire is more or less constant at Nkula since the building of the Liwonde barrage in 1965.

Look at Fig. 32. What feature of the river is shown here? At Nkula, the Shire makes a horseshoe bend giving a difference of 55 m between the upper and lower terminals of the bend. A tunnel, fully concrete-lined and partly steel-lined, was dug.

Nkula Falls hydro-electric station near Blantyre. From the surge chamber (the tall tower) the water passes into a valve house where the water supply to the individual turbines is controlled. From the valve house three steel penstocks lead the water down the hillside and into the power house

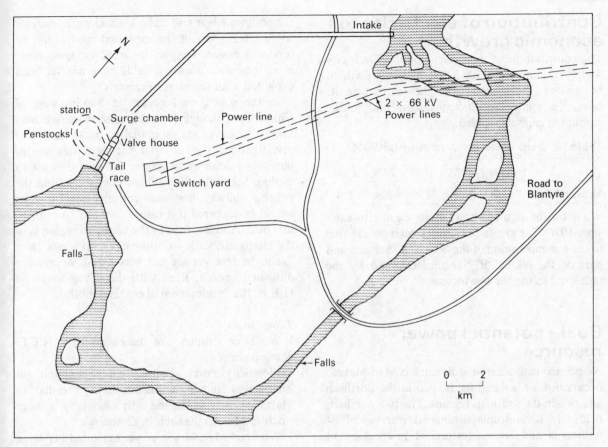

Fig. 32 Nkula falls H.E.P. scheme

It measures 1410 m long and is about 4 m in diameter. This conveys water from the upper terminal of the bend to a surge chamber over 33 m high and over 16 m in diameter (see photo p. 56). Where does the water go from this surge chamber? It is led into a valve house by three small tunnels and thence into three penstocks, each about 2 m in diameter to a power house set below ground level. The water's force turns huge turbines that in turn drive generators producing electricity. The electricity thus produced is 11 000 volts. Step-up transformers located in a switch yard higher up increase the voltage to 66 000 volts. How is the power conveyed to consuming centres from Nkula? This is done by overhead cables–high tension power transmission lines.

Nkula 'B' station came into operation in 1981 with an output of 36 MW. It is now in production and will be supplemented by new power trans-

mission lines to Lilongwe. The eventual capability of the plant will be 90 MW.

Tedzani scheme

What necessitated the development of the Tedzani Scheme? Greater demand for electricity by the manufacturing industries was the chief reason. Tedzani is 8 km south of Nkula. Of an estimated potential of 120 MW, 20 MW have already been developed and a further 20 MW are in the process of development. There have been estimates that a demand of the order of 10 to 20 MW, simply for bauxite mining on Mount Mulanje and an alumina processing plant, could be catered for by an extension at Tedzani or by development of one of a number of other suitable smaller hydro-electricity sites on the Shire River. Should this be inadequate, power from the Cabora Bassa Scheme on the Zambezi may be utilised for bauxite mining and alumina processing.

Contribution of electricity to economic growth

The contribution of the present public Electricity Supply Commission (ESCOM) to the growth of Malaŵi can be gauged from the increase in its sales, the number of its consumers and in the amount of capital involved.

Table 12 Sales of electricity units by ESCOM

Year	1976	1977	1978	1979	1980
Million kWh	252	265	274	308	354

What do the figures show about electricity sales since 1976? The greater increase in sales may be due to the commissioning of the Nkula 'A' Scheme and part of the Nkula 'B' Scheme. Demand by the industrial sector has also increased.

Coal – potential power resource

Associated with Karroo sediments, coal in Malaŵi occurs in four isolated fields, two in the northern and two in the southern regions. The two northern fields are Livingstonia (estimated reserves of 24 million t) and Nkana (estimated reserves of 14 million t). The latter, an extension of the larger Tanzania field, seems to offer the greatest possibilities for commercial production because the seam is shallower, the area less faulted and near to the Songwe River and Lake Malaŵi water systems so that transport of the exploited coal would be rendered easier. Despite these advantages, however, these two northern fields have not yet been exploited. Can you suggest reasons?

In the south, coal occurs at Sumbo west of Chiromo. Although it is the most extensive field known (reserves are estimated to be 45 million t) investigations showed that the field was so intensively folded as to render the coal difficult to exploit. Secondly, the field is some 80 km from the existing railway line and considerable expenses would be incurred if a railway was to be built to this field. Another field in the southern region is in the Thangadzi Valley southwest of Chikwawa. Here again the reserves are not very extensive and are difficult to reach. Even with the development of H.E.P., the development of coal is doubtful.

Things to do

1 What conditions are necessary for H.E.P. development?

2 Electricity costs about 2 cents per unit (in Zimbabwe) and 8 tambala (about 8 cents) in Malaŵi. Can you suggest why electricity is more costly in Malaŵi than it is in Zimbabwe?

3 Why has Malaŵi not as yet exploited her large deposits of bauxite?

4 Using electricity sales figures given in this chapter, show by a graph the increased sales between 1976 and 1980.

10   Industries and towns (Malaŵi)

Which part of the economy would you say is most important to Malaŵi in terms of cash: her manufacturing industry, farming, fishing or transport? Another question worth answering on this topic is: which sector of the economy has expanded the fastest? No doubt you stated that farming is the chief sector of the economy in terms of cash. This is quite correct. As we saw earlier, almost all Africans in Malaŵi derive at least part of their living from the soil, thus to all intents and purposes Malaŵi is an agricultural country.

You may have guessed that the manufacturing industry has grown the fastest. Those who know Blantyre well should know this from the number of new factories which have been established along Makata Road in the industrial area. From 1964 when Malaŵi became independent, the net output of all manufacturing industry has continued to increase at a compound growth rate of over 20% per annum. The number of employees in the manufacturing sector has equally risen by over 50%, half of whom are in the tea and tobacco industries.

Reasons for industrial growth

The expansion in industrial development can be attributed to the following factors:

1 The Malaŵi Development Corporation (MDC) was established in 1964 as the principal agency for economic development. It was initially financed by a K1 million grant from the government, and by 1969, this sum, together with other loans from overseas, was invested in some twenty-one subsidiaries and associate companies such as the Cold Storage Company, Nzeru Radio Company, the Commercial Bank of Malaŵi, etc.

2 The opening of several import-substitute industries after 1964. For example, sugar-refining at Nchalo, David Whitehead and Sons Limited–see photo (textile mill), Carlsberg Malaŵi Brewery, Chibuku Products, a plant manufacturing agricultural implements (Agrimal).

3 The opening of Nkula Falls Hydro-Electric Power Station (1966).

4 The government's desire (a) to reduce the country's dependence on overseas imports, and (b) to offer more employment with a view to raising the standard of living.

Until the above steps were taken, Malaŵi's industrial growth lagged far behind that of

The David Whitehead Textile factory

59

Zimbabwe. While Zimbabwean industries proved more attractive to foreign investors during the days of Federation, other economic factors also operated. Zimbabwean made goods would have been difficult to undercut; there was a lack of power, water or coal; the local market was very small because of a very low standard of living.

Structure of manufacturing industries

As a result of this heightened activity in industrial development, a significant change in the structure of manufacturing industries has taken place. Which of these firms do you think dominated Malaŵi's industrial sector before independence: mining and quarrying, soap making, tea and tobacco processing? If you guessed right, you said firms processing agricultural products dominated Malaŵi's industrial sector. With the growth of the manufacturing industries, the contribution of the manufacturing sector to the Gross Domestic Product (GDP) has steadily increased. By mid 1969, there were 140 fully licensed establishments in Malaŵi. This had increased to over 300 by 1980, over half of which were in Blantyre. What factors have attracted industries in Blantyre?

The Carlsberg Brewery, Blantyre

Classification of manufacturing industries

Sometimes, you will read about primary industry, secondary industry, and tertiary industry. Farming and fishing belong to the first group, flour milling, and fruit canning to the second and repairing of motor vehicles, teaching and banking are in the tertiary industry group. Geographers sometimes use the term heavy industries. If a manufacturing industry uses large quantities of raw material or produces bulky products such as large diesel engines, it is classified as heavy. On the other hand an industry involving the use of smaller quantities of raw materials, causing little or no atmosphere pollution and producing less bulky products, is generally referred to as light.

Table 13

Name of industry	Type or classification
	i.e. whether primary, secondary or tertiary
Breadmaking	
Soapmaking	
Transport	
Forestry	

Think of several industries located in Blantyre or in a town of comparable size in Zimbabwe or Zambia.

Agricultural processing industries

Malaŵi's secondary manufacturing is dominated by agricultural processing industries. Study the following figures for 1981.

Table 14

Description	Quantity sold (million kg)	Value (K million)
Tea	29·92	25·2
Tobacco	53·7	58·8

Source: Economic Report, 1981

Export performance was good with merchandise export receipts growing by about 16% per annum to K189·8 million in 1979/80. These statistics reveal that almost half the foreign revenue in 1979/80 was from tea and tobacco only. If to this were added groundnuts, rice and other agriculturally processed products, the picture would even better reveal the importance of agriculture to the Malaŵian economy.

Miscellaneous industries

Among others, the following belong to this group: the footwear industry, the clothing industry, sawmilling and furniture manufacturing, production of chemicals, printing and publishing.

Traditional craft industries

What are traditional craft industries? If you were a Malaŵian and you were at home in the evening, you could probably see your father, uncle or other relative making a basket from prepared bamboo or a net from string. Have you seen a wood carver fashioning wooden spoons and stools? These uncoordinated and, in most cases, small-scale undertakings are referred to as traditional crafts industries. These can be very useful both in preservation of culture and in promoting the industrial sector of the economy.

In an unpublished survey of cottage industries in Malaŵi conducted by the Ministry of Trade and Industry in 1969, an attempt was made to correlate the various activities and make recommendations as to those which could be exploited in the national interest. This survey revealed that the following crafts are commonplace in the Republic: basketry, wood and ivory carving, making of shields, spears and knives. Of special note is basket making which meets a small part of the demand of the tea industry. The survey revealed that over 40 000 tea-pluckers employed in the tea industry during the peak season use approximately 400 000 baskets a year, and that about 90% of these are imported from Mozambique. It was further estimated that about 90% of Malaŵi's population are skilled in one craft or another. The work produced can serve the people's own needs or be sold to the affluent class and to tourists.

Tourism

One industry that is showing signs of development is the tourist industry. Malaŵi has some of the finest scenery, fishing and water sport and game reserves in south central Africa. The towering Sapitwa peak on Mount Mulanje contrasts with the deep rift valley in which Lake Malaŵi lies.

Mt Mulanje. A great mass of syenite

National Game Park at Nyika plateau

61

Cape Maclear. Name the tourist attractions in this photograph.

In an attempt to boost the tourist industry, the government has a very ambitious programme of road building. Hotels and rest houses are being built and improved. Think of places in Malaŵi which tourists might like to visit and suggest factors which attract these visitors.

Major towns

The 1977 census in Malaŵi revealed that 9% of the population lives in urban centres. The major towns are Blantyre, Zomba and Lilongwe. These main urban centres have certain functions, administrative, commercial, industrial, social and recreational, to mention only a few.

Blantyre City: Population 250 000 (1980)

Study Fig. 33 and note the site of Blantyre and its position. Named after David Livingstone's birthplace in Lanarkshire, Scotland, Blantyre was founded in 1876 by a party of missionaries led by Henry Henderson. To which church did these missionaries belong?

In 1907, Limbe grew up some five miles south-east of Blantyre when the railway line from Nsanje reached the site. Later on, the headquarters of the Imperial Tobacco Company was established in Limbe. Both towns became mayoralties in 1948 and with the area between them becoming steadily built up, they were amalgamated in 1956. In 1959, the combined town was given the status of a municipality and on 6 July, 1966, Blantyre and Limbe became the City of Blantyre. A study of the 1:50 000 map sheet of Blantyre shows that the city is hemmed in on all sides by hills—Ndirande, Soche, Bangwe and Mpingwe and that it is situated at an altitude of between 1033 and 1066 m. An early trading centre and mission station, Blantyre is now the country's major industrial and route centre. The railway from Beira passes through Blantyre to its terminus at Mchinji near Chipata. Blantyre's importance has further been increased by the proximity of Chileka, at present the country's chief airport situated some 16 km away. Fast growing peri-urban areas are within easy reach of Blantyre. Look at Fig. 33 again and find these—Ndirande, Soche, Zingwangwa and Chilomoni. Blantyre has a very small central business district which is quieter and less built up than the comparable parts of either Lusaka or Harare.

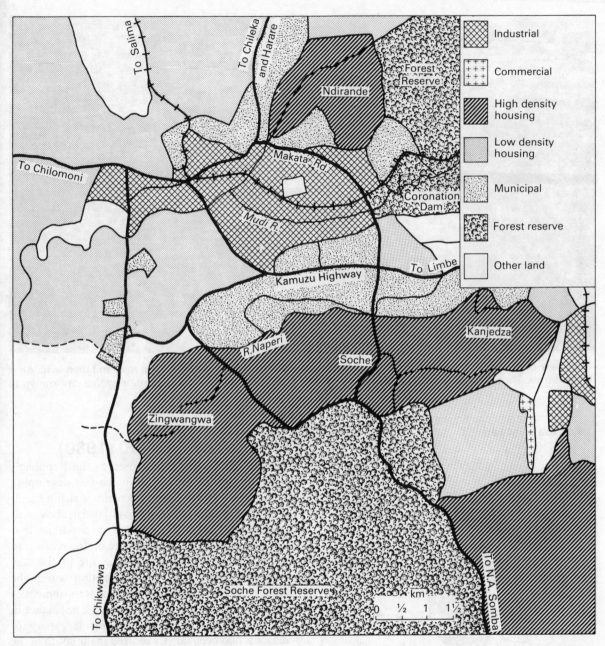

Fig. 33 Blantyre City

Zomba:
Population 24 000 (1980)

Study Fig. 34. Where is the municipality of Zomba situated with respect to the Zomba Massif? Zomba was chosen as a convenient site at the confluence of slave trade routes. The British Government was determined to exert all its efforts to put an end to slavery and Zomba provided a fine observation point for this purpose.

With the establishment of a British sphere of influence over Nyasaland, Zomba became the seat of government though not easily accessible from the rest of the country. The movement of the capital to Lilongwe and the building of Chancellor College has changed Zomba into a university town.

Aerial view of part of Blantyre city. Those of you who know the city should draw a street map and then mark on it the land uses. Those of you who have never seen the city should compare the street pattern with a city known to you

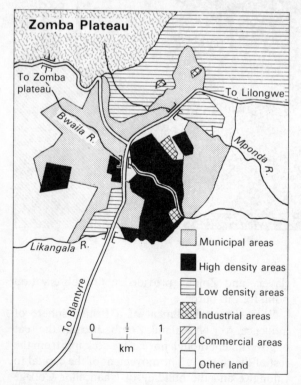

Fig. 34 Zomba

Lilongwe:
Population 125 000 (1980)

See Fig. 35. Since being chosen as the Republic's seat of government, Lilongwe is a fast developing town. It lies in the Lilongwe plain, a rich agricultural area, at an altitude of about 1 066 m above sea-level. Study Fig. 35 again. It is apparent that Lilongwe is a route focus. Where do the roads lead to? Lilongwe was chosen as the site of the new capital because of its central position within the country. It was considered that the establishment of a new capital would help to correct the imbalance in economic development which, for a variety of reasons, had been largely centred in the south of the country, particularly in Blantyre. The decision to resite the capital was substantiated by the passing of the Capital City Development Corporation Act in 1968 and the capital was officially transferred from Zomba on 1st January, 1975.

The resiting of the capital has been planned along with the Lilongwe Land Development Scheme, a huge enterprise concerned with improving agricultural production on some 400 000 ha of some of the best land in the country. It is hoped that these

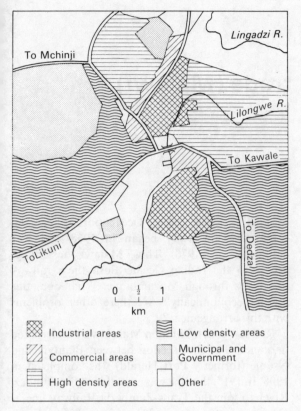

Fig. 35   Lilongwe

Legend:
- Industrial areas
- Commercial areas
- High density areas
- Low density areas
- Municipal and Government
- Other

developments together will provide a new growth point through attracting new investment and commercial and industrial expansion on a growing scale. It is expected that the population of Lilongwe will be 500 000 by the end of the century.

Liwonde

Some 50 km from Zomba on the M1 road to Lilongwe lies Liwonde where the Nacala railway crosses the Shire. Liwonde has bright prospects for growth. Already, it is the headquarters for the district adminstration of Machinga district (previously known as Kasupe district). Its situation in the Shire Valley is most ideal for expansion, and being on the main road to Lilongwe and on the railway line to Blantyre and Nacala, it is going to be an important route focus. Several tourist attractions will help Liwonde to grow. These include the hot baths near the railway station, the barrage, the game reserve and fishing on the River Shire. The Liwonde Brush factory, Admarc Warehouses and depot and similar establishments will further attract people to Liwonde.

Things to do
1 On a sketch map of Malaŵi, show the routes taken by raw materials (for agricultural processing industries) to reach Blantyre.
2 You are a visitor to Malaŵi. State, with the aid of a large sketch map, where you will go and what you will see.
3 Discuss the advantages of Lilongwe over Zomba as Malaŵi's capital city.
4 Discuss the problems which have hindered industrial development in Malaŵi.

11   Communications and trade (Malaŵi)

Like Zimbabwe and Zambia, Malaŵi is a land-locked country. What does this statement mean? Think of Malaŵi's external contacts and trade. What are the practical problems faced by a country without a sea-board? Consider the part played by water transport before and during the colonial era when roads were non-existent. The above considerations will help you to see that for a long time water transport played a vital role in the communications system of Malaŵi. Lake Malaŵi, the Shire and the Zambezi were major highways, despite sandbanks along certain stretches of the Shire and the varying levels of the lake in the 1890s. These problems made it difficult for boats to ascend the Shire to Chiromo. What did the Colonial Government do in an attempt to promote trade, economic development, efficient administration and adequate contact with the outside world? Other forms of transport had to be developed. What were these? First, the era of railway construction set in, to be followed later by tarred road building and air transport.

Railways

Look at an atlas map of the north-east United States of America and note the density of the railway network. What conclusion can you reach when you compare this map with that of Malaŵi?

Malaŵi is linked to the sea via the 3·6 km Zambezi Bridge at Sena. The Trans-Zambezia Railway connects the port of Beira with the southern end of the Zambezi Bridge at Sena and the Malaŵi Railway, together with its subsidiary the Central African Railways Company, continues from there to Blantyre and Salima.

Construction work on the rail link to connect Malaŵi with the Indian Ocean port of Nacala, some 1046 km away began in 1968 and was completed in 1970. Thus Malaŵi has direct access to the Indian Ocean. Both these railway lines pass through Mozambique. What does this involve economically? Are there other problems with this arrangement?

Railway construction in Malaŵi was undertaken in stages. The first section between Blantyre and Nsanje (formerly Port Herald) was completed in 1908. In 1915, this line was extended to the Zambezi River to join the Trans-Zambezia Railway line at Dondo junction some 30 km from Beira. From Blantyre, the line was extended to Chipoka in 1935 and later to Salima, some 16 km from the shores of Lake Malaŵi. There were plans to reach the lake, but these were abandoned. Why was this abandoned? To answer this question, look at an atlas map of Malaŵi showing relief features.

The Malaŵi Railways headquarters are at Limbe. The line is single track with a narrow gauge of 1·09 m. In 1970, there were 976 km of railways, 288 km of which comprised the Trans-Zambezia Railways. The line between Chiromo and Blantyre passes through steep gradients as it ascends the Shire Highlands from the rift valley below. It passes through the Nsanje/Chiromo districts. What is the main crop carried by the railways from these districts? Trace the route of the railway line and note two other districts it passes through before reaching Blantyre, and name the most important commodity carried from these districts. Further developments include realignment in the southern section, and the now completed Salima-Lilongwe-Chipata extensions (Fig. 36).

The tonnage hauled by Malaŵi Railways decreased from 210100 tonnes in 1976 to 200900 tonnes in 1978. Why do you think this took place? Hint: previously Zambia was extensively using the Nacala railway line before the opening of the Tan-Zam pipeline. What has been the trend in passenger traffic? Can you explain the likely cause of this trend?

Table 15 Traffic on Malaŵi Railways (1976–1980)

Year	Net tonne	Passengers
1976	210 100	953 700
1977	201 100	964 200
1978	200 900	1 083 800
1979	221 200	1 136 400
1980	228 300	1 238 000

Note the trends in both net tonnage and number of passengers carried on the railways since 1976.

Water transport

How did Arab slave dealers transport slaves from south central Africa to the Indian Ocean? You may have answered that the Arabs used Lake Malaŵi. Indeed the lake played a vital role in the transporting of ivory and slaves from this part of the world to the Indian Ocean ports on the African coast. With the inception of the Ilala by the British in the nineteenth century, the lake was more extensively used despite the hindrances referred to earlier. Today, Malaŵi Railways operated a passenger and cargo service on Lake Malaŵi using four motor vessels, five tugs, fourteen barges and a motor launch. The four main steamers are the Ilala, the Mpasa, the Nkhwazi and the Chauncy Maples. The Ilala and the Chauncy Maples are mainly passenger steamers while the remainder are cargo boats. Well over 75% of the total lake cargo is carried by the four steamers. What type of cargo do you think is carried from the northern region? What forms the bulk of cargo from the southern to the northern and central regions?

In 1964, the lake service moved 14 061 t of freight and 66 000 passengers. In 1968, corresponding figures were 18 358 and 108 000 respectively. Why was there an increase in either case? Previously, the Ilala was the only passenger ship on the lake. With the commissioning of the Chauncy Maples as a passenger ship, more people could be carried.

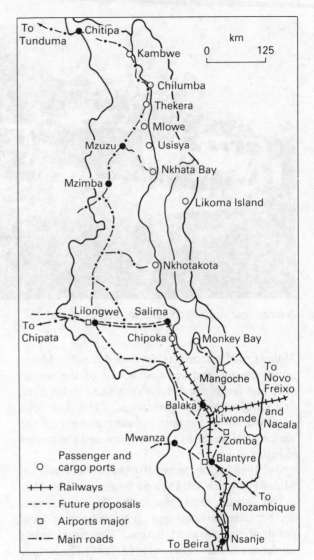

Fig. 36 Malaŵi transportation map

Prospects for the future

The Ministry of Transport and Malaŵi Railways are carrying out surveys and investigations for the provision of additional harbour facilities, the canalisation of the Shire River to Liwonde, and the further utilisation of the lake as a waterway. The conclusions of this study will take into account future plans for the Viphya pulpwood project.

Road transport

Road transport has certain advantages over rail transport. Can you name three advantages? The

67

A passenger steamer on Lake Malaŵi

Malaŵi road system has developed rapidly. Major improvements and re-construction of the secondary and feeder roads have continued to be given first priority by the government. This has been done mainly to support the development of the agricultural sector of the economy and the tourist industry.

By 1968, there were 10 688 km of roads in Malaŵi of which 480 km were bituminised, 992 km gravel and the remainder earth. The trunk roads are organised around and connected to the focal points of Blantyre and Lilongwe. What problem has hindered road development in Malaŵi? The answer is the hilly nature of the country but, despite this drawback, there are links with Mozambique, Zimbabwe and Zambia and trade between Malaŵi and these countries flows freely.

Air transport

Air transport is becoming increasingly important in Malaŵi. Air Malaŵi, which became an independent airline on 1 September, 1967, assumed full responsibility for all its services in January, 1968, when Central African Airways (CAA) ceased to operate as an airline.

Air Malaŵi operates internal scheduled flights from Blantyre airport at Chileka to Lilongwe, Mzimba, Mzuzu, Karonga, Chitipa and Zomba.

Regular external flights include those to Harare, Lusaka and Beira, while a number of international airlines also operate. These include British Airways, East African Airways (EAA). Air Zimbabwe, Zambia Airways and South African airlines.

Charter aircraft operate in Malaŵi and it is possible to fly to remote parts of the country at short notice and at tourist fares. Since 1967, Blantyre airport at Chileka has been developed and equipped with modern landing facilities. The table below shows how air traffic has increased at Chileka airport since 1964.

Traffic at Chileka Airport

The figures in Table 16 shows declines in both passengers and freight at Chileka in 1980. This trend is likely to continue now that Kanuzu International Airport at Lilongwe is fully operational.

Table 16

Year	Passengers	Freight (000 kg)	Mail (000 kg)
1977	179 798	14 557	246
1978	203 568	13 380	280
1979	216 780	20 530	323
1980	188 555	12 317	284

Chileka International Airport

Table 17 Trade statistics 1980

Export	% of total	Value (Km)
Tobacco	47	105·4
Tea	13	30·3
Sugar	16	36·3
Groundnuts	7	15·9
Cotton	2	4·5

Exported to	
U.K.	28
U.S.A.	17
Netherlands	8
South Africa	3
W. Germany	8
Zambia	2
Japan	2
Others	27

Proportion of imports	1979	1980	1981
Petroleum Products	11·7	13·9	15·9
Fertiliser	3·7	4·3	4·7
Consumer goods	14·5	11·2	14·1
Capital goods	35·6	38·3	30·0
Intermediate and other	34·5	32·3	35·3

Trade

The feature of Malaŵi's trade, and indeed of all developing countries, is that raw materials are exported to and manufactured goods are imported from the industrialised countries. As Malaŵi increases its tempo of manufacturing, this imbalance will change for the better.

Import statistics show the dominance of capital goods importation, though declining, followed by petroleum products steeply increasing. Similarly, there are increases in the proportion of fertiliser and consumer goods, while Intermediate goods remain a fairly steady proportion of the total. Most of Malaŵi's imports come from the U.K., South Africa, the U.S.A. and the Netherlands. Trade between Malaŵi and her immediate neighbours has not been fully developed. It is hoped this will improve in due course.

Things to do

1 Discuss the importance of a lake shore road to Malaŵi.

2 Visit your local shops and note the foreign goods sold. Find out their origin and locate this on a world map.

3 Draw a map of Malaŵi to show the main flight routes within the country.

69

12 Population (Malaŵi)

The population of Malaŵi has been increasing at a very high rate since the end of inter-tribal warfare. This increase has been so much that pressure on the land has become serious. This is because there has not been a corresponding increase in industry and commerce to absorb the increased labour supply. Consequently, living standards have remained low. In 1921, the country's population was estimated at 1 200 000. By 1960, this figure had swollen to 2 840 000. This shows that in forty years, the population had more than doubled. In 1966, Malaŵi's population was 4 042 400 and the census of 1977 gave the total as 5 571 567. What factors have contributed to this population increase?

A study of population growth shows that natural increase and immigration are two principal factors that contribute to population growth. Since the end of inter-tribal warfare natural increase has been greater. Increased medical facilities have arrested high death rates and this has resulted in increased longevity among adults.

Another factor that has been responsible for population increase in Malaŵi is immigration. Studies of population movements in central Africa have revealed that large numbers of people moved into Malaŵi from neighbouring Mozambique to seek employment on European estates, to settle in the better watered areas of Malaŵi during successions of droughts such as were recorded in Mozambique between 1925 and 1932, and to follow relations permanently resident in Malaŵi. Imagine you are a village headman or chief. A large number of families enter your village to settle. What problems are you faced with? How will you deal with these problems? Consider this

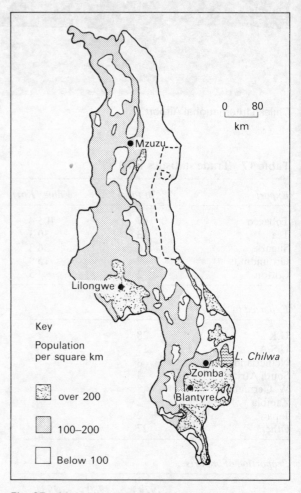

Fig. 37   Malaŵi population distribution

with respect to Malaŵi and reach your own conclusions.

Population distribution

Look at Fig. 37 showing Malawi's population distribution. Compare this map with that showing relief. How do the two maps compare? What conclusions can you reach? Study the density map from an atlas. Which areas are sparsely populated and why?

From the above maps and conclusions drawn from their study, it will be apparent that Malawi's population is unevenly distributed. The 1966 census showed an increasing population density from north to south with an average of about 20 persons to the square km in the northern region, 43 in the central region and 68 in the southern region, giving an overall population density of 44 per km²; by 1977 this was 48 per km² and is one of the highest in Africa, exceeded only by Ruanda (108 per km²), Burundi (95 per km²), and Nigeria (60 per km²). The neighbouring countries in central and eastern Africa show lower densities: Zambia 7, Mozambique 9, Zimbabwe 17, Tanzania 10, and Republic of South Africa 14.

Look at the relief map of Malawi again. What factors contribute to the density differences? In the Republic, density differences reflect the dominance of high uninhabited plateaus in the northern region and the relative inaccessibility of the area. The south, however, with earlier economic development and easier accessibility has the highest densities. The area north of Blantyre is the most densely peopled in Malawi. This area includes the Chileka Plain, which is agriculturally rich, and the Chiradzulu District. Densities here reach 360 per km². Other highly populated areas in the south are the Thyolo and Mulanje tea-growing areas with densities of over 80 per km², the Lisungwe River Valley and the Shire Valley, especially between Liwonde and Lake Malawi, and south of the Elephant Marsh where densities exceed 40 per km². Can you suggest reasons why these areas support higher densities?

In general, low densities in Malawi are found along the escarpment zones where soils are thin and poor, the plateaus of the Vipya and Nyika, where climatic conditions are bleak and communications difficult, and in the hills where there is a lack of water during the dry season.

Composition of Malawi's population

Of the population of 5·57 million people in 1977, there were about 10 000 Asians and 6 000 whites. What do these figures tell you about Malawi's population? The Asians are mainly traders and businessmen while the European population is mainly composed of missionaries, civil servants, farmers and a few businessmen. Of these two alien groups, 80% of the Europeans and 72% of the Asians live in the southern region especially in the urban areas of Blantyre and Zomba.

In 1977, only 9% of the total population were urban dwellers. This situation is typical of developing countries in Africa. The excess of females, 2·14 million as compared wiuth 1·9 million males, partly reflects the migration of males to the neighbouring African countries for employment. It was estimated that about a quarter of the male labour force is employed outside the country. This state of affairs can only change if Malawi can develop better paid jobs in commercial agriculture and in manufacturing industry.

Things to do

1 Construct a pie-graph showing percentage of total population by sex: 1911–1977.

Table 18 Selected population figures (%)

	1911	1921	1926	1931	1945	1966	1977
Males	44	46	47	47	46	47	48
Females	56	54	53	53	54	53	52

2 Which areas in Malawi are densely populated? Account for this.

3 Discuss the effect of the loss of able-bodied men to the economy of Malawi.

13 Location, geology, relief, water resources and climate

Features of geology and relief (Zimbabwe)

Geographers are keen to find out much about rocks as it helps them to explain such matters as relief and the distribution of soils, economic minerals and underground water. We should, then, ask ourselves, three questions about rock type in Zimbabwe. First, in what ways does this rock affect relief? Secondly, does it contain any economic minerals? Thirdly, does it have a distinctive type of soil? Fortunately for us, we do not need to consider every rock type in the country since many of the rocks have only a limited influence in these three respects. Fig. 38 shows those rocks which are significant to geographers and you will already know something about some of them. In making your own notes on geology it would help if you compiled a table like the one below and filled it in as you go along.

Table 19

Rock type	Relief	Soil	Minerals	Other points
Gold belts Granites				

The line in Fig. 38 marked by dashes divides Zimbabwe into two distinct regions. To the east lie the older rocks of which the most extensive is granite. Within the granite area occur several large patches of rocks called gold belts. Here, we find Zimbabwe's towns and cities founded by pioneers who sought to make their fortune in gold; through these gold belts pass the railway lines of the country and on them too, we find some of Zimbabwe's richest soils.

Gold belts

The gold belts consist of a variety of metamorphic rocks which do not all have the same resistance to weathering. Resistant rocks like banded ironstone make up kopjes and ridges as in Harare. Schists usually form low ground, frequently occupied by vleis or streams. There are many other rock types and all of them together give rise to a hilly relief, often a trial to the cyclist. In addition, the different rocks are associated with different soils most of which are red clays. The black soils of the vleis are the result of poor drainage and are not associated with any particular rock. Minerals, other than gold, mined in these belts include chromite at Shurugwi (this town is not on the Great Dyke), asbestos at Mashava and iron ore at Redcliff.

Granite

Granite occupies some 40% of the country and over this large expanse the relief is undulating despite the many kopjes and dwalas that are photographed and painted. Nonetheless, the Matopos and Domboshawa reveal granite hills and boulders in all their splendour (see photo on page 4). Overlying the granite are grey to pink, sandy soils which are not inherently fertile owing to their porosity which favours leaching. This means that all soluble plant foods like nitrates and phosphates are washed down below the plant roots quite readily. However, granite soils respond well to fertilisation.

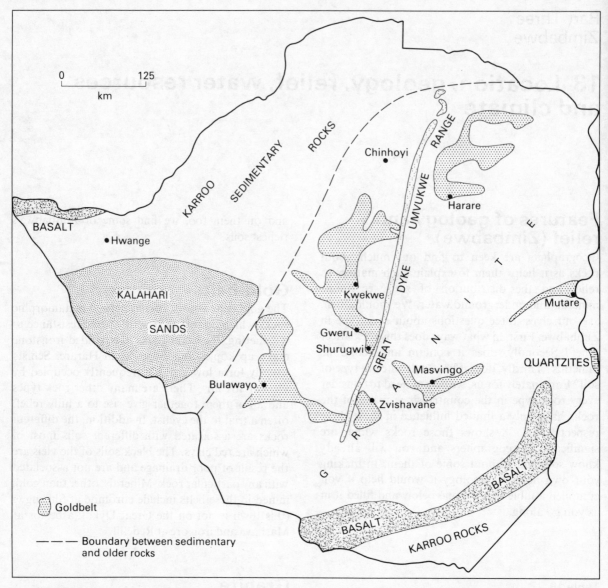

Fig. 38 Zimbabwe geological map

The Great Dyke

The Great Dyke is a prominent feature of the geology map because of its elongated shape and its length of over 515 km. Where the rocks of the Great Dyke are more resistant than the surrounding rocks, hills occur as in the Umvukwe Range. Further south, it does not form the skyline. Economically, the Dyke is rich in chromite and it also contains reserves of platinum. Soils of the Dyke are red clays which cannot support crops because of difficiencies of trace elements in the soil.

However, there are scattered areas of livestock-rearing.

Basalt and Karroo rocks

In the south-east of Zimbabwe lie rocks of Karroo age and one of these is basalt. It merits study because of the self-ploughing soil to which it gives rise. In the dry winters the clay soil contracts and it cracks severely: soil particles fill the cracks. In the wet seasons the clay expands rapidly after

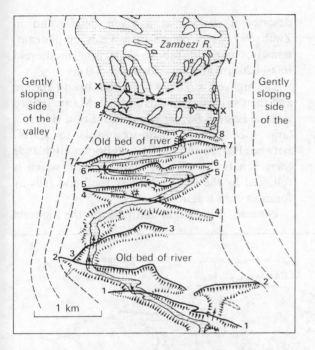

Zambezi R.

Gently
sloping
side
of the
valley

Gently
sloping
side
of the

Old bed of river

Old bed of river

1 km

Fig. 39 The present position of the Victoria Falls is marked by the line numbered 8. Other lines show earlier positions. Lines X and Y indicate future positions. Each of the numbered lines marks an east-west line of weakness which the Zambezi erodes into a deep gorge. At the lip of the Falls, erosion is greatest at the weakest point where a gorge is eventually cut. This gorge will follow a roughly north-south direction. At the next east-west line of weakness the river resumes the erosion of another waterfall.

rains and since it can only expand upwards it tends to turn over. This self-ploughing action can be labour-saving to the African wheat and cotton cultivators on the Chisumbanje irrigation scheme. Within the Karroo rocks are deposits of coal as yet unmined.

To the west of the dividing line Karroo rocks also outcrop. These rocks were laid down at the same time as those in the south-east; in fact, there were two huge lakes on either side of the present watershed. To the west of the line the relief is flattish. The resistant Karroo rocks form flat-topped plateaus, while the less resistant rocks like mudstones form the lower ground. Coal is the main mineral found and there are a few fields other than Hwange including the Maamba field north of Lake Kariba.

Basalt outcrops also appear at the surface around the Victoria Falls; indeed, the falls and gorges below them have been cut in six flows of basalt. The zig-zag course of the gorges suggests that there were lines of weakness in the basalt. Fig. 39 suggests a possible formation.

The Victoria Falls and some of the gorges. Compare this photograph with Fig. 39 noting the position of the former falls.

Kalahari Sands

The Kalahari Sands were deposited by wind and they give a level landscape. The associated soils are infertile and lack water because of their porosity. Yet, they support forest. Why? Turn to page 85 for the answer.

Relief

Zimbabwe is located on part of the Great African Plateau which covers much of Southern Africa. A plateau is an elevated surface which is fairly level but it can be deeply cut up. Veld is the word used to describe a surface at a given height and in Zimbabwe we recognize three velds or plateaus, namely, highveld (above 1 200 m), middleveld (600–1 200 m) and lowveld (under 600 m).

The highveld stretches from Plumtree to Harare and then swings eastwards through Maronderu to join the Eastern Border Highlands. From Harare a large lobe extends north-westwards to Karoi. Between Harare and the Eastern Border Highlands there is a bridge of land above 1 500 m which is followed by the Harare-Mutare road and railway for most of its length.

Because of its height and position the highveld

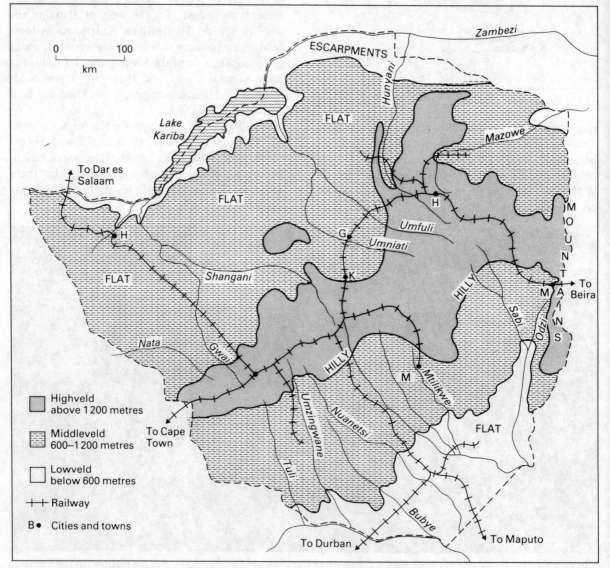

Fig. 40   Relief and drainage of Zimbabwe

forms the central watershed of the country. Most rivers drain to the Zambezi and Sabi-Limpopo and many short streams flow down the slopes of the Eastern Border Highlands. The following rivers should be noted:

(i)   rivers draining to the Zambezi: Gwai, Shangani, Umniati, Umfuli, Mazowe.
(ii) rivers draining to the Sabi: Odzi, Lundi, Chiredzi, Mtilikwe, Tokwe.
(iii) rivers draining to the Limpopo: Tuli, Umzingwane, Bubye, Nuanetsi.
(iv) rivers draining to the Makarikari Pans: Nata.

The surface of the central watershed is flat or gently undulating over large areas but usually one can see hills or kopjes. Granite landscapes are particularly well developed in the Matopos to the south of Bulawayo. The gold belts which occur on the highveld frequently give hilly relief because of the varying resistance of their rocks.

The Eastern Border Highlands comprise three sets of mountains as shown in Fig. 5, namely, the Inyanga Mountains, the Vumba and the Chimanimani Range. These mountains mask the edge of the Zimbabwean plateau and the main gap through the escarpment is the Mutare gap. Mountain scenery, softwood forests and varied crops such as tea, coffee and deciduous fruit give this area a distinctive character within Zimbabwe. The tourist industry is partially developed.

The middleveld (600–1 200 m) borders the high-veld and this plateau is considerably cut up or dissected by rivers. The rivers are in their middle courses and the relief is very marked in the Sabi-Limpopo basin. To the west of the central water-shed the middleveld is flattish over wide areas. The straightness of the railway line from Gwai to Dett indicates the flatness of the land which is due to the Kalahari sands.

The lowveld (below 600 m) is located along the northern border of the country, in the south-east and in a small pocket where the Mazowe River leaves Zimbabwe. The lowveld is undulating with a few isolated hills and numerous swamps near the larger rivers.

In Zimbabwe where rainfall decreases greatly from east to west and from north to south, relief plays a major part in soil formation. On the higher areas which are wetter, rainfall is heavy enough to help in the weathering of the rock to some depth. This leads to deep soils which are, however, well leached. On the lowveld where rainfall is low, the soils are generally shallow but not heavily leached so that plant foods are not carried downwards by water.

Water resources

While relief is an important influence on man's activities, it is the availability of water which has the greatest influence over most of Zimbabwe. As you read on page 6, high evaporation rates, unreliability of rainfall and its seasonal nature mean that farmers must conserve water. The government too must conserve or use water wisely in their financing of dam construction and borehole sinking.

Dam sizes vary greatly as is shown in Fig. 41 Broad shallow dams are inefficient since they lose much water by evaporation. Some rates of evaporation are given in the table below.

The majority of dams in this area were built in the 1960s and all are directed towards irrigation. On the other hand, the dams closer to the Central

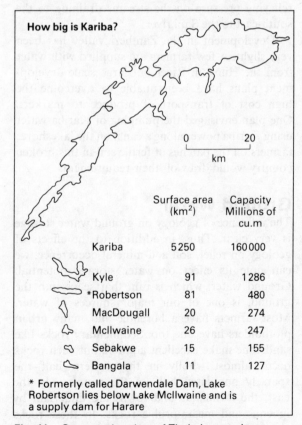

How big is Kariba?

	Surface area (km²)	Capacity Millions of cu.m
Kariba	5 250	160 000
Kyle	91	1 286
*Robertson	81	480
MacDougall	20	274
McIlwaine	26	247
Sebakwe	15	155
Bangala	11	127

* Formerly called Darwendale Dam, Lake Robertson lies below Lake McIlwaine and is a supply dam for Harare

Fig. 41   Comparative sizes of Zimbabwean dams

Table 20 Evaporation and rainfall at selected stations

Place	Evaporation (mm per annum)	Rainfall (mm per annum)
Binga	1 650	649
Beitbridge	1 625	332
Goetz (Bulawayo)	1 420	540
Lake McIlwaine	1 420	829

Watershed are used as reservoirs. Bulawayo, for example, has four dams for her industrial and domestic uses: Umzingwane, Ncema, Inyankuni, and Khami.

Some Zimbabwean engineers have suggested that new towns be developed off the Central Watershed in order that their water supplies may be more easily obtained. At present, most Zimbabwean towns on the watershed must have water pumped to them over considerable distances. Many argue that Bulawayo's supply should have been obtained largely from tributaries of the Zambezi, thus relieving pressure on the streams draining to the south-east to the Sabi river.

Development in the Zambezi valley has been very slight. A few farmers are supplied with water from the Hunyani River but large scale development plans have been unable to overcome the high cost of transport of produce to markets. One plan envisaged the pumping of Kariba water using Kariba power along a canal on the lakeshore; farmers on the patches of fertile soil in this broken country would draw off their requirements.

Ground water

The influence of geology on ground water storage is very clear. Thus, in addition to the effects of geology on relief, soil and mineral occurrence, we can note its effect on water storage ·potential. Ground water, which is rain that seeps into the ground, is one of our major sources of water. Most farmers have a borehole and many urban plotholders have one too. Sedimentary rocks like sandstone make excellent aquifers but such rocks occur almost wholly in the western half–the sparsely populated half–of the country. In the east, the farmlands and towns are underlain by igneous and metamorphic rocks. In these rocks the water is stored in cracks, joints and zones of decomposed rock. There is no water table in such rocks as the storage areas are not interconnected to any extent. Siting of boreholes is therefore a tricky business.

Despite these disadvantages, some of the crystalline (igneous and metamorphic rocks as contrasted with non-crystalline, sedimentary rocks) rocks yield copious water supplies. At the contact of the Great Dyke and adjacent rocks in the Midland and Lomagundi areas water supply is adequate. The greenstones which are metamorphosed igneous rocks underlie much of the Gatooma district and have given fair amounts. The greenstones of the Arcturus district, to the east of Harare, have yielded prolifically. On the other hand, the same kind of rock in the Bulawayo area lacks water.

A metamorphic rock which resembles a rotted slate in appearance is phyllite (pronounced fillight). This rock underlies Marlborough township, north-east of Harare, and each year the township pumps millions of litres from it.

Granites cover nearly half of Zimbabwe but unfortunately they vary greatly in their ground water potential. Where rainfall is heavier, in the north and east, the granites give favourable yields, but in the south and west of the country their supplies are very limited.

The Karroo sandstones in the west of Zimbabwe have been drilled by Zimbabwe Railways at several points along the Bulawayo-Victoria Falls line. High yields–over 45 000 litres per hour–were obtained.

The Kalahari sands, whose extent is shown in Fig. 38, are highly porous and for this reason are probably the country's finest aquifer. Their potential remains unknown because of their varied composition; in parts of the Hwange National Park and the Gwai Reserve the sands contain clay which renders them impermeable.

Alluvium one would expect to be rich in water and that in the lower Sabi valley has justified expectations. While most of the Sabi alluvium is sandy, there is some clay derived from decayed felspar. Yields from boreholes have been high. More recent alluvium in the channel of the Shashi River also proved to be rich in water.

Things to do

1 Note examples of how rock types influence relief, soils, mineral wealth and water supply.

2 Collect samples of the main rocks in your school and home area and have them identified. Label your collection and add to it during the year.

If you live in a granite area, collect specimens of granite which show differing degrees of weathering.

3 Using a jam jar or similar receptacle filled with water, measure the amount of evaporation which takes place in your school grounds during each month of the year.

4 Make a large copy of the simplified geological map. Add notes to the map to show how each rock type influences relief, soils, mineral occurrence and water reserves. Such an annotated map will be a summary of this chapter.

5 Study the geology map of a town or study a map contained in a Geological Survey Bulletin and note the ways in which the geology has influenced land use.

6 Draw sketches of kopjes, dwalas and hills. You will be surprised just how much you see when you draw. To look is not enough nor is a photograph as valuable as a sketch.

Climate
Temperature

Mean annual temperature of Harare is 19·4°C
Mean annual temperature of Port Elizabeth is
19·4°C

The above statements contradict the rule that temperature increases as latitude decreases. Can you explain why Harare is not hotter than Port Elizabeth?

A brief study of Fig. 42 shows the position of the hottest and coolest places in the country. The underlying cause of this difference is further brought out in the comparison of Livingstone and Harare, which lie on the same line of latitude, in the following table:

Table 21 Relief and temperature compared

	Height above sea level	Mean temperature of hottest month
Livingstone	963 m	26·8°C
Harare	1 469 m	21·4°C

Before the Second World War, the Zimbabwean highveld (and the Zambian plateau) was one of the few tropical areas which was regarded as suitable

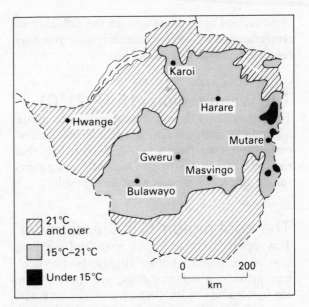

Fig. 42 Zimbabwe average temperature map

for the white man. The tropics were generally looked upon as areas of disease and of extreme discomfort only to be endured for the grand cause of empire-building. Today we may scoff at such false ideas which are noted here only to indicate that the environment appears to man to change as his knowledge increases.

Regional temperatures

You should compare the temperature and relief maps of Zimbabwe. Just as we can divide Zimbabwe into three relief regions so we may recognise three temperature regions, which in large measure correspond with altitude.

The hot region (21°C and over)

In this region are found the lowveld and part of the middleveld. Temperatures are high throughout the year and in the rainy season some people feel very uncomfortable because of the heat and high humidity. The lateness of development of this region makes an interesting topic for the thoughtful student! Even today, the Zambezi valley has not been opened up apart from a brief incursion at Chirundu by a sugar company. Low rainfall, paucity of minerals, disease, and difficulty of communications have all played their part in the late development of the region. The way in which these factors have operated and the influence of temperature itself will become clear after you have read the remainder of this section.

The warm region (15°C–21°C)

The remainder of the middleveld and nearly all the highveld lie in this region where the mean annual temperatures are from 15°C–21°C. It is here that the larger urban centres are located but temperature is only a minor reason for their position.

The cool region (15°C and under)

This region covers the highest parts of Zimbabwe, that is, the Eastern Border Highlands. The coolness provides a welcome change for people from the hotter areas of the country and, together with the scenic grandeur, has encouraged the development of hotels and holiday cottages.

The lower temperatures have led to the cultivation of deciduous fruit trees and seed potatoes. On the other hand, the greater risk of frost in this region has made the tea and coffee planters wary of certain sites.

Rainfall

What do you notice when you compare the seasonal distribution of rainfall at the following two stations?

Table 22 Rainfall comparisons (mm) between Harare and London (UK).

	Jan.	Feb.	Mar.	April	May	June
Harare	187·2	173·2	100·6	33·5	10·9	4·1
London	50·8	38·1	35·6	45·7	45·7	40·6

	July	Aug.	Sept.	Oct.	Nov.	Dec.
Harare	0·8	2·3	6·9	30·2	97·3	181·9
London	50·8	55·9	45·7	58·4	·63·5	50·8

The outstanding fact about the Central African climate is that most rain falls in one season. The heaviest rain is brought by the Congo airstream and it is convectional. The south-east trade winds also bring rain which falls mainly on the Eastern Border Highlands as orographic rain.

The Congo airstream rarely reaches the latitude of Masvingo where the average annual rainfall is some 620 m per annum while the south-east trades are limited chiefly to the Eastern Border. The directions of decrease can be seen in Fig. 43.

Fig. 43 brings out the influence of the relief on rainfall. It shows that the rainfall decreases in a certain direction and that the Sabi Valley lies in the shadow of the Eastern Border Highlands. Can you name the rain-bringing winds and the full name given to the Sabi Valley to explain its position in relation to the rain-bringing winds?

From this very brief survey of the facts of the climate, we can make up a simple table from which you should draw a map. First, try to complete the table.

Table 23

	Summer	Winter
Lowveld	Very hot : Slightly wet	Warm : Dry
Middleveld	.... : Wet	Warm : Dry
Highveld	.... :	...... : ......
Mountains	Cool : Very wet	Cold : Wet

Table 24

Season	22/23	26/27	38/39	46/47	52/53	61/63
Beitbridge	525·7	139·7	508·0	228·6	597·0	177·8
Bulawayo	514·3	394·7	785·5	199·4	930·1	464·1

Table to show rainfall in mm of some very wet and some very dry seasons at Bulawayo and Beitbridge.

While the rainfall map has enabled us to see the patterns of rainfall and to get some idea of the amount of rainfall, it does not tell us the whole story. If you are a farmer's son you should know that one of the missing facts is the variability of rainfall which is dealt with below. Other omissions from the map are the seasonal distribution and the intensity of the rain. The intensity of rain means the amount that falls over a given period, usually an hour. It is measured by a gauge in which the rain moves a pen over a chart fixed to a revolving clock drum.

Variability of rainfall

The mean annual rainfall totals shown in the climatic tables need to be regarded with caution. The reason for this is that the variability of rainfall from year to year is so large in parts of Zimbabwe

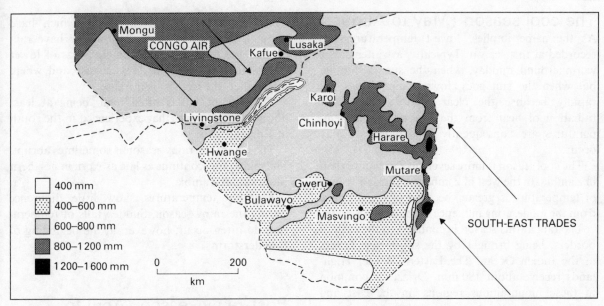

Fig. 43   Rainfall distribution over Zimbabwe

that the mean values do not really indicate what can be expected in any particular season. Figures of the following stations show considerable variability.

Intensity of rainfall

Most of you will have read a rain gauge which records the amount of rain which has fallen since it was last read i.e. 24 hours previously. The gauge which measures intensity of rainfall is made so that an exact record of how much rain and when it fell is kept. The highest intensity recorded in Central Africa is 340 mm per hour. Apart from records the significance of high rainfall intensity is its power of erosion. 40% of Harare's total annual rainfall is erosive, i.e. it falls at an intensity of above 25 mm per hour. Only 2% of London's annual rainfall is erosive and this big difference is one major reason for the emphasis placed by governments and other national groups on *soil conservation*, that is the wise use of soil.

When rain falls at a low rate of intensity, most of it will soak into the ground. High intensity falls, however, lead to a large proportion of the rain water flowing over the surface or collecting in pools.

Lake Kariba and rainfall

Frequently we hear that evaporation from Lake Kariba must increase the rainfall over Zimbabwe. This sounds very logical but the fallacy of the statement is quite simply that Kariba is too small to have any significant effect on Zimbabwe's rainfall. In any year some 1 900 mm are evaporated from the lake's surface and Zimbabwe is about 75 times the size of Kariba. A quick calculation shows that even if all the moisture evaporated did fall as rain over Zimbabwe there would be an increase of some 25 mm per year. But most of the moisture, in fact, is spread by winds into drier air and only within some 32 to 50 km of the lake can one expect any increase in rainfall, provided the winds are blowing off the lake.

The seasons

In the climatic tables it should be noted that the year begins in July. This is done so that the rainy season is not divided into two parts.

How many seasons would you say that there were in Central Africa? If we think only of rainfall distribution we would say two seasons, but if we consider temperature as well we should say four seasons, namely, the cool season, the hot season, the rainy season and the post-rainy season. Rather than read through the following description of each season, it is strongly suggested that you first try to describe each season on your own, using only the climatic data given on page 83.

The cool season (May to August)

As the name implies, lowest temperatures are recorded at this season. Typically, a winter day is warm around midday, when the sun is shining, but when the sun goes down temperatures fall rapidly because the clear night skies favour radiation of heat from the ground. Night temperatures are consequently low and frost may occur.

The cool season is more severe in Zimbabwe than in Zambia. In the west of Zimbabwe the daily range of temperature is greater because of the distance from the moderating influence of the sea.

The rain at this season is confined to the eastern borders, being brought by the south-east Trades of the Indian Ocean. The Eastern Border Highlands receive about 180 mm. Drizzle is common in these mountainous regions on the east and south-east facing slopes, and has been given several local names. In Zimbabwe it is called *guti*, meaning cold wind. Such drizzle does occur at other seasons but is less noticeable.

The hot season (September to mid-November)

The chief characteristic of this season is high temperature. Stations show a considerable rise in September and this rise continues during the first half of October. The highest temperatures are reached not at midsummer but before the rains begin. This is most noticeable in the north, while in the south, e.g., Beitbridge, the highest monthly temperature of 27°C is in December.

Occasional thunderstorms occur in the afternoon when temperatures are at their highest for the day.

The rainy season (mid-November to March)

The months given above in brackets to define the seasons are only roughly correct, and this is especially true of the rainy season which may begin in Zimbabwe in mid-November, but may be as late as the end of December. The rainy season begins earlier in Zambia than in Zimbabwe.

Rain is by no means a daily occurrence during this season. The rains are made up mainly of showers and storms, very unevenly distributed, from November to March. Places which have about 890 mm per year will probably have rain on half the days of the season. In areas of lower rainfall the number of dry days increase, and, where it is higher, the wet spells increase.

The rate of fall is often high, being at least double, for example, that experienced in the south of England.

The end of the rainy season is sometimes abrupt. The main rains continue as late as April in northern Malawi and Zambia.

Monthly temperatures show little difference during the rainy season. Sudden falls of temperature do often occur, however, at the beginning of thunderstorms.

Post-rainy season (April to early May)

A season between the end of the main rains and the cold season may be expected, lasting from April to early May.

Showery weather is quite frequent during April, especially towards the north, and early morning mists are common, as the ground is still damp. By May the ground is drying out and rain becomes a rare occurrence.

Temperatures fall fairly steadily.

Things to do

1 Using the temperature and rainfall figures given on page 83 for the nearest town or for your home town, draw a temperature graph and a rainfall column diagram. What are the advantages of showing the figures in this way?

2 From your atlas find out which countries have a climate like that of Zimbabwe.

3 You have been asked to collect temperature and rainfall figures for the Department of Meteorology of Zimbabwe:

   a) name the instruments which you would be issued with.

   b) describe the precautions you would take in siting these instruments

   c) state the daily readings you would take.

4 Describe what you would learn about the climate of Zimbabwe from daily temperature and rainfall data which you collected for one year. (Remember

to think of monthly differences as well as daily variations. Don't forget the seasons!)

5 Measure the amount of rain falling, noting the time taken to fall. Note how much of each shower soaks into the ground. Try to produce a rough scale to show what intensity is necessary before water collects on the ground. Note too, the conditions, e.g. a heavy downpour may occur just after a prolonged shower.

6 Discuss the influences of climate on agriculture in Zimbabwe.

Table 25 Climatic data for some stations in Zimbabwe (Note that the year begins in July)

		July	Aug.	Sept.	Oct.	Nov.	Dec.	Jan.	Feb.	Mar.	April	May	June	Totals
Beitbridge	T°C	16·7	19·2	22·3	25·7	26·3	26·5	26·1	26·1	25·2	23·5	20·2	16·7	
	mm	2·0	1·3	6·6	21·6	46·7	64·5	75·4	51·8	37·8	15·2	6·1	3·3	332·3
Kadoma	T°C	15·4	18·2	21·4	24·3	22·9	22·1	22·0	21·7	21·3	20·6	18·4	15·5	
	mm	—	0·3	3·0	24·1	81·5	175·0	178·8	170·7	100·3	24·9	4·8	1·0	764·4
Inyanga	T°C	8·9	11·1	13·6	16·3	16·3	16·2	16·1	16·3	15·4	14·3	11·9	9·4	
	mm	16·8	15·5	11·9	42·7	127·0	221·7	249·4	237·2	143·3	47·0	17·0	15·0	1 144·5
Harare	T°C	13·5	16·0	18·9	21·6	20·9	20·1	19·9	19·9	19·2	18·3	16·1	13·3	
	mm	0·8	2·3	6·9	30·2	97·3	181·9	187·2	173·2	100·6	33·5	10·9	4·1	828·9
Stapleford	T°C	8·7	10·3	13·5	16·0	16·6	16·6	17·1	17·1	16·2	14·6	11·3	8·9	
	mm	32·5	40·9	31·2	73·2	181·4	310·1	395·0	339·6	250·4	89·4	37·1	37·3	1 818·1
Mutare	T°C	14·2	15·8	18·6	21·2	21·3	21·2	21·7	21·2	20·7	19·2	16·7	14·5	
	mm	6·4	8·9	10·2	26·2	95·3	159·5	195·8	146·1	115·8	27·2	10·4	7·9	809·7
Hwange	T°C	13·9	16·9	21·4	24·9	23·4	22·7	22·4	22·1	21·4	20·5	16·9	14·2	
	mm	—	0·3	2·3	22·9	64·5	139·1	166·4	154·4	76·5	25·9	4·3	0·5	657·1
Masvingo	T°C	13·4	15·9	18·9	22·4	21·9	21·6	21·3	21·4	20·2	19·1	16·5	13·4	
	mm	2·3	2·0	4·6	19·3	73·4	146·1	141·7	112·5	86·6	18·5	6·9	7·1	621·0
Binga	T°C	20·1	22·4	26·3	29·3	27·9	26·1	25·7	25·0	25·7	25·1	22·6	20·4	
	mm	—	0·3	0·8	11·7	52·1	158·5	176·3	151·9	73·4	19·8	3·8	0·5	649·1
Bulawayo	T°C	13·4	15·9	19·2	22·1	21·6	21·4	20·9	20·8	19·9	18·8	15·9	13·3	
	mm	0·8	0·8	4·06	23·4	128·3	128·3	143·3	107·7	79·0	19·8	9·1	1·8	540·4
Gweru	T°C	11·6	14·3	17·3	20·6	20·0	19·8	19·6	19·6	18·6	17·4	14·7	11·8	
	mm	0·5	0·8	6·1	22·6	96·0	155·5	147·6	137·2	87·9	20·3	6·9	4·3	685·7

14   Vegetation and forestry (Zimbabwe)

Timber in Zimbabwe

About 55% of Zimbabwe is under savanna wood-land or forest, but only a very small proportion of this area contains commercially valuable timber.

Some of this timber is indigenous to Zimbabwe (trees native to a land) and some of it, known as exotic, has been introduced to Zimbabwe from foreign countries.

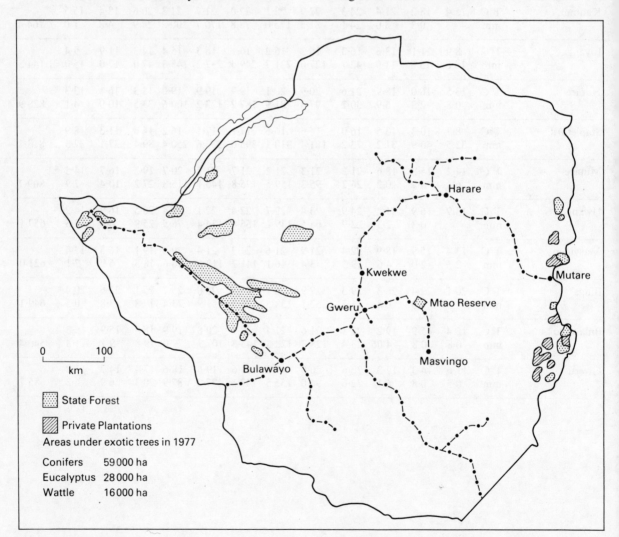

0   100
km

▓ State Forest

▨ Private Plantations

Areas under exotic trees in 1977

Conifers	59 000 ha
Eucalyptus	28 000 ha
Wattle	16 000 ha

Fig. 44   Distribution of major plantations growing exotic trees and State forests. Indigenous trees grow in the forests to the north-east of Bulawayo

The names of some indigenous and exotic trees are:

INDIGENOUS TREES   Zimbabwean teak, mukwa, mchibi or Zimbabwean copal-wood

EXOTIC TREES   Conifers, eucalypts, wattle

The above list is of economically valuable trees. The flamboyant and jacaranda, for instance, are omitted although they are exotic trees which you may have noted.

Study Fig. 44 and describe the distribution of indigenous and exotic trees.

Uses and values of timber

Make a list of these before consulting the diagram.

Forests provide

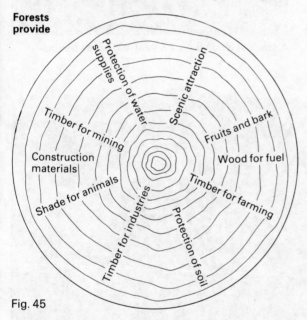

Fig. 45

Savanna woodlands

This is a convenient name for the indigenous trees that make up the woodlands of the country.

Value of timber in savanna woodland is limited because:

a) trees are usually small;
b) trees are often fire-damaged;
c) timber is often not durable;
d) volume of trees per hectare is small;
e) rate of tree growth is slow.

The drier areas need suitable trees to meet the requirements of the subsistence and commercial farmers.

The woodlands consist of hardwoods except for the Mulanje cedar and the Yellowwood, both softwoods, which grow in very limited quantities in the Eastern Border Highlands.

A few trees in these woodlands are felled for commercial uses, for example, the mahoganies of the riverine forests in the Urungwe-Sipolilo districts.

Indigenous forests

The location of these has already been described. The trees tap the water supplies stored at depth in the sands. Indeed, it is the water-holding capacity of the Kalahari Sands which explains why forests grow in this area of low rainfall.

Within the forests railway sleepers are made at the sawmills. Otherwise, the trees are transported by the nearest railway to Bulawayo.

Table 26   Timbers in Matabeleland

		Bulawayo factories
Rhodesian teak		parquet flooring blocks
mukwa	—by rail→	plywood
mchibi		furniture veneers

The regeneration rate of hardwoods is slow. What is the danger economically? Foresters have experimented, so far unsuccessfully, to increase the rate. Therefore, at present, the only solution is to reduce the existing scale of exploitation if a continuous supply of these valuable timbers is to be ensured.

While we have dealt with the uses of timber we have not covered the uses of forests. Is the idea of using a forest strange to you? Recently, the forests have been used for honey production, game ranching, cattle grazing, hunting and photographic safaris in an attempt to utilise the resources to the full.

Exotic forests

1 SOFTWOODS The less pronounced winter drought of the Eastern Border Highlands favours coniferous plantations and the Government began planting softwoods in the Stapleford Forest Reserve in 1928. The photograph of the estate gives an idea of its great extent and its hilly relief. Stapleford had 4 000 ha under pines in 1979.

About 70% of the total area under pines in Zimbabwe is devoted to one species, the Patula pine, which grows quickly and average 27 m in height after 25 years.

The first seed was imported from Mexico but after the Second World War, South Africa was the source. Recently, seed from locally grown, selected trees has been used. There are only two other species of pine commercially used.

The Forestry Commission, through its research services, are constantly testing new species of softwoods and other exotic trees for three reasons. Can you think of them?

1 The new tree may be a better variety yielding more timber or better timber. At present, for instance, no local pines produce the better grade of softwood.

2 A particular site may need a tree that is highly frost-resistant or adapted to a rather shallow soil.

A small sawmill with 27-year-old pines behind

The Stapleford Estate

3 The new species may be more resistant to fungal or insect attacks than varieties already planted.

Central America and the Caribbean Islands are regarded by some experts as one of the homes of the pine. Furthermore, Mexico with its great range of altitude–over 3 600 m, and its moderate to heavy rainfall which has a seasonal trend, bears similarities to the Eastern Border Highlands. For these reasons, therefore, this region has been the source of many species of pine for testing in Zimbabwe.

The pines are felled at about 30 years of age, although three or four thinnings of the plantations are carried out in the first 24 years of the life of the trees. The area under softwoods on privately owned estates exceed that of State plantations, and it is expected that some two-thirds of the required softwood cover in Zimbabwe will be controlled by private concerns. It is estimated that the area required to meet local demands is 121 000 ha.

Thinnings from the softwood plantations of the Eastern Border Highlands produce most of the pulp used in the Mutare Board and Paper Mills. Also located in Mutare are mills producing plywood, woodwool, floring parquet, boxes, block-board and laminated timber.

Along the Central Watershed between Mutare and Harare there are several small softwood plantations which supply wood for local sawmills, e.g. at Marondera.

2 WATTLE The demand for tannin, a dye obtained from the highly scented wattle tree has fallen off in recent years. Tannin is a dye and softener in the leather industry, used for tanning hides, and the Zimbabwean extract has a very light colour. This trend is reflected in the decreasing areas under wattle, e.g. 20 000 ha in 1967 and 16 000 in 1977. Softwoods have replaced wattle on many of the estates which are located between Inyanga and Mutare, Chimanimani and Chipinge.

Wattle trees are planted on a ten-year cycle, which means that ten years after germination the tree is large enough (about 6 m high) to be stripped of its bark. The bark is taken to the factory, chopped into small pieces, and boiled to extract the tannin, of which it contains a high percentage. The tannin liquid is concentrated sufficiently to produce a brittle, toffee-like substance on cooling,

Patula Pines pruned to a height of 7 metres

which is exported in sacks. The trees, having no further use, are burnt, some of the seed falling to the ash-fertilised ground. New rows of trees spring up, to be thinned out by hand after a years or so.

At Silverstream factory the bark is processed for part of the year and the same machinery is used to extract sugar from locally grown cane in the remaining months.

3 EUCALYPTS With the exception of the Mtao Forest Reserve, the eucalypt plantations are located in the Eastern Border Highlands. In 1922, the government wanted a gum plantation to meet the needs of the country. Mtao was selected rather than the Eastern Border Highlands. Why? Fig. 44 will help you. (Look at the position of Mtao relative to the whole of Zimbabwe and note communications). Mtao supplies transmission poles, fencing posts, mining props and tobacco barn frames.

Gum poles, as Eucalyptus is commonly called, were planted by the first settlers in the late nineteenth century and many farms have their small plantations in order to supply the demand for fencing timber, tobacco barn timber, fuel and timber for other purposes.

Australia, the home of the Eucalyptus, and South Africa are the main sources of Eucalyptus for testing by the Forestry Commission.

Hazards to forestry

Fungi, insects, cyclones, localised whirlwinds and fire are the main hazards to forestry. In addition, the old argument that trees take away water from adjacent farm land is still being used although the evidence is inconclusive.

Fungus damage has led to the discontinuance of one pine species and this danger illustrates the necessity of experimenting with several species of a tree. Insects have attacked the Patula pine but the outbreaks have so far been small and successfully controlled. Damage by fire renders the pines particularly susceptible to insect attacks.

In March 1962, considerable damage was caused to some stands of pines on Stapleford estate by cyclone 'Kate'. Extensive damage to plantations by wind is not a common occurrence and the extent of the damage is thought to have been due to lack of thinning of the forest during the Second World War. More common are localised whirlwinds which occur where winds are confined as in gullies. At Tilbury estate, south of Chimanimani, for instance, whirlwinds have snapped off pines some 1·2 m above the ground. In Zimbabwe, a very efficient system of fire-watching and fire-fighting exists in government and private plantations to cope with the annual outbreaks.

The main threat to forests is fire. The large extent of these forests and the high proportion of grass in the ground cover make it very difficult to extinguish a fire. Despite a fairly comprehensive system of fire lookouts and fireguards, plus a firefighting force, annual fires in forests are common.

Woodlands in African rural areas

As population grows pressure on the woodlands increases and the communal lands become stripped of trees. Whereas commercial farming areas have a good tree cover, the communal areas are comparatively bare of trees as a visit will show.

In 1975, it was estimated that 44 per cent of this area should be set aside as natural woodland if the demands for firewood and timber for other uses by people are to be met. This proposal is not practicable but it does give some idea of the size of the problem.

The collection of firewood is very strenuous and it is a job carried out mainly by women. On average, the firewood is collected in bundles of 36 kilograms within two kilometres of a kraal, two or three times a week. As the kind of wood needed for burning is used up near to the kraal greater distances have to be travelled and Scotch carts are frequently used.

Two solutions to the evergrowing shortage of wood for domestic uses in the rural areas have been suggested. The first is the planting of kraal or village woodlots. A second answer to the problem may be the planting of clumps of bamboo. The bamboo can be cut after only four years. Both schemes require further investigation before any large-scale plans can be made.

The wood fuel shortage affects all countries of Africa in the savanna region mainly because of population pressure. People need wood for cooking and keeping warm and they will continue to clear the woodlands until alternative fuels are available.

Read pages 154–155 on natural woodlands and the interests of forestry department.

Things to do

1 Veneers, plywood and blockboard are three of the more complex timber products. Find out more about them from your woodwork teacher.

2 Discuss how the development of forests assists in soil conservation.

3 Trees have much more than a monetary value. Discuss.

15 Agriculture (Zimbabwe)

Natural farming regions

Of all the physical factors influencing agriculture in Zimbabwe, rainfall is the most important. Any division of the country into natural farming regions must therefore take into account this dominant factor.

The five farming regions shown in Fig. 46 are based on effective, not annual, rainfall. The effective rainfall is that part of the rain which plants can use. For instance, an annual rainfall in Zimbabwe of 600 mm may allow only 400 mm for plant growth. The remaining 200 mm are lost through run-off, seepage below the root zone and evaporation. These proportions differ from those given on page 76 because here we are concerned with water available to plants and not water that can be stored.

Another significant point about these farming regions is that they do not reflect existing farming systems. If present types of farming were to be shown we would expect to see two national farming systems namely, commercial and subsistence.

The main object in delimiting natural farming regions is to show how the land could be used considering only the physical factors of rainfall, soils and relief. (This explains why the word 'natural' appears before farming region.) The influence of markets and the farmer's wishes are not considered because they change. Physical factors do not alter over ten or twenty years and therefore the survey has a long-term value for planners so vital in our rapidly developing country.

A summary of the characteristics of each of the five natural farming regions is given in the following paragraphs.

Region I

Variations of relief and climate characterise this region. The Chimanimani Mountains pass into the rolling hills or down country of Chipinge and the flat-topped plateaus of the Vumba. Rainfall varies greatly with aspect while temperatures change with altitude differences. With such a variety of physical conditions the recommended farming systems are equally wide in scope, namely, intensive livestock and diversified production. The latter type of production implies types of land use not always related. For instance, tea plantations, coffee farming, production of seed potatoes and deciduous fruits, and afforestation with wattle and softwoods. Intensive livestock production includes both dairying and beef production. Effective rainfall in Region I exceeds 635 mm.

Region II

Covering almost 20% of Zimbabwe this region has much less variation of relief and climate than Region I. Gold belts and the Great Dyke introduce some of the greatest relief differences. Rainfall is enough to favour intensive farming based on crop production. The degree of intensity of land use and the crops grown are matters for the farmer to determine within wide limits. Thus, maize might be a main crop with numerous sidelines like beans, sunflowers and soya beans. Such cash crops provide valuable residues which can be fed to dairy and beef cattle and pigs. Intensive beef or dairy production are alternative farming systems. Effective rainfall varies from 500 to 635 mm.

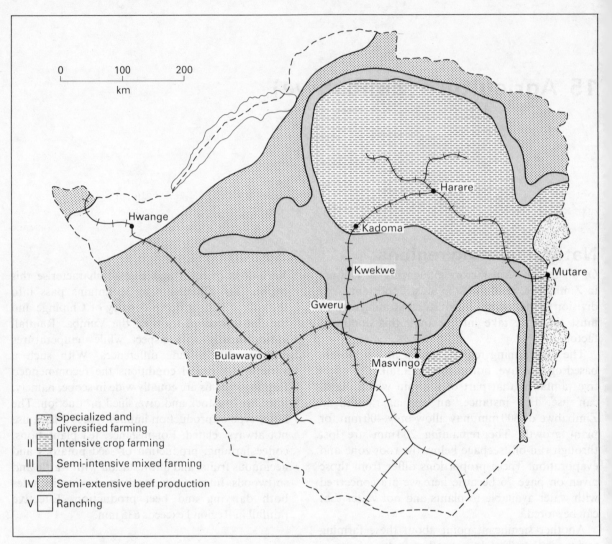

Fig. 46 The natural farming regions of Zimbabwe indicating the types of farming best suited to each region. The facts in the text refer to commercial farming. Most communal farming areas are in Natural Regions III to V.

Legend:
I   Specialized and diversified farming
II Intensive crop farming
III Semi-intensive mixed farming
IV Semi-extensive beef production
V   Ranching

Region III

With an effective rainfall of only 400 to 510 mm and a high probability of drought, farming must be less intensive than in Region II. Semi-intensive mixed farming is recommended, that is, a cash crop like maize, a drought-resistant crop such as sorghum and livestock. The latter are essential since the farmer could not make a living from crop production alone.

Region IV

Effective rainfall of between 350 and 450 mm together with mid-season spells of drought make cash cropping uneconomic. Crops grown should be for beef cattle fodder mainly, with limited areas planted to cotton, millet or sorghum. Such a farming system is termed semi-extensive beef production.

Region V

Including the Zambezi Valley and much of the Sabi-Limpopo lowveld, this area is mainly flat on the valley floors becoming very broken where escarpments of the Zambezi are approached.

Effective rainfall is very low (less than 400 mm) and unreliable. Without irrigation, most crops cannot be grown in most years and the farmer depends on the veld grazing. Therefore, ranching or extensive beef production is practised. The carrying capacity of the veld in this region varies from 1 beast to 8 ha to 1 beast to 20 ha. It is essential to provide well distributed watering points for the cattle. A survey is to be made of the area below the Zambezi Escarpment, north of Sipolio, to determine its potential for both dryland farming, e.g. cotton, and irrigated farming.

This summary of the natural farming regions has not included soils. Nonetheless, you should be in a position to answer the following questions. If you cannot give the correct answers, read through the summary again.

1 What is effective rainfall?
2 Try to define a natural farming region.
3 Describe the relief of natural farming Region I.
4 Describe a system of mixed farming.
5 In what region would you expect to find extensive beef production?
6 Practise drawing Fig. 46 so that you know it fully.

Commercial and communal farming in figures

Over 75% of the population depends directly on farming for a living. This figure includes communal land peasant farmers, 261 000 workers on commercial farms and the 5000 owners or lessees them-

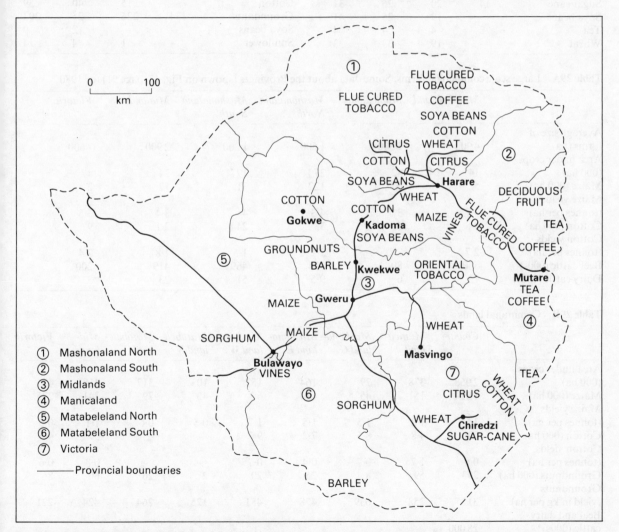

Fig. 47 Commercial crop distribution. Compare this map with that showing the natural farming regions in Fig. 46. Note the regions where crops are grown.

selves. In 1980, about 80% (by value) of gross agricultural production came from communal lands, a fact which emphasises their significance.

Tables 27 and 28 should be studied and then compared. Reference to Fig. 47 should also be made.

Tables 29A and B show the huge economic

problems of the communal lands which arose from neglect in the past.

Now we will look at some statistics which will enable us to get an overall picture of farming in Zimbabwe. The first tables show changes in the areas of crops in recent years. As you read the table put the changes into words.

Table 27 Areas under various crops (figures in thousands of ha)

Commercial farms	1965	1972	1976	1980
Flue cured tobacco	85	45	65	62
Maize	176	300	227	228
Cotton	14	60	58	75
Sugar cane	14	20	26	31
Soya beans	—	19	25	41
Tea	2	4	4	4
Wheat	—	19	33	33

Table 28 Areas under various crops (figures in thousands of ha)

Communal area farmers	1965	1972	1976	1980
Maize	592	644	767	1 014
Sorghum	142	188	236	218
Millet	359	441	511	395
Cotton	—	15	40	59
Groundnuts	134	226	325	293
Soya beans	—	—	2	9
Sunflower	—	1	4	24

Table 29A Large scale commercial farms. Some data about the Provinces (shown on Fig. 47, page 91) for 1980.

	Matabeleland	Manicaland	Mashonaland North	Mashonaland South	Midlands	Victoria
Average size of farms (ha)	4 900	1 300	1 600	1 200	2 900	7 600
Area under crops (000 ha)	14	42	270	177	24	47
Maize (000 ha)	5	6	122	71	12	2
Maize yields (tonnes per ha)	3·7	3·7	4·3	4	3·4	3·5
Cotton (000 ha)	0·8	6	33	24	2·1	9
Cotton yields (tonnes per ha)	2·7	2·1	2·1	1·5	1·8	2·4
Beef cattle (000s)	560	80	374	469	419	200
Dairy cattle (000s)	13	6	9·5	51	23	3

Table 29B Communal lands

	Country	Manica-land	Mashona-land C.	Mashona-land E.	Mashona-land W.	Matabele-land N.	Matabele-land S.	Mid-lands	Victoria
Area under crops (000 ha)	2 068	378	79	164	157	103	317	418	486
Maize (000 ha)	1 014	151	45	114	67	43	79	241	275
Maize yields (tonnes per ha)	1	1·2	1·5	1·5	1·7	0·5	0·6	1·1	0·5
Cotton (000 ha)	59	4·8	8·5	7·2	9·7	—	—	37	4·5
Cotton yields (tonnes per ha)	0·8	1·7	0·7	0·4	0·7	—	—	0·8	0·6
Groundnuts (000 ha)	293	59	8	25	20	2	20	60	86
Groundnuts (yield in kg per ha)	312	258	639	478	451	125	264	424	221
Beef and dairy cattle (000s)*	28 000								

* Provincial breakdown not available

Major marketed crops

The purpose of this part of the chapter is to give full details of the major marketed crops; that is, maize, cotton, tobacco, wheat, soya beans, sugar, groundnuts, citrus, potatoes, sorghum, tea, coffee and barley. What a long list it is, but you can easily learn the facts by using the right approach. To do this, carefully read the facts on one crop. Then try to write down the answers to the following questions:

a) What are the growing conditions?

b) What points are to be noted about cultivation, diseases or reaping?

c) Where are the chief growing areas (a map is essential)?

d) Are any geographical principles illustrated? Such principles may be economic or physical.

Finally, learning isn't easy – try to relate the new facts to some of your daily life. For instance, you may see mealies growing in a patch on your way to school, or you may think of a machine that would harvest sugar cane; cooking oils may suggest soya bean oil. Tea and citrus are frequently consumed, and your clothing probably contains some cotton. These 'fact-springboards' should lead you to recapitulate what you have learned.

A fine maize cob. Each hair is attached to a seed

Maize

Maize is a summer rainfall crop grown mostly on the highveld and middleveld. It likes hot, humid conditions for most of its growing season which is 130 to 180 days, according to variety.

Since the early 1960's considerably more maize than was needed had been produced so that large quantities (e.g. 500 000 t in 1978) were exported to the United Kingdom, West Germany and other countries. The prices obtained on the world market are not high, therefore some governments subsidise the crop. In some years South Africa, Zambia and Malawi have to import from Zimbabwe if their own crops are insufficient, but in good years all three countries are able to export part of the crop.

The following table shows two good seasons.

Table 30 Two good years for maize production

	Thousands of t	*T per ha*
1965–1966	663	3·47
1980–1981	1 717	5·96

The 1963–64 season was poor owing to drought, with little for export. In that season Zimbabwe produced only 220 000 t, and Zambia 60 000 t.

Bulk storage of grain in large silos is done at such places as Concession, Banket, and Lions Den.

Yields of maize on commercial farms are on the increase. On good dryland farms 7·5 t per hectare are common although the Zimbabwean average is about 4 t per ha on account of lower yields from poorer areas. The yield in communal lands is about 0·7 t per ha but better farmers get over 1 t per ha.

Cotton

Zimbabwe has a surplus of middle grade cotton, i.e. cotton whose fibre length (called staple) is between 27 and 30 mm. For comparison, India produces short staple (below 25 mm) and Egypt

Picking cotton

long staple (28 to 44 mm). Sea Island cotton is the longest staple in the world at 44 to 57 mm. In Zimbabwe the crop has had a very chequered career. After a promising start at Kadoma from 1923–26, attacks by the jassid pest caused a drastic cutting back in 1927. Then the Kadoma Research Station tested a jassid-resistant strain from Uganda, called U4, and this was issued to farmers in 1928. Yet production did not increase partly because of

the ravages of other pests like the bollworm. Some farmers persisted with cotton and the discovery of DDT during the Second World War enabled bollworm to be controlled. In 1952, production rose to 3·4 million kg of seed cotton but declined to 0·09 million kg in 1957. Another strain, Albar 637, became available at Kadoma and this together with a range of pesticides, led to a rapid increase in production. From a return of 5·9 million kg of seed cotton in 1964 output jumped to 126 million kg in 1972. Growing areas are many but on the highveld the main ones are Kadoma-Chegutu, Shamva, Darwin, Bindura, Glendale and Gokwe. In the lowveld growing areas are increasing. Here a cotton called Deltapine was produced as it was suitable for machine picking. Now Albar is widely grown because of its higher yields. Ginneries were built at Bindura, Banket, Mutare, Shamva, Glendale, Chegutu, Triangle and Gokwe because of distance from the ginnery at Kadoma.

The deep, red clays, the maize soils, favour cotton which, in Zimbabwe, requires a minimum of 600 mm rain during its growing period. Naturally, the water demand varies; high yields per hectare can only be realised where rainfall is higher or where

Grading and packing cotton. Cotton is the major African cash crop and production is increasing rapidly in many areas

94

Weighing cotton

irrigation is available.

Yields vary from 2 200 to 2 600 kg per ha on irrigated land to an average of 1 600 kg per ha on dry land. Communal area farmers average 1 000 kg per ha.

There is no doubt that cotton areas will increase and that entry into the world market on a larger scale will take place. Both small and large-scale growers will benefit from such expansion.

Tobacco

In Zimbabwe tobacco farming is concentrated in the extensive arable areas near Harare, Chegutu and Marondera, and in the Lomagundi district, northwest of Harare. These areas correspond closely to the higher, more reliable rainfall regions. Virginia flue-cured tobacco has been the only type grown until recently, when Oriental and Burley tobaccos were introduced. The production is still mainly Virginia, although many farmers are now growing Burley. Prices for Burley tobaccos are usually as high, if not slightly higher than for Virginia, but the crops have certain disadvantages such as a high seasonal labour requirement. Details of cultivation and curing are given on pages 34 to 36.

Production

In 1965 tobacco accounted for 50% of total agricultural production by value, but by 1980 this

Oriental tobacco shed and racks. This tobacco is cured by the sun. At night, or when it rains, the racks are slid along wires into the shed.

figure was only 20% because of the need to concentrate on grain production during the period of international sanctions.

Table 31 Sales of tobacco in thousand tonnes

	1977	1978	1979	1980	1981
Virginia-					
flue-cured					
Zimbabwe		83	83	112	123	67
Zambia		5·6	3·7	4·6	4·1	2·4
Malaŵi	20	21	25	26	20	
Virginia					
fire-cured					
Malaŵi		19	16	12	10	—
Burley					
Zimbabwe		2	2	3	3	2
Zambia		0·3	0·2	0·4	0·6	—
Malaŵi		10	11	15	17	19

Tobacco farmers produce a good quality crop and this has enabled them to weather the problems of recent years. Scarcity of wood compelled farmers to turn to coal. More recently, a rise in the minimum wages for farm workers has been a big input cost since tobacco is a labour intensive crop. Of greater significance for production in the long term is the publicity given to the hazards of smoking. For instance, health warnings must be printed on cigarette packets in the UK.

Exports

The 1980 crop was consigned to the following areas in the quantities indicated:

Western Europe	51%
Eastern Europe	2%
Middle East	19%
Far East	13%
Americas	2%
Africa	9%
Oceania	1%

Local consumption of tobacco takes up some 4% of the total production. Overseas buyers come to Zimbabwe between March and October when the tobacco is auctioned in Harare. Each bale produced by the farmer is auctioned individually and the auction floors have long been a tourist attraction largely because of the speed at which the auctioneer speaks.

Wheat

Nearly 1·5 million bags of what a year are consumed in Central Africa at present, and this figure is expected to rise steadily owing to the increased appetite for bread instead of maize porridge.

In 1965 only about 4% of this requirement was grown within Central Africa. The reason for this is chiefly climatic. All attempts to grow summer wheat have been hampered by the high summer rainfall together with fairly long cloudy periods, which usually allow *stem rust* to appear on the plants with disastrous effects.

One way in which wheat production is being increased is by growing it as a winter crop under irrigation. Queleas present a problem but bigger difficulties are the cost of irrigation and the shortage of irrigation equipment. Even so, production increased to 195 000 tonnes in 1978. Since then it has fallen to 155 000 in 1980.

In 1966 at Mkwasine (managed by the then South-Eastern Development Company) in the lowveld (see map page 107) 970 ha of wheat were planted and the harvest exceeded the total Zimbabwean production of 1965. Planned extension made Mkwasine the granary of Zimbabwe with the highveld occupying second place. In 1975 some 6 000 ha were put under wheat at Mkwasine, making Zimbabwe self sufficient.

Wheat

Harvesting wheat at Mkwasine. The same sight can be seen on those parts of the highveld marked 'wheat' in Fig. 47, page 91.

Soya beans

Only in recent years has soya bean production become considerable. They are used widely as green

Soya beans

shelled beans and dried beans for human consumption and the whole seed may be fed to livestock. The high protein content makes soya bean flour valuable, especially in the Far East where protein foods of animal origin are in short supply. Soya bean oil, like palm oil, has many uses depending on its quality, e.g. in the manufacture of margarine, candles, paints and insecticides. Moreover, the oil meal which is the product remaining after oil extraction makes a very rich animal feed.

Only recently have Zimbabweans realised the value of the soya bean. There is an increasing world demand for soya bean oil which, in turn, means a big profit to the grower!

Maize, cotton and winter wheat are common Zimbabwean crops and soya beans are an excellent crop to be grown in rotation with them. Soya beans prefer a loam or clay and do less well on sands. Rainfall of over 500 mm per annum or irrigation is required and this means that the crop can be grown on any of the three velds. Different varieties of soya beans vary in their reaction to day length and temperatures.

The crop has a high degree of resistance to most diseases that attack legumes in Zimbabwe and it is attacked by few pests. It can be sown by planters designed for maize or wheat and is easily harvested.

Yields of about 1·1 t per ha are necessary for a fair profit to be made by the grower and it has been found that with a reasonably high standard of management yields of 2·3–2·8 t per ha are obtained.

Sugar

Sugar cane is a perennial grass which grows to a height of some 3·6 m. It has for long been associated with islands like Cuba and Mauritius and continental margins such as Natal, Queensland and south-east Brazil. All of these places are close to the tropics because the crop requires high temperatures of over 18°C for successful growth. In addition, sugar cane needs copious water supplies from sources which you should try to state.

Zimbabwe has at least one marked advantage over the above-named producing areas in that she is not subjected to severe storms or hurricanes or floods. On the positive side, Zimbabwe has large areas of level land in the lowveld underlain by fertile loams as on Triangle and Hippo Valley Estates; the sugar cane takes only 14 months to mature as against 18 months in South Africa and elsewhere and yields per hectare are high.

Sugar production in Zimbabwe is in the hands of large companies who must deal with wide fluctuations in world sugar prices. Most sugar is sold at a price negotiated by producers and buyers. Better prices are paid under international sugar agreements, e.g. Lome Convention II, under which Zimbabwe is granted a quota equal to some 12% of her production. Some 12% of production of Triangle Estates is used to make ethanol which makes up one-fifth of the petrol blend sold in the country. What are the advantages of growing our own fuel?

Groundnuts

Facts about this crop of which 85% comes from Africa are given on pages 42 and 44. Production in Zimbabwe has recently increased in communal lands and high yields have been obtained under irrigation.

Citrus

The basic climatic requirements of citrus fruit-growing are moderate rainfall of at least 760 mm per year, freedom from heavy frosts and risk of hail damage. In Central Africa the climate is not altogether suitable on account of the long dry winter. Where provision can be made for irrigation facilties, however, this disadvantage is easily overcome. Mild frosts on the highveld do not constitute a drawback, although at the Premier Estate near Mutare it was discovered some years ago that the presence of extensive tree windbreaks prevented the dispersal of cold air which accumulated in the valley at night by temperature inversion. Removal of trees permitted free movement of winds in the valley, which has reduced the frost incidence considerably. Severe hailstorms are relatively rare in Central Africa, therefore their bruising effect upon the fruit is seldom experienced.

A good crop of groundnuts which contain protein

For the fresh fruit there is a fairly large local market within Central Africa, which is fully supplied during the season, but important export products from the estates are orange and lemon juice concentrates, and peel oil essences. For instance, $2 million worth of concentrate and oils were exported by the Mazowe Estate in 1981. There are exports of fresh fruit from Premier Estate and Hippo Valley.

Mazowe Citrus Estate

In 1967 this estate had some 290 000 citrus trees planted on 1 540 ha. Note the word *estate*. What makes an estate different from a farm? Another crop normally grown on estates is tea.

The Mazowe Dam wall was completed in 1920 and 63 000 trees were planted steadily over the years. Although more trees could have been planted, this was not done until the fifties when competition from world markets became strong. Why were more trees planted to meet this competition? Further expansion became possible when the dam wall was raised in 1961.

Products from the estate in addition to fresh citrus fruit for local markets is varied and includes:
orange and lemon juice both natural and concentrated;
orange and lemon oil for use in the pharmaceutical and cosmetic industries;
citrus pulp which is a cattle-feed partly used for cattle kept on the estate.

The estate is located 48 km north of Harare on a main road to Bindura.

In recent years Mazowe Estate has diversified its production. On the hilly ground of the estate cattle are reared, the beef herd including Sussex and Afrikander breeds. A large area under sprinkler irrigation double crops annually with wheat in winter and either maize or soya beans in summer. Another part of the estate is planted in non-irrigated cotton, maize and soya beans.

Premier Estate

Sixteen km west of Mutare, this estate has a smaller area than Mazowe, and is irrigated by a canal from the Mutare River. No great expansion is contemplated there in the near future.

Rice

Rice is grown by Africans in all three nations for their own consumption and as a cash crop. In Zimbabwe, rice was grown under irrigation in the Zimbabwe Lowveld. From a small production in 1967 the crop became so popular that by 1970, the country's requirements of polished rice were met. However, declining prices forced producers to change to wheat and other crops and little is grown now. This step led to grave shortages in the early eighties.

Potatoes

In 1980 production of potatoes in Zimbabwe was of the order of 1·5 million pockets (15 kg in a pocket) but this figure must be treated with the greatest caution since many growers use their own seed. Seed from Inyanga Research Centre is exported to other countries of southern Africa.

In Zimbabwe potatoes are planted in every month but it is customary to recognise three crops:
a) The summer crop planted from October to February. This crop is unfortunately liable to late blight. To counter this, various blight-resistant strains have been developed through research in Zimbabwe.
b) The winter crop is divided into the first irrigated crop (March to May plantings) and the second irrigated crop (June to September plantings). The first of these crops benefits from the tail-end of the summer rains and the residual moistness of the ground.

Harare and Inyanga are centres of important potato-growing districts and frost is a limiting factor.

Sorghum

Sorghum is a drought-resistant crop and its production on commercial farms is about 27 000 tonnes. As a subsistence crop on African lands it ranks a poor second to maize. The Africans sow mixed seeds of sorghum and *munga* (a type of millet) so that if the rainfall is high the munga will give a good crop and if the rains are low he can reap his sorghum. Therefore, sorghum is an insurance against a dry season and is regarded in the same light by the commercial farmer. In recent years, the popularity of sorghum for malting of cloudy beer has increased and the country is self sufficient.

Tea

In Zimbabwe, as compared with Malaŵi, the tea industry is only small scale on account of climatic conditions. About 4 000 ha are planted of which about 2 000 ha are to be seen on two estates, Tanganda and Zona. The chief production areas are all in the Eastern Border Highlands.

New Year's Gift (Tanganda) estate stands on the Tanganda River, a tributary of the Sabi, not far from Birchenough Bridge on the road to Chipinge. This is the biggest of the Zimbabwean estates with 610 ha planted, all under irrigation. This makes the estate a rarity in the world of tea. The Tanganda River supplies the water and also gives its name to a well-known brand of Zimbabwean tea.

Jersey and Zona are two estates near Mount Selinda, which lies south of Chipinge. The high rainfall here has not only made this area suitable for tea, but also resulted in one of the few rainforests in Central Africa.

Ratelshoek and Southdown are irrigated estates on the downs east of Chipinga.

The Inyanga area has proved suitable for tea production. The scheme at Holdenby has already produced tea for the export and local markets. Honde Valley Estates are also producers.

It should be noted that whereas most of Malaŵi's tea is exported, some of Zimbabwe's production is consumed internally. The total production in Zimbabwe is 9 million kg a year.

As both Malaŵi and Zimbabwe are well-placed geographically to compete with other tea-producing countries, there are good prospects for expansion with large markets readily available in the long term.

Recent switches to coffee by tea growers is a result of poor prices for the latter caused by falling consumption and overproduction.

Coffee

In the last few years coffee has become a very important crop. Zimbabwe grows the *arabica* type which fetches a higher price than *robusta* on the world market.

Coffee trees need some 1 140 mm of rainfall per year (or irrigation) and moderate temperatures of

Tea plucking at Aberfoyle Estates, Inyanga. Few trees are to be seen. Contour ridging is clearly visible

Coffee tree laden with berries

Coffee farm near Chipinge

from 15 to 21°C which remain uniform. The seasonal nature of Zimbabwe's rainfall favours coffee which prefers a dry flowering season.

In 1965 the government financed a settlement scheme under which four farmers were each given 400 acres for coffee-growing. The farms were near Chipinge where there is a coffee experimental station and a mill where the berries are processed. The coffee farms are on hilly land and at an average altitude of 950 m. Coffee trees give good yields after four years. The Vumba is the only other major coffee-producing area. High world market prices encouraged extension of coffee growing to areas near Chinhoyi and north of Harare.

Barley

Barley for brewery malting purposes is grown mainly in the Kwekwe region of Zimbabwe, as a winter crop under irrigation. It does not grow very easily in Central Africa (in Malaŵi there was no marketed production at all in 1965) and the cost per ha to the farmer is high. In recent years while there has been no increase in the area cultivated, production has been maintained by raising the yield per ha. In 1982 Zimbabwe was self-sufficient in barley which is bought by National Breweries.

South-eastern Lowveld

This area is treated separately because it shows how man has altered the environment for his own benefit by irrigation. Imagination, planning and determination of those concerned have evoked the enthusiasm of Zimbabweans. Yet, this part of the lowveld was only developed in the late 1950s, apart from the sterling efforts of Tom MacDougall, an early rancher and cane farmer, in the late 1920s. There were several reasons for this late development and some are listed below.

a) The altitude of the lowveld is below 600 m.

b) The area was malarial and infested with tsetse fly.

c) The lowland was isolated since the main Beitbridge to Masvingo road skirts the region.

d) There was no gold to attract white settlers which, in turn, meant an absence of a market.

e) What natural farming region does this area lie in? What are the limited farming activities that can be carried on?

On the other hand, the highveld offered various attractions to the whites. You should write down these attractions which are the opposite of most of the facts stated about the South-eastern Lowveld above.

Overhead irrigation in the Lowveld

Table 32 Some statistics and information about farming in the Sabi Lowveld

Name of scheme	Area irri-gated (in ha)	Crops grown	Type of irrigation	Soils	Livestock	Type of farming
Triangle estate and settlers	13 700	Sugar Cotton Maize Wheat	Overhead water from Kyle Dam, Bangala Dam and Esquilingwe Weir	Sandy clay loams	Cattle fed on sugar cane tops, cottonseed cake and molasses. 6·1 beasts per ha.	Estate. 8 farmers. Approx. size of holding is 8 240 ha.
Hippo Valley Estate and settlers	11 500	Sugar Citrus Cotton Wheat Maize	Flood and overhead. Source of water same as for Triangle but with extra from Siya Dam.	Sandy clay loams. Black basaltic clays.	Cattle as on Triangle. Citrus pulp also fed.	Estate. 42 farmers. Approx. size of holding 120 ha of which 80 ha is irrigable.
Mkwasine Estate and settlers	6 750	Wheat Cotton Sugar Coffee	Overhead water from Lake MacDougall and Siya Dam. Flood irrigation also.	Sandy clay loams		Estate. 10 farmers.
Middle Sabi Estate and settlers	6 600	Cotton Wheat Maize Coffee Soyas	Overhead water from Sabi River and Lespapi Dam.	Sandy clay loams and alluvium		23 large-scale farmers. 47 small-scale farmers.
Chisumbanje Estate and settlers	2 500	Cotton Wheat	Flood water from Sabi River and Ruti Dam	Black basaltic clays and alluvium		250 farmers and estate farming

102

Opening up of the Lowveld

Having just given good reasons why the Lowveld (with a capital L this word refers to the South-eastern Lowveld) was not developed before the Second World War it may seem odd that the circumstances should change so much as to encourage the opening up of the area. Nevertheless, the Federal Government wanted to stimulate the economy of the country by initiating an agricultural venture which would be viable and imaginative. Irrigation schemes offer greater profit than dryland farming projects since two crops can be grown annually. In the end, the South-eastern Lowveld was selected as being the best proposition. Why was the Zambezi lowveld not chosen? Perhaps distance from a railhead, the tsetse fly and the high temperatures were the main disadvantages. In 1947, a report by a firm of consultants had pointed out the advantages of developing the South-eastern Lowveld and, the results from experimental stations set up were very promising.

Furthermore, the government were convinced by Tom MacDougall that sugar could be grown successfully in the region. In 1919, this pioneer planned to grow sugar. After some amazing feats, he milled his first cane in the early thirties. Then, in 1945, he sold Triangle to the government. Water for irrigation was the first essential and the government constructed the Esquilingwe Weir in 1947. Later, the Triangle Estate was sold to private enterprise.

In 1956, Sir Ray Stockil and several farmers bought Hippo Valley Estates in order to grow citrus fruits; sugar cane was planted after some years because of the exceptionally high price on the world market. The entry of a private company into the Lowveld was a major factor in the government's decision to proceed with further development. The completion of the Bannockburn railway line to Maputo in 1956 was another inducement to development.

Existing irrigation schemes

There are five major irrigation schemes in the

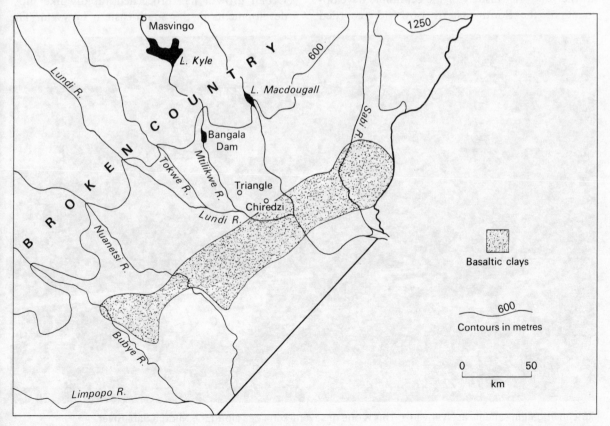

Fig. 48   Some physical features of the South-eastern Lowveld

South-eastern Lowveld and these are listed below:
    Triangle Estates;
    Hippo Valley Estates;
    Mkwasine Estate;
    Middle Sabi Estate;
    Chisumbanje Estate.

Schemes of an area of about 400 ha include the African areas along the Sabi River. They are Nyanyadzi, Mutema-Tawona, Chisumbanje, Devuli and Chibuwe. In addition, there are smaller African irrigation schemes along the Lundi, Sabi and Limpopo Rivers. Most of these are isolated, depending for sale of their surplus to surrounding dryland African farmers.

Some facts about the major irrigation schemes are given in the table on page 102. You should show most of them on your copy of the map showing existing irrigation schemes.

The Agricultural and Rural Development Authority

In the very brief history of the economic development of the South-eastern Lowveld recorded above, you may have noticed that no mention was made of any body responsible for overall planning. It was only in 1965 that such a body, the Sabi-Limpopo Authority was set up. Its major objectives were to conserve and utilise the water of the rivers within its area in order to promote the economic development of the area in the national interest.

In 1982, the Agricultural and Rural Development Authority was set up incorporating the Sabi-Limpopo Authority. ARDA is responsible for promoting agricultural development in all areas of Zimbabwe. The Sabi-Limpopo Authority did, in fact, develop three estates using Government loans. These three estates are the Mkwasine Estate, the Middle Sabi Estate and the Chisumbanje Estate. The first of these companies was formed to take over the Nandi Sugar Company which was forced into liquidation in 1965 because of the dramatic fall in the price of sugar on the world market.

Towns and industries

Urban growth has proceeded rapidly like most developments in the South-eastern Lowveld. The

African irrigation scheme at Nyanyadzi. This is one of several schemes along the Middle Sabi River. Note the flatness of the flood plain.

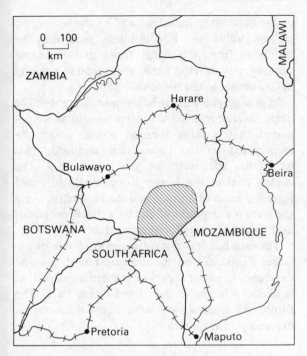

Fig. 49.1 Sabi Limpopo Authority area

largest settlement is Chiredzi, established only in 1962 by Hippo Valley Estates. Apart from providing the necessary services to the estates, such as maintenance of machines and vehicles and banking, the town also has schools, hospitals, various depots and a weekly newspaper. Triangle was developed about ten years before Chiredzi as the first company town of the Lowveld. Its functions resemble those of Chiredzi. Both towns are served by railway and tarred road and they have air transport available at Buffalo Range, near Triangle. A daily air service links the area with Harare, Bulawayo and Masvingo.

Rutenga is a small village which owes its existence to the junction of rail routes and a major road.

Industries in the Lowveld are based on the agricultural products of the developed estates and the town attracting most industries is Chiredzi. Three mills produce unrefined sugar from the sugar cane. One mill is located on the Triangle Estate and two on Hippo Valley Estates. The second mill at Hippo Valley is an old one and has a capacity of 80 t of cane per hour as compared with 250 t per hour of the two larger mills. Sugar mills must be located in the growing areas because (1) sugar cane deteriorates rapidly after harvesting and this means losses of sugar; (2) at least 7 t of

sugar cane are required to make 1 t of sugar, which means that transport costs must be kept to a minimum.

In the mill, the sucrose is separated from the rest of the cane plant and is then railed to the refineries at Bulawayo or Harare. During the processing, several by-products become available. Bagasse, the remains of the sugar cane after extraction of the sucrose and molasses, is used as a fuel to generate electricity for the mill. Molasses is a thick liquor left after the sugar crystals have been removed. At Triangle, it is made into a rich cattle feed while at Chiredzi the molasses are processed in a special plant to yield alcohol, carbon dioxide and dry ice. The carbon dioxide is used to make dry ice and liquid carbon dioxide.

On the Hippo Valley Estates a canning and processing works has been established for the production of orange and lemon concentrates, canned grapefruit and orange oil. Triangle is the site of the Lowveld's first cotton ginnery, opened in 1968. The ginnery processes the Deltapine cotton grown in the area. At Triangle and Chiredzi there are several light industries. Triangle has a maize mill and various engineering industries associated with vehicle and machine maintenance. Chiredzi has the same industries as well as the following: tyre retreading, soft drink bottling, brewing and dairying.

From these details you can realise the limited degree of industrialisation within the estates: at the same time, you should appreciate the potentialities. At some distance from the Chiredzi-Triangle growth point are two small plants on the land of the Mkwasine Estate. One plant is concerned with the drying of rice while in the other venison is canned. The ethanol distillery is mentioned on page 98 under 'sugar'. This will play a major role in the future of the Lowveld.

Mining

The full extent of the mineral wealth of the South-eastern Lowveld is not yet known and the existing development of mining has been limited. To date, gold is extracted at the RENCO mine and iron ore is mined at Buchwa; coal has great potential. Small deposits of wolfram and copper together with occurrences of limestone, molybdenite, nickel, phosphate, beryl, calcite, chromite and gold illustrate the variety of the mineral deposits of this area. Of course, whether it would be an economic proposition to mine them is another matter. Suppose that you were asked how you would use the coal deposits and iron ore of Buchwa, what suggestions would you make? Here are the facts about the coal and iron other than their location which is shown in Fig. 49.2. The Lower Sabi coalfield has shallow seams of from 0·6 to 3·6 m in thickness and the coal has a fairly high ash content. The Lower Bubye field has seams of 2·4 m in thickness and they contain a good quality coking coal. At Buchwa, the iron ore occurs in a hill that rises some 910 m above the surrounding country. The ore contains between 40 and 60% iron. A branch line from the main Maputo railway was constructed to the iron deposits and before UDI, some of the ore was exported to Japan. If you positively cannot think of how these deposits can be profitably used, the answer is given below.

The future

The planned irrigation schemes are shown in Fig. 49.1. By 1970, the Sabi-Limpopo Authority expected to have over 303 000 ha under irrigation. Some 40 000 ha were irrigated by 1970 which compared with 80 000 ha under irrigation on European farms on the high and middle veld. The government is eager to develop the estates and settler farms of this area, but the investment required is very large.

Table 33 shows that maize and wheat do better on the highveld than on the lowveld. Wheat does not yield so well under high temperatures and maize also yields less. Cotton, however, flourishes and sugar, of course, cannot be grown profitably on the cooler highveld.

Table 33 Comparison of crop yields on highveld and lowveld

	Unit of measurement	Lowveld	Highveld
Maize	t per ha	·9	6·0
Cotton	kg per ha	3 360	1 215
Wheat	t per ha	2·8	4·5

Two implications arise from the higher yields of the Lowveld. First, investment is made more attractive and secondly, the need for external markets is underlined. The future expansion of agriculture will lead to an increase in the output of the processing industries and to the setting up of new industries. For instance, jams may be produced from the citrus fruits and vegetable canning may develop based on vegetable growing in Chisumbanje and the Middle Sabi.

In mining you will probably have thought of the likely developments. A firm of consultants suggested that a large thermal power station be constructed on the Lower Sabi coalfield. This would use effectively the low quality coal. The coking coal of the Lower Bubye coalfield could form the basis of an iron and steel industry, using the iron ore deposits of Buchwa. Such proposals as these are of a very long-term nature.

Tourism is a less distant prospect. Some of the larger dams, still on the drawing board, may be developed as national parks but the main attraction is likely to be the Buffalo Bend Game Park. The future of ethanol will affect any decision on expansion of sugar estates.

Gletwyn Farm

This farm lies on the eastern outskirts of Harare on the Enterprise Road. From Fig. 46 you can see that Gletwyn is located in Natural Farming Region II. Do you remember the farming system recommended for this region? If you do, you will not be surprised to find that Mr Ross, the owner of Gletwyn, has a varied farm production which includes seed maize, commercial maize, soya beans, sorghum, winter wheat and fattened cattle. Gletwyn is 1 200 ha in size and of this area some 320 ha are cultivated. Mr Ross believes that still more will be made arable. The remaining 880 ha are used for grazing; some of it, however, is too rough for any profitable use.

On the farm map, you can see that the relief is quite hilly. What is the direction of slope of Gletwyn Farm? The lower ground in the north forms vleis which are used mainly for grazing. This land is affected by frost in winter; so to avoid frost damage, Mr Ross plants his wheat in late May rather than earlier in the month. The annual rainfall figures kept by the farmer include the following which show considerable variation:

1978–79	730 mm
1979–80	767 mm
1980–81	1 164 mm
1981–82	619 mm

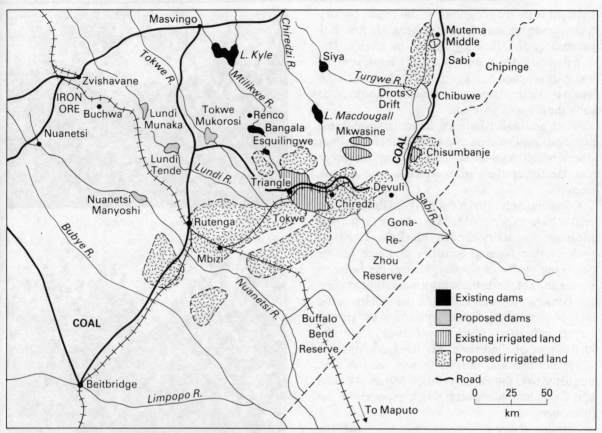

Fig. 49.2   Some present and future developments in the South-eastern Lowveld

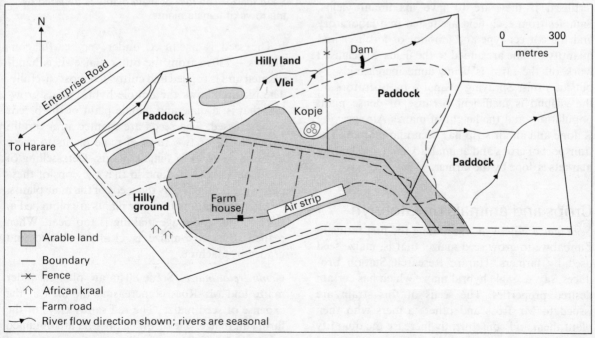

Fig. 50   Gletwyn farm

Drought years are uncommon in this region but dry spells during the summer are frequent. Mr Ross has guarded against these by sinking boreholes. The water obtained not only provides supplementary water in summer but also permits the growth of wheat in winter. More water is needed, however, to solve the dry spell problem.

Wind and hail combined have flattened some maize on Gletwyn in past years. It is the late summer storms which cause the damage, since in November and December the maize, which is still young, recovers.

Knowing only the location of Gletwyn, we might have expected Mr Ross to be a market gardener or a dairy farmer. Mr Ross, however, prefers other farming activities as noted at the beginning of this case study. Hence, the farmer's wishes and not the distance from markets determine the farming programme. In the past, dairy cattle and pigs were kept and tobacco was grown, further indications of the possibilities of farming in this part of Zimbabwe. Mr Ross employs one white assistant and thirty Africans, as well as a mechanic to maintain 6 tractors, 3 lorries, 4 trucks and 2 combine harvesters, which represent a big investment.

Farming today is a highly scientific business. For example, every year lands must be limed and fertilised if they are to give maximum yields. Samples from each field are tested in a laboratory and the correct type and amount of fertiliser and quantity of lime are added to the fields. Specialised work on the farm is being done increasingly by outside firms. Spraying of maize by operators on the ground is inefficient because of dense plant populations and the height of maize. Air spraying is done and an air strip has been marked out. The transport of crops and animals to and from Harare markets is done by the farmer.

Crops and animals on Gletwyn

Seed maize: Gletwyn was among the first farms in Zimbabwe to grow seed maize, that is, maize seed used by farmers. Harare Research Station produces, say, a single hybrid maize which has certain desired properties. The seeds of this strain are issued to Mr Ross and other farmers who then plant them and consequently increase the quantity of seed. This process is called bulking up.

Part of the maize crop at Gletwyn

Seed maize. The row of male plants is dwarfed by the rows of female plants

The seed is produced under very carful conditions – 730 m from the other maize; it is hand-planted and is rogued and cultivated most carefully. The picture shows the double hybrid seeds growing, that is, a male and female plant of the breeds to be crossed. The seeds are planted in a certain pattern: one or two rows of male plants to every three or six rows of female plants. Detasselling of the female plants is done so that the cobs of these plants are pollinated by the seeds of the male plants.

After pollination, the male plants are ploughed in since labour for silage making is too dear. When reaped, the seed maize is cleaned, shelled and graded by machine.

Commercial maize: Some 80 ha are planted under maize and Mr Ross is increasing the area at the expense of seed maize. The red sandy clays of the farm suit maize. Yields of 7·8 t per ha are obtained as a result of heavy fertilisation, spraying and regular cultivation. Machines are used whenever possible on this maize as they are more efficient than hand labour.

After harvesting, the maize plant is ploughed in as this returns food to the soil. The same maize lands are put under maize year after year, a practice called monoculture. Pests like stalk borer and aphids are common while cutworm is a nuisance. All are controllable and the cost of control is one of the expenses of cultivating the crop.

Soya beans are a useful crop in the farm's rotation which is soya beans, wheat and seed maize. Soya beans have been an established crop on the farm and are grown for their seed. Mr Ross cannot grow commercial maize near to his seed maize and soya beans are cultivated in those fields. An average yield of 2·7 t per ha is obtained.

Sorghum: This crop has proved to be profitable and is grown next to seed maize.

Cattle: The cattle-maize combination is profitable. Each season some 150 to 200 yearlings are bought at cattle sales. They are fattened for one year and sold to the Cold Storage Commission. The fattening is done in two stages. During the summer, the veld grass is grazed. Three paddocks are fenced off and the cattle graze these in rotation each year. For three months of the winter, they are fed in pens on silage made up of the male rows of maize plants. Then in July, the beasts are sold. Ticks on the cattle are dealt with by dipping once a week.

The calendar given below shows the cycle of a farmer's life. Mr Ross has one light working period during February and March but at other times he must be on the farm. The calendar begins with October as this month marks the beginning of the farming year.

October: Reaping of wheat. Final land preparation for summer crops. Groundnuts planted.

November: Onset of rains; planting. Cultivation and spraying with herbicides.

December: Soya beans and sorghum planted. Cultivation.

January: Cultivation. Detasselling of seed maize.

February: Cultivation. Detasselling of seed maize.

March: Cultivation. Detasselling of seed maize.

April: Silage making completed. Soya beans and sorghum reaped. Seed maize reaped at end of month. Cattle in pens now fed. Ploughing for wheat started.

May: Seed maize reaped. Wheat planted. Land ploughed. Cattle feeding.

June: Commercial maize and seed maize reaped. Ploughing.

July: Commercial maize and seed maize reaped. Ploughing.

August: Commercial maize and seed maize reaped. Ploughing.

September: Commercial maize and seed maize reaped. Ploughing.

Construct a circular calendar by drawing concentric circles, putting the months on the outside circumference and the activities of each month inside the circles.

Future plans include the construction of a large dam in the northwest of the farm. Water will be pumped to arable land near the air strip. Some 80 ha will be irrigated and this will offset to some extent mid-season drought.

Things to do

1 Draw a map of the natural farming regions of Zimbabwe. Give the meaning of effective rainfall.

2 Describe land use in Natural Farming Region I, noting the conditions under which the crops are grown.

3 Cotton, maize and cattle are the chief supports of Zimbabwe farming today. Discuss this statement.

4 Practise drawing the map showing the distribution of crops in Zimbabwe.

5 Topics for class discussion:
water conservation; changes in the farming landscape; comparison of farming methods on Gletwyn and any other farm; new crops.

6 Try to keep a record in the form of a calendar of a single crop grown on a farm known to you. Then try to find out how the farmer fits in the work done on the crop with the other farm work.

7 Discuss the economic value of the Sabi-Limpopo area to Zimbabwe.

8 Contrast any large drainage scheme with the South-eastern Lowveld.

9 Draw bar graphs to show the areas under maize and cotton (see Table 29 on page 92) in each province.

16   Fisheries (Zimbabwe)

Despite Zimbabwe's distance from the sea, fishing has become important to the country in three ways. It yields a significant source of protein to the African who, as you may have seen at the beginning of Chapter 8 – Fisheries (Malawi) – eats much starchy food like maize. Fishing has encouraged business and thus contributed to the nation's wealth; it is also a popular recreational pursuit. Of interest is that fishing is done largely in man-made lakes and small streams of the Eastern Districts. In 1981, the commercial catch for Lake Kariba was 11 000 t, a big increase over the 1977 catch of 9 000 t.

Commercial fisheries

The largest area of water in Zimbabwe is Lake Kariba. In Kariba is concentrated Zimbabwe's commercial fishing, controlled by several business enterprises. The business firms catch fish and also buy from the fishermen, transporting the fish by refrigerated truck to the urban markets. Some African traders compete in the latter markets as well as selling in the communal lands. Some 60% of the fish caught are saro therodon (bream), 15% labeo (mudsucker) and the balance comprises mainly barbel and tiger fish. Of the 2 000 t per annum which are caught, 50% are marketed as fresh fish and 50% as dried fish.

The Fisheries Research Officers have been disappointed by the low production from Lake Kariba and they believe that the failure of one type of bream to populate the open waters partly accounts for this. However, a freshwater sardine

Sardine fishing at night on Lake Kariba. Note the use of bright lights to attract the fish.

The giant Malaysian prawn is cultivated in ponds at Kariba. Industry is thriving and provides local employment

Off-loading sardines on Lake Kariba. In 1981 almost 10 000 tonnes of Kapenta were loaded as compared with 1 200 tonnes in 1977.

has been stocked by the Zambian authorities and this has led to open-water fishing. Sardines, or kapenta as they are called, are caught at night, the fishermen using lights to attract the fish to the boat and nets.

On Lakes McIlwaine and Robertson the main catch landed is bream with barbel second. Poachers are a menace here no doubt because of the nearness of the Harare market where they can sell their catch.

Lake Kyle and the other dams of the Lowveld were stocked with the bottle nose and barbel and the exotic yellow fish and black bass. Bream are caught by the commercial fishermen.

Commercial fisheries are also located on Mazowe Dam and other privately owned dams. The smaller farm dams are cropped by gill and seine nets and yields are of the order of 160–180 kg per annum. In communal lands many dams are fished by rod and line, basket traps and nets.

Fish ponds have increased recently in popularity. They are best run along with poultry or pigs whose waste can be used as a fish food. The ponds are fished daily by rod and line and traps. Experiments have shown the economic success of rice culture and fish, and this combination may increase.

In the Eastern Districts considerable quantities of trout are produced in hatcheries and then put into the local streams and dams. Brown, rainbow and brook trout are all hatched and these are enough to make for commercial as well as private fishing.

Recreational fishing

The annual International Tiger Fishing Contest at Lake Kariba attracts many anglers. In addition, that there are many serious anglers in the country. Trout fishing has recently gained greatly in popularity. All of this means a rising demand for tourist facilities, an added incentive to foreign travellers to visit the country and a demand for fishing tackle.

Things to do

1 Discuss some of the advantages of a fishing industry to Zimbabwe.

2 If you are a fisherman write down where you fish and why you select certain spots to fish.

111

17 Mining (Zimbabwe)

Study the map above and answer the following questions which will assist you to describe the distribution of mines.

1 Name the geological features around which most of the mining is carried on (compare Fig. 51 with the geological map, Fig. 39).

2 Name two of the minerals mined in the west of Zimbabwe.

3 Name the minerals mined in the south-east of the country.

4 Name the minerals extracted north-east of Harare.

The next step for you is to practise drawing the map of the mining areas. You will find this task easy if you insert the railway routes and the Great Dyke as first steps.

When you have drawn a good copy of this map, you should compare it with the geology map of Zimbabwe. Try to name the different minerals associated with the gold belts, the Great Dyke and the sedimentary rocks.

Table 34 Mineral production ($ thousands)

	1970	1980
Gold	12 000	145 000
Asbestos	18 000	70 000
Nickel	17 000	56 000
Copper	25 000	35 000
Coal	9 000	28 000
Chrome ore	5 000	18 000
Iron ore	1 000	15 000
Silver	250	13 000
Tin	3 000	10 000

Uses of minerals

What follows is a list of uses and derived products of the main minerals mined in the country. Some you will find interesting but others that don't appeal at first should not be ignored. The best approach to these initially uninteresting facts is to think how they affect you in your daily life, e.g. asbestos and brake linings. We use so many things made of metal that we should find this easy.

Asbestos

This mineral is valuable because it is resistant to heat and can be easily spun into yarn. Fireproof materials such as sheets, brake linings, fireproof paints and firemen's clothing are typical products. Most asbestos, however, is used in the manufacture of asbestos cement products such as roofing tiles and corrugated sheeting.

Copper

Next to silver, copper is the best electrical conductor, and because of this property the electrical industry consumes some 50% of all copper produced. The metal is used in the form of wire for cables and in winding transformers, generators and electrical motors of all kinds.

Copper alloys absorb the bulk of the remaining copper production. Of the many alloys, brasses are by far the most important. The properties of brass, which is made from copper and zinc, depend on the proportions of these two elements. Thus, cartridge brass makes fine cartridge cases and headlamp reflectors, while clock brass is used in the making of the working parts of watches and clocks.

Bronze, an alloy of copper and tin, has a wide application in engineering, ornamental work and ordnance manufacture. Copper's resistance to

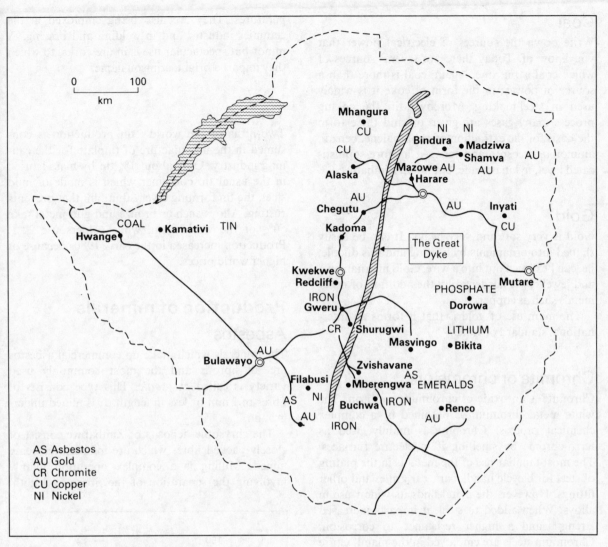

Fig. 51   Chief mines of Zimbabwe

corrosion, malleability (the property of being hammered into a sheet) and heat conductivity were appreciated by early man, who made copper cooking utensils. Modern uses which take advantage of these properties include gas and water piping, car radiators and copper roofing. The Harare Cathedral has a copper roof.

Nickel

This metal has many desirable properties including a high resistance to corrosion, heat-resistance, great strength and ductility. Like chromite, nickel is added to steel to produce alloys possessing different properties. When 5% of nickel is added,

the steel is hardened; the addition of over 24% causes the steel to become highly resistant to the conduction of electricity, a very valuable property for heating coils of electric fires and toasters.

The main use of nickel is in stainless steel which contains 18% chromite and 8% nickel. Other nickel alloys are widely used in gas turbines, undersea mining, in space vehicles and in petro-chemistry.

Pure nickel has long been used in electro-plating. Invar is an unusual steel which neither expands nor contracts at ordinary temperatures. Such a property is vital in measuring tapes and rods. The word *invar* is an abbreviation of the word *invariable*.

Coal

Write down the sources of electrical power that you know of. Today there are several sources of which coal is but one. Again, coal is more than a source of power; in the form of coke it is widely used in steel-making. Moreover, in the coking process many gases are given off and these form the basis for the extraction of naphthalene, benzol, ammonia, creosote and tars. At a more sophisticated level, nylon is made, but not in Zimbabwe.

Gold

Gold is very soft and very heavy. It can be easily shaped into ornaments by heating and it is ductile, i.e. can be drawn out into a wire. Gold in ornaments and jewellery is hardened by the addition of other metals such as copper.

The main use of gold is that it forms an international standard of value.

Chromite or chrome ore

Chromite is an oxide of chromium and iron. The white metal chromium is obtained by a complex chemical process. Chromite is mainly used as ferro-chrome by smelting it in electric furnaces. The most familiar use of the metal is in the plating of steel for bicycle handlebars, car grilles and other fittings. However, the metal finds its widest use in alloys. When added to steel, it imparts increased strength and a higher resistance to corrosion. Chromium steels are employed in the manufacture of automobiles, aircraft and railway carriages, where their lightness and strength prove ideal. Stainless steel kitchen units, cutlery and other domestic equipment are all made from stainless steel which has a higher content of chromium. To produce these alloys the chromium is added in the form of ferro-chrome since this is cheaper to produce than the pure metal.

A second major use of chromite is in refractories or furnace linings. In this case, the chromite is embodied in bricks and cement.

Lithium

Lithium compounds are used in making lubricating greases that can withstand high and low tem-

peratures. They are also being employed in the ceramics industry and in welding and brazing. A minor but spectacular use is in fireworks, to which they impart a bright, crimson flame.

Tin

Two-fifths of the world's tin production is consumed in the manufacture of tinplate for the canning industry. Only about 1% tin by mass is used in the usual tin container which is made of mild steel, the tin forming a very thin film that prevents rusting. Alloys such as bronze and gun-metal take 50% of the world's tin, while solders use 22%. Production increased in the early 1980s because of higher world prices.

Production of minerals

Asbestos

The minerals which make up commercial asbestos are all fibrous and the most commonly used variety is called *chrysotile*. This type consists of fibres of 2 mm or less in length. It is mined underground.

The chrysotile deposits of Zimbabwe consist of closely packed fibres which are milled after being mined. Milling is a complex operation mainly involving the separation of the fibres by length.

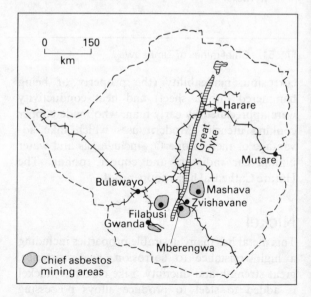

Fig. 52   Chief asbestos mining areas

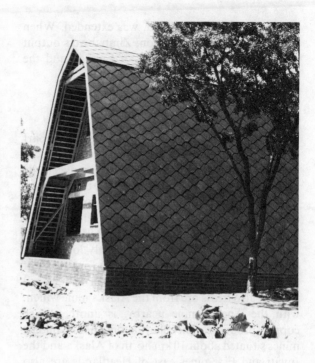

Some asbestos products. Try to name them

Asbestos, unlike the metals, is not a single commodity, but comprises a series of grades which are distinguished by the length of the fibres. The fibres are separated by screening, and air suction removes them with the minimum damage.

Note the names of the main mining areas which are shown in Fig. 52. How would you describe the position of these areas in Zimbabwe and relative to the Great Dyke?

Zimbabwe led the world in the production of top grade chrysotile fibre. Canada and Russia produce much more asbestos than Zimbabwe but their output of top grade fibre is less.

Asbestos was first discovered in the country at Zvishavane in 1906. An initial obstacle, as in the case of other minerals, was the absence of a rail link with Beira. Through which port is asbestos exported today? Until the line from Bannockburn to Maputo was opened in 1956, asbestos was railed through Beira.

When demand for a commodity exceeds supply, the price of that commodity rises. This is a basic economic principle and you should try to think of examples to illustrate it. In the case of asbestos, an illustration is given in the figures at the top of the next column.

1948 17 asbestos mines
1952 52 ,, ,,
1953 19 ,, ,,

After the dramatic increase in the number of asbestos mines in 1952, there was almost as great a decline in 1953. Can you suggest a reason?

Zimbabwe could not and cannot compete easily with Canada on overseas markets. If you think of the relative position of the two countries in the land hemisphere and their comparative accessibility to the sea you will find the answers. Nevertheless, some mines in Zimbabwe are managing to compete successfully for markets for 'shorts'. Zimbabwean industry consumes only a very small proportion of the total output. The largest markets were the United Kingdom and the German Federal Republic.

About 75% of the production is controlled by a large company, Turner and Newall, which also makes a variety of asbestos goods in Canada, the USA and the United Kingdom. The small mines have been forced to close down in face of economic difficulties which larger concerns can solve by spending big sums of money on improved production methods and general efficiency.

Vanguard, Pangani and Bos mines closed in 1981.

Shabani, on the other hand, was extended. When the new mill is in production, Zimbabwe's output will be comparable with that of Canada and the USSR.

Copper

Note the copper mines from the map and, apart from two of them, note their scattered distribution. The Mangula mine is the largest producer, its output in 1965 amounting to 15000 t of copper. The ore is concentrated at Mangula, and the concentrates are fire-refined at the Alaska refinery. Fire-refined copper has a purity of 99·9%, that is, higher than blister copper but slightly lower than electrolytic copper. (Study page 179 for details of blister and electrolytic copper.) Alaska smelter and refinery also treats ore from the Alaska mine which, with the Angwa mine nearby, is another large copper producer. The Shackleton and Avondale mines situated about 10 km north of Alaska and the Inyati and Era mines east of Headlands are also important currently operating copper mines. The Shamrock, northeast of Karoi, was a large producer for several years before closing down in 1978.

The copper content of the ores is low when compared with those of the Copperbelt (see page 175. Mangula averages 1·37% and Alaska 1·9%; these are still above the USA average of 0·8%.

Nickel

Do you remember the uses of this metal? Only in the late sixties was serious attention given to nickel deposits in this country. In 1968, Canada produced about 50% of the world's nickel, most of it coming from the Sudbury district. Consuming countries have been concerned for the past ten years about the continuing supply of this metal. Labour problems in Canada aggravated the position and led to the development of prospecting and exploration for new nickel sources throughout the world.

Zimbabwe's deposits, associated with the ancient rocks of the gold belts, were examined. Quite dramatically, this examination led to the setting up of the Madziwa near Shamva, the Trojan near Bindura and the Shangan between Gweru and Bulawayo. The Empress near Kadoma was partly developed and it expanded with the upsurge in demand. It is planned that each mine will have a

costly metallurgical plant to produce pure nickel.

Copper is a by-product of nickel production and a small amount comes from the Zimbabwean Nickel Corporation (which owns the Trojan, Madziwa and Epoch mines) at the Trojan Mine. In 1975 a rich prospect was opened at Shangani and in 1976 the Epoch mine was opened at Filabusi. In 1982, The Empress mine closed because of falling prices caused by world recession.

Chromite

Production of chromite increased fairly steadily from 1907 to 1960 apart from a drop in the early thirties. What was the economic condition in the UK and USA in the early thirties? From 1960 to the present, output has fluctuated in response to changes in the world demand and it has suffered severely from the dumping by the USSR of large quantities of chrome ore on the world market.

Zimbabwe is a leading world producer of chromite and some 90% of this output is of high grade, suitable for use in alloys.

Occurrence of chrome ore

1 *Parallel seams of Great Dyke*

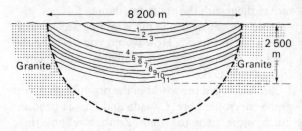

Fig. 53   Parallel seams of the Great Dyke

Look at Fig. 53 which shows a fascinating geological structure. In theory, miners beginning at either end of, say, seam No. 1, would meet in the middle! You can visualise the structure of the Great Dyke as you go along the road from Harare to Banket. Count the seams in the diagram.

The seams vary in thickness from a few mm to 35 cm. The photo shows one seam being worked in an inclined shaft. Originally, the seams were worked by open-cast operations but this method limits the extent of mining.

Miners examining a chrome seam

2 *Large lens-shaped bodies at Shurugwi and Mberengwa* It was at Shurugwi that chrome was first discovered and today the output from the mines in this area makes up over 40% of the country's production. It is much cheaper to mine chrome ore in these bodies than in the other types of deposits in the country. Thus, when demand on the world market falls, the first mines to suffer will be the small ones.

3 *Eluvial deposits* This is another interesting kind of deposit which occurs in the northern portion of the Great Dyke. In poorly drained, flat areas the source rock of chromite decomposes in place. The chromite is not removed and accumulates in the soil to a depth of about 40 cm.

While nearly all chromite is exported an increasing amount is consumed locally at factories in Gweru and Kwekwe.

Gold

The early development of Zimbabwe owes much to gold. Can you think of the reasons?

In the first place, stories of large deposits of this metal lured men over the Limpopo. Gold also gave the stimulus to railway construction since it could bear the cost of a long rail haulage and sea journey (gold is carried by air today) to Great Britain and, thirdly, there were no marketing problems.

Gold paid for the railways which in turn greatly facilitated the exploration of base metals and generally helped to open up the country to a cash economy.

Try to draw a map of Zimbabwe showing the gold belts and the railways. Make notes on gold production below this map using the following headings:

> Uses of gold;
> Importance of gold to the economy;
> Occurrence;
> Production.

The metal occurs in veins, commonly in quartz, and it is usually invisible to the naked eye. More romantically, gold is found in river beds and a picture of an old prospector panning material from a river bed is brought to mind. Such deposits are called *alluvial* or *placer* which is gold that has been transported by water from exposed veins and deposited downstream. The lower Angwa River was the scene of one panning operation. Can you think of another very valuable mineral which was found in river beds in South Africa?

When we look at the number of mines producing gold in 1964 we find the staggering figure of 285. However, almost 75% of the output came from only 14 of these mines; and it is these same mines which have been the mainstay of gold-mining for many years. The main problem facing gold producers was that while the basic price remained at $25 per fine ounce costs of production increased. This situation hit the small worker more than the large company. Why? The official gold price is no longer the controlling one and Zimbabwean mines sell their gold on the free market where the price varies greatly but is always considerably higher than the fixed price of $25.

The government helped the small worker by providing a roasting plant at Kwekwe which extracted the gold from ores which the miner himself could not treat. This plant has been shut down because the small worker found it more and more difficult to produce gold at a fair profit.

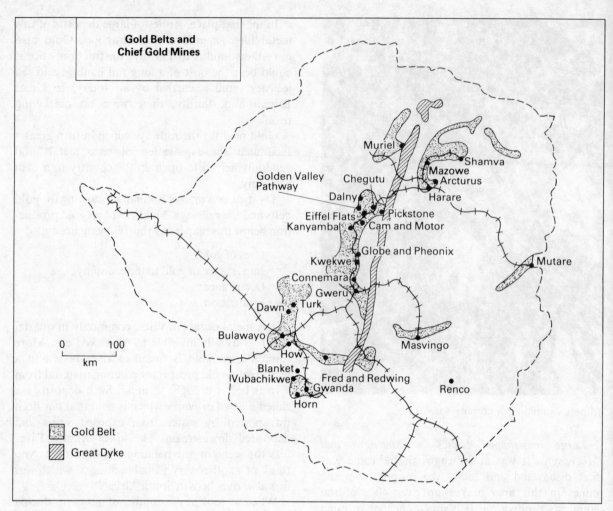

Gold Belts and Chief Gold Mines

Muriel
Shamva
Mazowe
Golden Valley
Pathway
Chegutu
Arcturus
Dalny
Harare
Pickstone
Eiffel Flats
Kanyamba
Cam and Motor
Globe and Pheonix
Mutare
Kwekwe
Connemara
Gweru
Dawn
Turk
Bulawayo
Masvingo
How
Blanket
Vubachikwe
Fred and Redwing
Gwanda
Renco
Horn

0   100
km

▒ Gold Belt

▨ Great Dyke

Fig. 54   Location of gold mines

Among the regular producers are those near Harare, namely the Arcturus, Mazoe, Muriel and Shamva mines, the Dalny, Golden Valley and Patchway mines near Chegutu and the Blanket, How and Vubachikwe mines south-east of Bulawayo.

Rio Tinto's RENCO gold mine near Masvingo is also a large producer and could become the largest in the country by the end of 1982.

The yield of gold from the different mines varies considerably and is of a low order, e.g. in 1965 it varied from 4 to 8·5 grams per t.

Coal

Do you remember what type of rock coal is? We believe that the coal of Hwange area was laid down some 250 million years ago when the area was swampy and covered with a dense vegetation. On the edges of a huge lake trees and ferns were submerged as they died. Later, this mass of vegetable matter which accumulated over a period of several million years, became covered by sediments and was compacted into bituminous coal.

In the Hwange area one seam reaches a thickness of twelve m and it is called the Hwange Main Seam. In Nos. 2 and 3 collieries at Hwange the main seam averages six m in thickness. The lower half of this seam is mined during the development or advancing stage while the upper half is extracted during retreat.

In Europe generally there are several thin seams rather than one very thick seam. Can you think of the way in which several thin seams might be formed? In Zimbabwe, there would seem to have been a fairly luxuriant forest and fern growth which continued over one long period.

Hwange coal is bituminous and is excellent for steam-raising and coking. Try to write down the by-products obtained from the coking process. The coal rests on a layer of fireclay which makes fine firebricks used for furnace walls.

The Hwange Colliery is the major coal producer in Central Africa. Cecil Rhodes, fully aware of the significance of coal to the economy of a country, diverted the proposed Cape to Cairo railway so that it passed through Hwange. It was in October, 1903, that the first trainload of coal was sent to Bulawayo.

Production increased steadily and in the 1920s the development of the Copperbelt and expansion of industries generally foreshadowed the heavier demands on the colliery. In 1927, No. 2 colliery was opened up, and during this year, for the first time, production exceeded one million tonnes.

After a decline in output in the early thirties, due to the world-wide trade depression, production was raised. The post-war boom in industry justified the opening of No. 3 colliery in 1953. The three collieries could meet the anticipated demand of 5 million t in 1956. This demand, however, did not materialise and a search was begun for overseas markets. In 1958, coal consumption fell and in 1962 it was only 3 million t. What event occurred in 1960 in the field of power to hasten this decline?

What steps would you suggest be taken to solve this problem of falling demand?

One answer is to reduce output and No. 1 colliery was closed down in 1958. Since 1970, however, four open cast mines have been opened, partly to cope with fluctuations in demand because coal is obtained more cheaply and partly to obtain coal with different properties. The rock and soil, that is, the over-burden, above the coal seam is first removed in order to expose the coal. After drilling and blasting the coal is loaded on to trucks which tip it on to a conveyor system feeding the coal preparation plant.

The underground collieres functioning are Nos. 3 and 4. No. 2 colliery was hit by tragedy in June, 1972 when over 400 miners lost their lives as a result of underground explosions. A cause of these explosions was the large accumulation of methane gas.

After this disaster No. 4 colliery was opened. This is a highly mechanised colliery but faulting of the coal seam has hindered production. In 1977, No. 4 colliery was put on care and maintenance the demand for coal being met by No. 3 underground colliery and the four open cast mines.

The main markets for coal are the iron and steel industry at Redcliff, thermal power stations as at Umniati, Mutare, Bulawayo and Harare, and general industry. Many tobacco farmers have turned to coal firing their barns because of the shortage of wood. More coal is consumed in high density townships for cooking as well as for heating during winter.

By-products of coal include ammonia liquor, benzole and tar. The ammonia liquor is used in the mining industry and also in the making of fertilizers. Benzole is added to petrol.

Lack of export markets is due to (1) the inland position of Hwange, which lies nearly 1 500 km from Maputo, (2) the cost of railing the coal to the seaboard, and (3) the highly competitive nature of the current markets which include the Far East and South America.

Two adverse factors affecting coal production in the sixties were the opening of Kariba and the dieselisation of railways. On the other hand, the iron, steel and the metallurgical industries, as well as the manufacturing industries expanded. The required extra energy will come from a thermal power station already built at Hwange. Stage 1 of the project giving 480 MW will be ready in 1983. coal will be carried to the station by a conveyor belt some 4 km in length. This coal has a high ash content but with modern technology it can be used in furnaces. Stage 2 of the power station will yield a further 400 MW in 1985. Even so, more power will still be required and this will probably be hydro-power derived from either the Mupata or Batoka Gorges.

Iron ore

The only iron ore deposits that are at present worked in Central Africa are at Redcliff, 14 km from Kwekwe and at Buchwa, near Mberengwa. There are many other iron ore occurrences in Zimbabwe, several of high economic value; Redcliff was selected for development because of the proximity of iron ore, limestone and manganese.

Recently, the reserves of high grade iron ore at

Redcliff have become so depleted that ore has been railed from Buchwa or obtained from the nearby Ripple Creek deposit. The story of ZISCO can be found on this page and pages 121–123.

Lithium
Zimbabwe is one of the leading producers and the amount produced depends on the demand of overseas markets.

Where is lithium mined in Zimbabwe? While the map of the mineral producing areas shows the main area to be near Masvingo, there are smaller mines near Goromonzi, east of Harare and near Odzi.

Tin
Don't you find it surprising that tin is mined in the west of the country at Kamativi? Although surrounded by sedimentary rocks, the tin is extracted from metamorphic rocks which have been partly exposed by erosion.

Limestone
Not mentioned under uses of minerals but nevertheless very important. It is, in fact, used in the making of cement and the main deposits are quarried at Colleen Bawn, near Gwanda, at Redcliff, at Sternblick outside Harare and at Alaska near Chinhoyi.

Other minerals
Since 1958, emeralds have been mined in the Sandawana area near Mberengwa. Very little is published about this mineral because information could well influence the price.

Iron pyrites and phosphates
Iron pyrites is mined at Iron Duke mine some 48 km north of Harare and is used in the manufacture of sulphuric acid. Phosphates are extracted at Dorowa, south of Inyazura. The Dorowa deposits were developed by African Explosives and Chemical Industries who own Rodia factory in Harare.

Factors influencing mining
The four major factors influencing mineral production are listed below, but perhaps you might have deduced them from your reading of this chapter. The factors are:

> Overseas markets;
> Railways;
> Port facilities;
> Power supplies.

Before continuing to read further, jot down the ways in which these factors influence mining.

Overseas markets
Mineral production is geared to overseas markets. Why? Think of the small quantities used in Zimbabwe. As the metallurgical industries expand, this dependence on external markets will decline. Low prices mean closure of smaller mines, stockpiling of minerals and less exploration.

ZISCO Iron and Steel Works – a case study
The works of the Zimbabwean Iron and Steel Company, abbreviated to ZISCO, are located sone 14 km from Kwekwe in a broad valley. Driving from Kwekwe, we see the township of Redcliff set on a wooded hillside. A red gash in the hill suggests the origin of the name. Then we see the works, a complex of chimneys, gas tanks and strange-shaped buildings. The oddest shape is that of the blast furnace. Close to the works' entrance by the road is a shallow quarry and a few hundred m distant is a red scar on a stepped slope. Our guide, a young metallurgist, meets us at the entrance and gives us a brief talk on the raw materials. From the quarry comes limestone which acts as a flux in the blast furnace. The red scar close by is an open cast iron ore mine. The iron ore (haematite) has a purity of about 60% which is very high by world standards. Some of the ore is so fine that it must be treated before it can be fed into the blast furnace. Since there are three blast furnaces it is not possible to use this fine ore all the time. Ore from other deposits nearby—such as Ripple Creek and the Buchwa, some 190 km distant—is also used. At the Dan deposit manganese is mined.

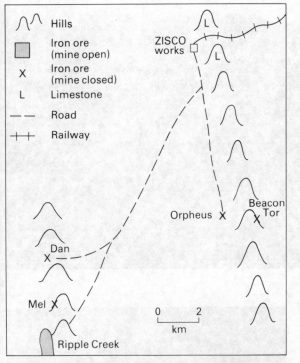

Fig. 55   Location of ZISCO and the local iron ore and limestone deposits

Apart from a few materials of which only a small quantity is necessary, only coal is lacking in the company's land. The coal is railed from Hwange, the only worked coal deposit in the country, and converted into coke at ZISCO. This is far more economic than buying coke direct from Hwange because in making coke a great deal of gas is produced; in fact enough to heat most of the plant at ZISCO. In addition, coke gas produces many valuable by-products such as tar, benzole and ammonia. Benzole is collected by bowsers and is added to petrol. Coke is much harder than coal and contains more carbon. If coal were tipped into a blast furnace it would be crushed under the mass of the other constituents which are mainly iron ore and limestone. Coke, iron ore and limestone are loaded into skips which charge the blast furnaces. We can smell sulphur as we approach the blast furnaces and our clothes become speckled with 'kish', a compound of graphite and sulphur, which resembles Christmas glitter. From a vantage point we watch the slag flow into a pit to be collected and dumped later.

Experiments have been done to find a use for

The works of the Zimbabwean Iron and Steel Company. Limestone is obtained from the pit marked A while the iron ore is obtained from the hill at B.

Iron ore mine

the slag. Until recently, a Bulawayo cement works took some as it contained a large percentage of limestone. Today, the slag is forming hills near the works and we are assured that the company is aware of the danger to natural beauty of such dumps. The heavier iron in the furnace is tapped at a lower level than the slag and is led into giant ladles mounted on rail trucks. These trucks are pushed by locomotives to the open hearth furnaces where the pig iron is poured into a mixer or huge storage tank. When required, the pig iron, still molten, is charged into the open hearth furnace. Some scrap steel is also added to the charge.

The state of the charge in the furnace is constantly checked, using both instruments and physical sampling. We see one sample being taken with a long-handled spoon. Through specially tinted glasses we look into the boiling cauldron where the flames and bubbling steel are shades of red and white. From the sample the metallurgists can tell how much carbon should be removed or how much manganese should be added. Each charge, of course, varies depending on the end use of the steel. For instance, Zimbabwe Railways need high silicon steel for spring steel clips which are fitted to concrete sleepers. The steel is poured into ingots and from these various shapes are produced.

The reducing of blooms—15 cm square rods—is a most fascinating sight. The blooms are passed through rollers which gradually thin them out and

A blast furnace

Molten iron being taken from a blast furnace

plane them. Workers move the blooms and rods with great dexterity from one set of rollers to another and all the time these rods are red-hot. One rod which was crumbled against a roller now stands in front of the ZISCO offices and resembles a piece of modern sculpture.

In the rolling mills large quantities of water are used for cooling the rollers. The Company owns a dam at Cactus Poort and, in addition, can obtain extra supplies from the Kwekwe Municipality.

From Fig. 51 you can see the central position of Redcliff which favours distribution of the finished products. ZISCO has led to the establishment of several industries like the two in Kwekwe. These produce wire of all kinds and rods for reinforcing buildings as well as seamless steel tubes. At Gweru, pig iron is used in the production of cast iron piping and in both Bulawayo and Harare

ZISCO iron and steel are widely used in engineering industries.

Railways

There is a very close relationship between railway routes and the location of mines. From a study of Fig. 51 you can list the minerals which have attracted railways.

After the Second World War mineral production increased to such an extent that the port of Beira could no cope. Then, in 1956, the line from Bannockburn to Maputo was opened. This relieved the pressure until the mid-sixties. In the early 1970's a line from Rutenga on the existing line to Maputo to Beitbridge was constructed to provide a direct link with the South African rail system.

Shortage of trucks has also been a nagging problem since the end of the Second World War. Remember that seasonal agricultural products like maize and cotton compete with minerals for trucks.

Port facilities

The docks of Beira and Maputo are scarcely adequate for the traffic of the seventies. What are possible solutions?

Things to do
1 Visit your nearest mine and collect the following information:
   a) mineral mined;
   b) uses of the mineral;
   c) how it is extracted;
   d) processing of the mineral;
2 a) Draw a map of your district plotting the mines. Alongside each mine stick a piece of the mineral extracted.
   b) At the side of the map make up a table using the headings given below:

Mineral	Uses	Exported to

3 Make a list of the metals you see very often. Note which ones are found in Central Africa.
4 Discuss the importance of railways and roads in the development of mining in Zimbabwe.

123

18 Power (Zimbabwe)

We scarcely notice how important electricity is in our lives. Only when lighting, television sets, factory machinery, irrigation sprinkler systems and lifts in buildings cease to function because of power failure to do we realise just how vital electricity is in our daily round.

Generation of electricity

Electricity may be generated in either thermal power stations or in hydro-electric plants. In thermal stations wood, coal or oil is used to heat water. The steam produced turns turbines which activate huge generators. In hydro-electric plants, water is usually dropped from a great height through pipes to turn water turbines which are connected to generators.

Before 1936, Bulawayo, Harare, Mutare, Gweru and Kadoma had thermal power stations to meet their electricity requirements. Mines, villages and farms depended on small generators which frequently failed. In response to general demand in the country, the Electricity Supply Commission (ESC) was set up in 1936 in order to control the supply and distribution of electricity to other areas besides Bulawayo and Harare which have their own thermal stations. Today, the ESC obtains most of its power from Kariba but there are several other sources, which will be considered in the following paragraphs.

Kariba

Officially opened in 1960, Kariba was constructed to supply the increasing demands of the Copperbelt mines and the fast-growing needs of Zimbabwean manufacturing industry. Estimates made in 1955, assessed the probable power demands in the Central African Federation by 1960 at a figure far beyond the capacity of stations then built and planned.

The site of Kariba on the border between Zimbabwe and Zambia was expected to have had some unifying effect on the two countries.

It is important to appreciate that a hydro-electric plant has several advantages over a thermal plant. Try to make your own list before reading further. Advantages are as follows:
1 A hydro-electric plant has lower maintenance costs; for example, the equipment in a hydro-electric station will last longer.
2 A hydro-electric plant requires fewer staff than does a thermal plant of comparable output.
3 Water conveyes itself to the hydro-electric plant, whereas coal has frequently to be railed long distances from the mine to the thermal station.
4 Rivers are ageless while coalfields become exhausted.
5 Thermal stations cause more air pollution than hydro-electric stations.

These reasons among others led to the decision to proceed with the construction of a hydro-electric station. Transmission lines and towers have added new elements to out landscape. Fig. 56 shows the location of the grid which covers some 1 600 km and which is maintained, like the Kariba power station itself, by the Central African Power Corporation – CAPCO. The Central African power Corporation also controls the output of the thermal power stations connected to its transmission system

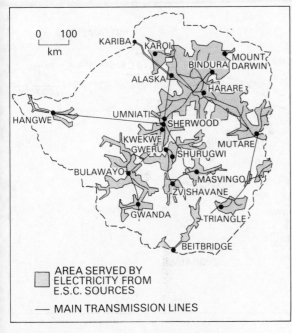

Fig. 56 Areas served by Electricity Supply Commission

and sells power to the ESC and to the cities of Bulawayo and Herare.

The importance of Kariba to Zimbabwe is illustrated in Fig. 56. The other sources of power used by ESC are dealt with below.

Table 35 Power purchased by ESC in 1980–81

	Energy—kW hours
Kariba System	5 100 million
Hippo Valley and Triangle Ltd.	0·6 million
Zambia Electricity Supply Corporation	1·1 million
Messina (Transvaal)	10 million

Before we leave Kariba it is convenient at this point to note that work on the North Bank power station i.e. on the Zambian side of the river was completed in 1976. This station generates up to 600 MW compared with 705 MW on the South Bank Station and all power is fed into the existing grid.

Those of you living in Harare, Bulawayo or Mutare may have noticed the thermal power stations functioning regularly in recent years. More power will have to be produced if manufacturing industries, mining and other sectors of the economy are to grow. A very likely development will be an increase in the generating capacity of Kariba's South Bank Station.

Central African Power Corporation supplies power to both Zambia and Zimbabwe as well as to Zaire as shown in Table 36.

Table 36 Sale of Power by CAPCO (Z$'0000)

	1976	1977
Zambia	22 000	16 000
Zimbabwe	25 000	30 000
Zaire	340	—

Messina

The Messina copper mine in the Northern Transvaal transmits power to Beitbridge which is so isolated from the main transmission line.

Victoria Falls

The hydro-electric station between the third and fourth gorges below the Victoria Falls is connected to the Hwange–Kamativi power line since the thermal station at Hwange coal mine cannot always cope with increasing demands within the area.

Hippo Valley and Triangle

These two stations, using bagasse which is waste material produced during the milling of sugar, provided the power for the Sabi-Lundi irrigation schemes.

Thermal stations of Ummiati, Zvishavane and Mutare

Thermal stations owned by Bulawayo, Harare and the E.S.C. (Ummiati and Zvishavane) are interconnected with the CAPCO grid. In addition we should note the Chipinge station which is a diesel plant. It assists the Lusitu River hydro-electric plant at peak load periods and supplies the nearby tea estates as well as Chipinge township. The Mutare station was noted above and was not used in 1981.

Lowveld power supply

For the first years the Sabi-Limpopo area developed, the thermal plants at Hippo and Triangle proved adequate. With newer and bigger schemes,

125

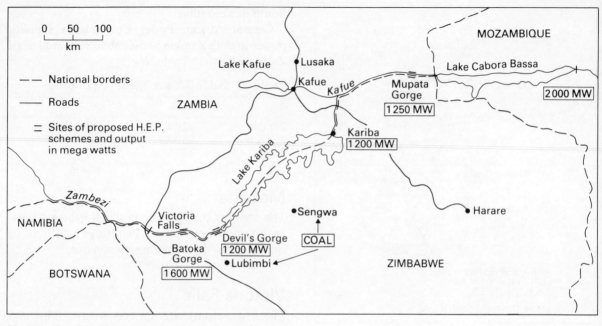

Fig. 57 Proposed hydro-electric power schemes

the planners had to ensure a much greater source of power. What would be your solution to this problem? Several possibilities presented themselves, namely,

1 to link up with the Kariba grid at Zvishavane.
2 to build a thermal plant on the coalfield near Hippo and Triangle and use the local coal
3 to use Hwange coal in the existing thermal plants
4 to construct a transmission line from Mutare.

The Lower Sabi coalfield contains a coal that has a high ash content while the transport of Hwange coal to the lower lowveld thermal plants would be very expensive. The other possibility which was rejected, namely, the link with Zvishavane, would have been unsuitable in 1970. In the 1980s when the Zvishavane area is served wholly by Kariba power, such a link will be made. Meanwhile, on the short term basis, the link with Mutare proved the most economical. A 240 km transmission line from Mutare to Mkwasine has been constructed. This line transmits 40 MW of power which is distributed from a sub-station at Mkwasine and another at the Middle Sabi. The line from the Middle Sabi to Chipinge and to Melsetter covers much of the Eastern Districts including Tilbury Forests and Southdown Tea Estates.

This survey has not included generating plants which are privately owned except for those at Hwange and Redcliff.

Power for the future

In order to determine how best to meet the power needs of Zimbabwe in the eighties, the Government of Zimbabwe employed a group of consultants to study the situation and put forward recommendations. The consultants proposed several hydro-electric schemes and thermal power plants. The major projects are located on the map (Fig. 57) above. The only schemes left out of the map are coalfields in the South East Lowveld.

Government decided to proceed with extensions of two 150 MW generators at Kariba south, and at the same time to go ahead with Hwange power station Stage 1 (see page 119) which will yield 480 MW by 1983. Stage 2 of Hwange will give a further 800 MW by 1985. This power should make Zimbabwe self-sufficient and independent of imports from neighbouring countries such as Mozambique (Cabora Bassa), Zambia (Kariba north) and Zaire (Inga).

Should demands for power exceed those forecasted, then one or more of the other schemes recommended will be implemented. A major difficulty facing development of the coalfields at Sengwa and Lubimbi is isolation. Locate these coalfields on the map and suggest rail routes to existing lines.

Solar and wind power were also examined by the consultants but were not regarded as practicable on a sufficiently large scale.

Things to do

1 Referring to Table 35 on page 125 calculate the percentage of power purchased from each source.
2 Study Table 37 and describe the changes which have taken place in the amount of electricity sold to the different consumers.
3 Represent the data diagrammatically.

The network shown in Fig. 56 has several large gaps in it and comparison of this map with Fig. 61 on page 145 shows that the communal lands are scarcely served at all. ESC are extending electricity supplies to the communal lands where the business

Table 37 Sales of electricity (millions of kWh by use)

Year	Mining	Manufacturing industries and transport	Agriculture and forestry
1969	486	687	109
1970	595	804	144
1971	674	912	157
1972	704	1 050	176
1973	867	1 720	251
1974	948	2 000	195
1975	990	2 200	252
1976	1 000	2 500	298
1977	1 200	2 500	330
1978	1 230	2 700	428
1979	1 220	3 000	536
1980	1 300	3 500	500

centres are close to an existing transmission line. The Commission is also supplying African townships wherever this is economically feasible e.g. Chitungwiza outside Harare.

19 Industries and towns (Zimbabwe)

In Africa south of the Equator, Zimbabwe's output from manufacturing industry is second in value only to that of South Africa. The industries are located in the larger towns along the central watershed as well as in Masvingo. From the table below, you can see the comparative importance of the towns as based on the number of manufacturing establishments.

Table 38 Industrial establishments in main urban centres.

	Number of establishments	Percentage of total establishments
Harare	771	
Bulawayo	368	
Kwekwe	25	
Gweru	41	
Mutare	53	
Kadoma	14	
Marondera	11	
Masvingo	73	
Total	1 369	

The second column has been left for you to complete so that you will appreciate the dominance of the two cities.

Although there is a variety of industries in each centre some specialisation has occurred.

1 Mutare has pulp, paper and board mills associated with the coniferous plantations of the Eastern Border Highlands.

2 Redcliff, Kwekwe and Gweru have iron and steel industries based on the iron ore deposits of Redcliff and the production of iron and steel from that place.

3 Kadoma is associated with cotton spinning and weaving mills which were set up originally because the town was the centre of a cotton growing area.

In all three places industry has been attracted by raw materials.

The attraction of the market has obviously been weaker.

Types of industry

Most industries are based on the processing of primary products, that is, the products of farms and mines, while the remainder use local or imported materials for working up into consumer goods.

Farming products which are changed so that their value is increased (do you recognise the definition of manufacturing industry given on page 22) include maize, wheat, groundnuts, sunflower, cotton, tea, coffee, tobacco, citrus fruit, sugar and cattle.

MAIZE is milled in most of the larger centres and is also made into stockfeed.

WHEAT, some of which is imported, is made into flour at mills in Harare, Bulawayo, Gweru and Mutare.

The oil from GROUNDNUTS and SUNFLOWER is expressed and converted into cooking oils and cake at Harare, Bulawayo, Marondera and Rusape.

TEA-blending and packing are done in Harare, Mutare and Marindera, while COFFEE is ground and blended at Harare and Marondera.

TOBACCO-packing is carried out near to the tobacco auction floors in Harare and all Zimbabwean cigarette manufacturers are located here.

Mazoe and Chiredzi are the two places where ORANGE juice is canned and Chiredzi, Shamva and Harare can segments of GRAPEFRUIT. Mazoe Citrus Estates also produce oils from orange peel which is then made into cattle feed.

SUGAR is refined at Harare and Bulawayo and is used very widely in other food industries. Molasses, a by-product in both sugar-milling and refining, goes to make a cattle feed.

MEATS of all kinds are packed and canned at Harare and Bulawayo and at the recently opened plant at Kadoma. A smaller meat-canning plant is situated at West Nicholson.

FISH, chiefly from Lake Kariba, are frozen, dried or smoked in Harare. The main variety is bream.

The processing of ores includes smelting, refining and the making of alloys. In 1965, 87% of the mineral output was exported and the remainder was used in domestic industry. The iron and steel industry at Redcliff is the largest industry based on mining and it has given rise to a host of ferrous industries at Kwekwe and Gweru in particular. A variety of alloys using several local minerals like chromite, copper and manganese is made at Gweru. Copper is refined at Alaska and asbestos is mixed with cement to give sheeting and piping products.

Many of the engineering and electrical industries use varying amounts of imported raw materials. Plastics, vehicle parts and many chemicals are also imported.

Importance of manufacturing to the Zimbabwean economy

When we compare the percentage contribution of manufacturing industry to the economy with the contribution of some other sectors we find the position shown below.

Table 39 Contribution to economy by some sectors (%)

	1970	1975	1977	1980
Agriculture and forestry	15	17	16	14
Mining and quarrying	7	7	7	7
Manufacturing	29	24	22	24

Manufacturing, then, contributed over 24% to the economy by value in 1980 which is more than that of agriculture and over three times that of mining. Not shown clearly in the table is the adverse effect of the Unilateral Declaration of Independence in November, 1965, and the steady rise from 1966 to 1969, due largely to the in-

dustrialists' response to sanctions imposed by the United Nations Organisation, together with the government's control of imports and raising of tariff barriers. These protective measures enabled industrialists to establish immediately the necessary import substitution industries. Difficulties of quality control, deliveries and establishing new brand names were not sufficiently great to cause a reversal of the upward trend of output. Zimbabwe thus saved foreign exchange.

Dependence on the export of primary products like maize and chromite is unhealthy, since world prices of these products fluctuate greatly. It is therefore to the benefit of Zimbabwe to have a fairly well-developed manufacturing industrial sector which permits the export of processed goods and, at the same time, lowers the need for importing manufacturered goods from foreign countries.

Manufacturing industry in 1980 employed 159 000 persons compared with 66 000 employed in mining and 327 000 in agriculture. While the output by value of manufacturing is increasing, the labour required is decreasing because of mechanisation and higher efficiency. Nevertheless, some industries need more labour than others and the Tribal Trust Development Corporation suggested that such industries be located on the borders of communal lands. In these areas ample manpower is available but adequate roads are frequently lacking and other essentials for industrial location are also non-existent. Consequently, the corporation concentrated on developing projects on borders of communal lands on the central watershed. At Seki, some 25 km from Harare, garments of all kinds are being sewn while at Zimunya, near Mutare, handbags and other leather goods are being made for tourists.

These industrial schemes have been taken over by ARDA (see page 104).

Problems of development

Try to think of them before reading further.

1 Landlocked position of Zimbabwe. This has meant increased costs of exporting overseas and therefore greater difficulty in competing with those countries having a seaboard.

2 Small size of the domestic market. Market size and profitability go hand in hand and, of Zimbabwe's 6½ million people, some 5 million are living

at subsistence level. To raise the income of the 'have nots' of the community is the most difficult economic and human problem facing the country. In 1977, Africans in the communal lands produced the equivalent of $27 per head. This figure compares with $220 per head earned by Africans in the money economy.

3 Competition from industrialised nations which use mass production techniques. By raising tariff barriers and by controlling imports, the government has, for the present, virtually eliminated competition on the domestic market. On the external markets, however, Zimbabwe has to compete on price, quality and delivery dates. This she has done in textiles and clothing as well as in furniture (to South Africa) and in several farming and mining products that have been processed.

4 Many goods used in Zimbabwe cannot be made locally, e.g. machinery. The reasons are the lack of a Zimbabwean market large enough to make such manufacturing profitable and secondly, a shortage of skilled manpower.

Things to do

1 Visit your local shops and find out where the various items on sale have been manufactured. Draw a map of Zimbabwe and on it show the towns where each of the Zimbabwe-made items are produced.

2 Name three crops and three minerals in your locality which are processed. Note the products.

3 Name the products obtained from cotton, sugar and groundnuts.

4 a) Draw sketch maps to show the location and site of a factory which you have studied.

   b) Note the following points about the factory:

     i)   location of factory, i.e. in which town it is, and any reasons you can name for this location;

     ii)   site and any reasons for the choice of that site;

     iii) sources of raw materials;

     iv) layout of buildings, noting relations to roads or to railway siding or to storage of raw materials and finished products;

     v)   methods of production in brief;

     vi) problems of production;

     vii) distribution of product;

     viii) location of markets;

     ix) labour supply.

Tourist industry

Tourism is a labour-intensive industry and is, therefore, well-suited to Zimbabwe. This country has much to offer tourists, especially as variety is important. To those tourists from Western Europe and North America, the sunshine is a great attraction, but the same people are likely to wish to view game, play golf and so on. Our Tourist Board encourages private enterprise to offer diverse attractions and not to depend upon the unique Victoria Falls.

Traffic rights have been granted recently to French, German, Swiss and Australian air lines. This step should encourage more Europeans to visit Zimbabwe. Air fares from Europe, however, are a major restraint to potential tourists. Attempts are being made to lower the costs of travelling by air to Harare and to introduce package deals. For example, special cheaper fares may be offered if tourists visit Kenya, Zambia and Zimbabwe.

Recently published figures show that Zambians are visiting Zimbabwe in much greater numbers

Chinhoyi Caves

(largely on shopping trips) but most visitors (120 000 in 1980) come from South Africa. A favourable sign is the recent marked increase of visitors from overseas. The tourist attractions of Zimbabwe are probably well known to you but have you tried to classify them? One suggestion is that the scenic views and the lakes be grouped together. What other headings would you use in classifying these attractions? Undoubtedly the climate is a great asset with long hours of sunshine and lengthy spells of dry weather, a contrast to climatic conditions over Western Europe.

Attractions without the requisite tourist facilities, cannot, however, be exploited by tourist agencies. Airports, such as the recently opened one at Hwange Game Reserve, roads, administration and accommodation within the Game Reserves, are government's responsibility, as is the publicity material advertising the attractions of the country. Camping grounds and caravan parks are set up and maintained by town councils while private enterprise has built hotels and established car hire firms and travel agencies. Siting of these facilties is interesting to geographers. Away from cities, hotels are located near places of historical interest or they command scenic views. Motels are found most commonly on the outskirts of the larger towns or at road junctions, apart from a few at several holiday resorts. Within the towns, travel agencies are located near the hotels; in Harare, the airway's bus terminal, a large travel centre and hotels border the same street-front which is close to the city centre. The table below summarises some information about tourists to Zimbabwe:

Table 40   Some facts about tourists to Zimbabwe

Year	Total receipts (million $)	Visitors on holiday
1977	10	108 000
1978	10	97 000
1979	7	64 000
1980	24	214 000
1981	32	269 000

In order to improve facilities, a hotel grading system was introduced in 1968. Other inducements to tourists include fishing competitions, trade fairs and agricultural shows. Visitors to these are likely to take the opportunity to tour the Victoria Falls and other attractions.

Things to do

1 Write down the places around your home which you would like to show a tourist. For each place named, state the attraction which a tourist would find.

2 Make a list of the facilities available to tourists in any town in Zimbabwe. Use a newspaper and tourist brochures to help you.

Towns

Types of towns What kinds of towns are there in Zimbabwe? Copy the following headings into your notebook and then insert the towns you know of under the appropriate headings.

Mining	Industrial	Commercial	Administrative

For the purpose of the tabulation, you should select the main activity of each town. Even this is difficult, but the exercise will make you ponder.

Town size

Below is a list of some of the towns of this country arranged in order of size of total population. With the aid of a 1:1 000 000 map of Zimbabwe, you might locate them. On a sketch map or tracing, you might show the population of each town by appropriate symbols.

Table 41   Total populations of major urban centres

Harare	686 000	Kadoma	36 000
Bulawayo	400 000	Chinhoyi	38 000
Chitungwiza	300 000	Marondera	30 000
Gweru	78 000	Masvingo	24 000
Mutare	74 000	Zvishavane	21 000
Kwekwe	62 000	Redcliff	20 000
Hwange	33 000		

Functions of towns

Above we dealt with the activities of a town. We could substitute the word FUNCTION for activity. This is linked with land use in a town, e.g. the commercial function is normally found in the centre of a town, while the industrial and residential functions are located elsewhere. Fig. 58 shows the location of different functions in Masvingo and

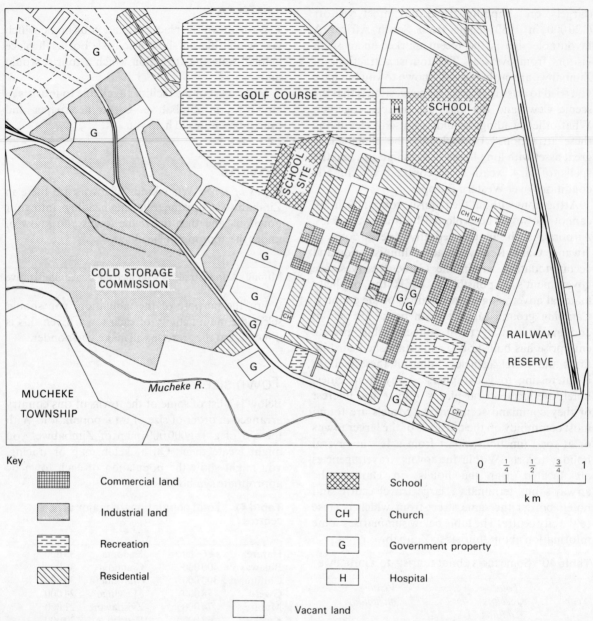

Key

▦ Commercial land		▨ School
▨ Industrial land		CH Church
▤ Recreation		G Government property
▨ Residential		H Hospital
	☐ Vacant land	

0 — ¼ — ½ — ¾ — 1 km

Fig. 58 Masvingo

a clear pattern is visible. Even if you do not live in this town, study the map and think of the pattern of land use in your own town.

Situation of a town

Situation means the same as position or location, that is, where the town is relative to other features. A mining town is situated near to a mineral. Many

Zimbabwean towns are situated on a railway and offer services to the surrounding farming areas.

Site of a town

The site of a town is the land on which it is built. Factors influencing the site include water supply, suitable ground for building, defence, freedom from disease (malaria, for instance) and aspect.

The expanding central business district of Harare. CDB in centre of the photograph is separated from heavy industrial sites by the wooded slopes of Harare Kopje.

Think about the site of your own nearest town. What has influenced where the various buildings are placed? Are there vleis (*dambos*) to be avoided or drained?

Harare

This city is the capital of Zimbabwe, and like other capitals of the world it has a large number of civil servants, and has attracted the head offices of many firms and banks.

When the settlers arrived in 1890 at the present site of Harare, they chose it on account of its good water supply, and the *kopje* which could be easily defended. It was the riches of the surrounding countryside, however, together with good rail links and its choice as capital, which ensured Harare's subsequent growth.

Many industries on the city's two large industrial sites reflect the character of its wealthy farming hinterland. Over $70 million worth of tobacco is

sold annually on its two auction floors, making Harare the greatest single tobacco-selling market in the world. Other important agricultural industries represented include cattle-slaughtering, foodstuff-manufacturing, sugar-refining, grain-milling, dairy product manufacturing, brewing and cigarette-making.

Part of the mineral wealth of Zimbabwe is used in Harare to make asbestos cement products, copper cables, and a variety of iron and steel products.

Many products are assembled in Harare, using both imported and locally-made components. The products include commercial vehicles, and electrical machinery. Several factories manufacture clothing and other textile goods, furniture and plastic goods.

Factors favourable to industrial growth include a pool of labour, a large population to provide a market for goods, good rail and road connections and Kariba power. Also, Harare has an inter-national airport.

The business district of Bulawayo. The grid pattern of streets is very evident

Bulawayo

Bulawayo was the first large settlement to be linked by rail with South Africa. Before the coming of the Europeans, Lobengula's kraal (the capital of Matabeleland) was situated nearby and this determined the situation of the city.

The extension of the railway to Harare and across the Zambezi ensured Bulawayo's supremacy in the southern part of the country, and today it is the major route centre of Central Africa. Naturally, the city is the headquarters of Zimbabwe Railways, and, partly for this reason and partly because of its proximity to the raw materials and markets of South Africa, Bulawayo has become the main engineering centre of the country. Manufacturing industries include radios, which are produced on a large scale for markets both at home and abroad, and tyres, made in the Dunlop Company factory.

The textile and clothing industry ranks second to engineering and is followed by food processing, brewing and soft drink manufacture.

Around Bulawayo there are cattle ranches and forests of Zimbabwean teak which have given rise to such industries as meat canning and the making of parquet floor blocks. The latter are exported to Britain and the USA.

Mutare

This town is situated in the main gap of the Eastern Border Highlands and lies in line with a ridge that continues westwards through Harare. Mutare is therefore a natural entrance for the railway and road from Beira, some 290 km distant; and because of its proximity to Beira, importation of materials to Mutare is cheaper than to Harare. This was one major consideration which led British Leyland to establish a car assembly plant there. A new market was created by the plant for locally produced glass and carpets.

The economic advantage of Mutare's position largely determined the location of the oil refinery too. Unfortunately the oil pipeline has been blown up several times in Mozambique. Industrial growth in Mutare may be stimulated in the future by the availability of by-products from the refinery, but market demand will be the limiting factor for some time to come.

Mutare Board and Paper Mills use large quantities of local pine for mechanical pulp which is processed into paper, cardboard and newsprint. Timber from the Eastern Border Highlands is also used in the making of plywood and boxes.

Other local resources processed in the towns are tea, fruits and vegetables, while coffee holds promise as a basis for another industry.

Power for the town and its industries is drawn from the Kariba grid but there is also a thermal power station.

Gweru

Centrally situated in the country, Gweru is the commercial, educational and industrial focus of the Midlands. It has attracted customers for the more durable consumer goods like furniture and clothing from both Kwekwe and Redcliff although this attraction will diminish as Kwekwe's central shopping centre develops. Gweru also possesses many schools and two teacher training colleges. The city is well-known for its air force base at Thornhill where many pilots were trained during the Second World War.

A variety of light industries is to be found in Gweru including clothing and light engineering. The heavy industrial sites contain a large ferro-chrome (see p. 114) works which process chromite from the Great Dyke. Iron from Redcliff and cement from Matabeleland are used in the manufacture of cast iron fittings and concrete products respectively.

Kwekwe

This town owes its origin to the development of the Globe and Phoenix gold mine which, together with other smallworkings on the same gold belt, was exploited in the 1890s. Kwekwe lies in the middleveld and the main railway-line leaves the highveld to tap the resources of the area. The government gold-roasting plant is located on the outskirts of the town. Expansion of the iron and steel production at Redcliff, 14 km distant, led to the establishment in Kwekwe of a wire, bar and rod mill, a piping plant and a firm making wire ropes and spring steel wire among other steel items. This concentration on metal manufacturing led to a large firm opening up a ferro-chrome plant on the industrial sites. The same firm owns the chromite mines at Shurugwi.

In 1975 a malting plant was built to treat the locally grown barley, the product going to large breweries in Salisbury and Bulawayo.

Chitungwiza

Situated 25 km south of Harare, Chitungwiza has an established population of 300 000, making it the third largest town in Zimbabwe. Officially declared a municipality in 1981, Chitungwiza embraces St. Mary's, Zengeza and Seki townships together with an industrial site. Unlike the urban centres just described, Chitungwiza is not a self-contained town. The industrial site has only 13 factories which employ less than 3 000 of the total workforce of about 13 000. Most workers travel daily by bus to work in Harare; a few use cars or 'pirate' taxis. Shopping facilities are seriously limited in the town, and roadside stalls where prices are much higher

135

than in Harare, are a common sight.

Chitungwiza could well become independent of the capital as its industries grow and its infrastructure develops. It seems likely, however, that a railway to the town will have to be constructed if industries are to be attracted there instead of to Harare. In addition, industrialists will have to be given strong incentives to set up factories in Chitungwiza.

Rural service centres

There are no towns in communal lands and Government is investigating the establishment of service centres of different sizes in rural areas. Such centres will

1 relieve land pressure caused by rapid population growth and dependence on farming. Rural service centres will provide jobs in commerce and administration as well as supply housing;

2 assist the economic growth of surrounding rural areas by providing the necessary infrastructure such as electricity, water, roads; and

3 offer facilities for credit, banking, repair of machinery and a focus for extension services.

Other important towns

Redcliff was established in 1948 to accommodate some of the workers in the Zimbabwean Iron and Steel Company. The site of Redcliff relative to the steel works is shown on the map (Fig. 59).

HWANGE and ZVISHAVANE owe their existence to coal and asbestos respectively.

KADOMA, as has been noted, is the cotton spinning centre of the country and in 1970 the Cold Storage Commission opened a main abattoir and meat processing factory in the town. A cheese factory started operations in 1979.

MASVINGO is situated in a rich cattle-ranching area and its economic activities are primarily agricultural, e.g. Cold Storage Commission plant. Nearby is the famous Great Zimbabwe so the tourist industry is expected to increase as the several development schemes associated with the Kyle Dam are completed. On the other hand, the town

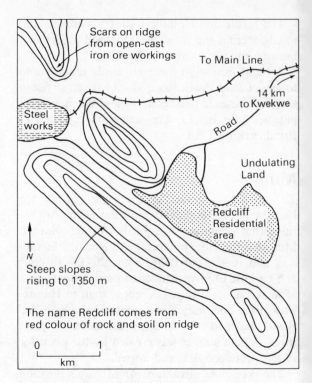

Fig. 59   Redcliff and the steel works

did not develop as expected when irrigation schemes got under way on the South-eastern Lowveld. It would seem that Chiredzi and Triangle have assumed most functions needed by the lowveld companies and settlers.

Things to do

1 Write down as many reasons as you can think of why people like to live in towns.

2 Draw an outline of your home town. Draw in the main route leading out of the town. Note the kind of development which has taken place along this route, that is, residential, commercial or industrial.

3 During one term, keep a record of all plot and house sales as recorded in the daily newspaper. Plot the locations and the value of the properties and describe the picture that emerges.

20　Communications and trade (Zimbabwe)

The inland position of Zimbabwe led to the early extension of the railways from the port of Beira. The link with Maputo came only in 1956. Why was it comparatively late?

The inland position of Zimbabwe, the location of the gold belts and the broad elements of relief, as well as Rhodes' dream of a railway line to the north, have all influenced the early development of railways and roads. After UDI (1965) the political factors became very important, and a direct rail link with South Africa, through Beitbridge, was built in the 1970s.

Railways

Look at an atlas map of Zimbabwe and note the density of the railway network. Compare this density with that of the southern Transvaal and reach your own conclusion. Secondly, compare a map showing railways with the one of population distribution in Zimbabwe (Fig. 61). Can you explain why the railway routes do not pass through all of the densely populated areas of the country?

Throughout Central Africa the railway line is single track with a narrow gauge of 1·06 m. This gauge was chosen to conform with that of the South African Railways and means reduced speeds, particularly on curves. Consequently, traffic is slowed down. However, the straightening and regrading of lines which were originally laid as cheaply as possible, has speeded up trains.

The following three factors have determined the routes followed by the railways:

1　Location of minerals

The relation between mineral deposits, especially the gold belts, and railway routes was stressed in the chapter on mining. The line to Zambia was routed to pass through the Hwange coalfield. The line from Bulawayo to Harare leaves the highveld to tap the gold mine at Kwekwe and then passes through the gold mines at Eiffel Flats and Chegutu, both of which lie on gold belts. Branch lines to West Nicholson (originally gold), Fort Victoria (gold and lithium), Shurugwi (chromite), Zvishavane (asbestos) and Shamva (gold) bring out the very close relationship between mines and railways.

In 1969, a branch line was constructed to the Trojan nickel mine near Bindura. Large trucks with trailers could have been used to move nickel or any other mineral over long distances but the necessary road improvements and terminal facilities would have been as costly as laying a branch line.

2　Position of the watersheds

It is no coincidence that the main lines follow the watersheds. The ridge separating two river basins, called a *watershed* or *water parting*, provides a much more level surface than does the country, broken up by river valleys, on either side of the watershed. The contractors, therefore, followed the watersheds wherever possible.

3　Position of Beira and the Mutare Gap

The railway line from Beira was built through Mutare because of its situation in a gap in the mountainous rampart of the eastern border. Mutare, moreover, lies in line with the watershed running westwards to Harare. The actual town had to be moved to the existing site since old Mutare was difficult to reach by rail.

When the British South Africa Company took over the administration of Zimbabwe, Rhodes planned to push a railway north. He was fully aware that the economic development of the country depended on railway communications, and that Rhodesia needed a link with the eastern seaboard.

The railway from South Africa via Botswana reached Bulawayo in October, 1897, and at the same time a line was being laid from Beira to Harare. In 1899 the latter line reached Harare only after many workers had died from malaria and blackwater fever. By 1902, it was possible to travel by train from Beira to Bulawayo.

The line from Bulawayo to Zambia via Hwange reached the former border in November, 1909.

In 1956, a line was constructed from Bannockburn to Chicualacuala to join the Mozambique railway from Maputo. In this way a much needed second outlet to the Indian Ocean was provided.

Sugar initiated the branch line from Mbizi, on the Bannockburn to Maputo railway, to Nandi. This line was completed in 1965, and it serves Triangle and Hippo Valley Estates. There has been speculation that the line is to be extended northwards along the Sabi River Valley to the Harare to Mutare railway. Although a pipe dream, it is a fascinating prospect for the geographer to contemplate, especially in conjunction with the recently completed Beitbridge rail link. The economy of the Eastern Border Highlands could be influenced by SADCC and South Africa.

The rapid increase of railway traffic since the Second World War made it imperative that the efficiency of the railways be improved. How would you have tackled the problem?

Zimbabwe Railways adopted the following measures which have been financially profitable.

1 Steam engines are less economic than diesel engines since thay have less power and must stop frequently for watering, coaling and de-ashing. The maintenance of such service depots is costly. Also expensive is the labour involved in clearing the grass bordering the track in order to reduce fire hazard.

Diesel-electric engines, on the other hand, can pull heavier loads because of their greater power and can carry large quantities of fuel. One major disadvantage, however, is that their fuel must be imported. In 1982, there were 114 steam engines as compared with 277 diesel electrics.

Electrification of the railways is expensive but the opening of the Hwange thermal power station has made the scheme feasible. The line from Harare to Dabuka (9km south of Gweru) is electrified and the next stage is to electrify the line from Dabuka to Chicualacuala and to Beitbridge, and Somabula to Bulawayo.

2 Regrading and straightening of the track is being carried out and high-level bridges are replacing the old low-level ones. In such ways, traffic will be speeded up.

Because the line is single track, passing places are essential. More have been constructed recently.

3 Improved signalling not only increases the speed of trains but also raises the safety factor. Zimbabwe Railways now operate CTC (Centralised Train Control) on the main line from Mutare to Livingstone and from Somabula to Beitbridge. This system enables control of trains from a certain point, e.g. a controller in Harare can watch, on a board, the route of a train as far away as Headlands. From the control room, signals are then transmitted electrically and the engine driver acts accordingly.

4 A big marshalling yard, Dabuka, just south of Gweru, was opened in 1979. This step eased the job of making up goods trains of different types of trucks and has facilitated inspection of all railway trucks.

5 Liner trains have been introduced. These are trains of wagons of the same carrying capacity (about 50 tonnes each) which shuttle between two given points. There are two liner trains in the country, one carrying coking coal from Hwange to Redcliff and the other taking iron ore from Buchwa to Redcliff.

The increasing popularity of air travel and the greater use of private motor cars have led to a serious decrease in the number of passengers travelling by first and second class rail accommodation. On the other hand, the number of rail travellers requiring fourth class passenger accommodation rose during 1969 and at some peak traffic periods not all of these could be accommodated. Such trends are watched carefully as they strongly affect the economy of the railways.

Zimbabwe Railways also operate the Road

Motor Services (RMS) which act as:

  a) substitutes for rail transport between places on a line of rail in order to save rail resources as at harvest time,

  b) a means of transport in rural districts to link up with the nearest railhead,

    and

  c) carriers on special goods trips. These include

    i) seasonal traffic like maize, wheat, tobacco, cotton, fruits and also fertilisers;

    ii) fairly regular traffic like livestock which is delivered to Cold Storage Commission depots and timber and minerals; and

    iii) short-notice, non-regular traffic such as materials required for a new mining undertaking.

The RMS could yet serve the communal lands where there are no scheduled services.

After the unilateral declaration of independence the Zambian and Zimbabwean railway systems were faced with immense problems. Copper traffic, the major source of revenue, all but ceased, having been diverted to other outlets such as Lobito Bay. Tobacco, another lucrative item was badly hit by sanctions. Maize and cattle produced within Zimbabwe were not affected but both of these are carried at low rates. Nevertheless, in 1969, the Zimbabwe Railways made a profit and not a loss as in 1968. Zambian copper is railed through Zimbabwe to South Africa ports.

The construction of a direct link with South Africa was a controversial matter in 1966 when a commission was appointed to look into it and came out in favour of a link from Rutenga, on the existing Somabula to Chicualacuala line, to Beitbridge. This route, rather than the alternative one from Jessie Junction on the West Nicholson line, was preferred since it was considered to be more suited to the country's economic needs. It was opened in 1975.

Most rail traffic is generated in the area east of Somabula and it is there that most Zimbabwean exports to South Africa are produced and that the greater demand for imports arises.

South Africa will provide a growing market for Zimbabwean agricultural products because, with its rapid economic and population growth and its lack of agricultural resources it must import foodstuffs. These are produced in Zimbabwe mainly in the area east of Somabula.

Road transport

The competition between road and rail transport is not exclusive to Zimbabwe. It is in varying degrees common to most countries of the world. In the United Kingdom, for instance, the railway system was streamlined in order to compete with private road haulage contractors. Containerisation and liner trains were two improvements introduced and these methods of transportation are now used here. Nonetheless, in Zimbabwe, road transport has certain definite advantages over rail transport. These include:

1 a faster door-to-door service,

2 better and faster passenger services and

3 fewer breakages and losses because of less handling and no shunting.

As we noted above, Zimbabwe Railways are unable to utilise to the full their first and second class accommodation; and in the not so distant future other classes of accommodation will also become redundant. African bus services may carry those passengers and better facilities at terminals will be required in order to cope with the larger numbers.

Another problem facing road users is the traffic congestion at certain periods in Harare and Bulawayo. Peri-urban dwellers and smallholders are those chiefly affected. It is certainly clear that the African townships will have to be better served if movement to town and industrial sites is not to be slowed up.

While the main traffic arteries outside the urban centres are adequate, changes can occur rapidly; the rise in private car ownership by Africans is one example. Increasing demand for road transport will eventually bring about the situation prevalent in some European countries where the motorist's speed is determined by that of the lorry ahead.

Generally, Zimbabwe has an adequate road network which is utilised competitively by numerous road hauliers. However, most of the communal lands lack the type of road associated with densely populated areas on the watershed, a reflection of the lack of traffic generated at present.

Air transport

Air transport is, apart from several small private firms, in the hands of Air Zimbabwe. The fleet of aircraft is still small, compirisng seven Viscounts

The airport at Masvingo

(700 series), one Douglas DC3, three Boeing 720s and three Boeing 707s. Two further 707s are on order (1982).

Though small, Air Zimbabwe's fleet is adequate to cover the internal and the external flights which it controls.

South African Airways was the only other airline to fly into the country until 1980.

In that year, the year of Independence, Air Zimbabwe and BA began weekly flights to the United Kingdom. Regular flights by other national airlines were resumed after a break of some fifteen years brought about by UDI. Harare Airport cannot handle passengers from more than one aircraft at a time, but there are definite plans to extend the airport facilities over the next few years.

Inside Zimbabwe air communications are likely to expand. Long distances between urban centres. mean that much time is wasted in travelling. Quite a number of farmers use private aircraft to travel between farm and town, and several Government departments also use aircraft to reach distant parts of the country.

In 1975 Air Zimbabwe carried some 452 000 domestic passengers while in 1980 the comparable figure was one million. These figures include tourists

from outside Zimbabwe most of whom travel on the Bulawayo-Victoria Falls-Hwange-Kariba route. More businessmen have been using the Harare-Bulawao flight which reflects the improvement in the economy and the desire of businessmen to avoid spending a night away from home.

Trade

In spite of sanctions, trade increased rapidly during the seventies and a favourable balance of trade was maintained. In 1980, the first year of independence, total exports increased by 27% in value, and imports rose by 47% in value. The general position of trade is shown in the table below:

Table 42 Summary of external trade in Z$million (gold sales excluded)

	Total Exports	Total Imports	Balance
1975	531	462	69
1976	557	383	174
1977	551	388	163
1978	609	404	205
1979	716	549	169
1980	909	809	100

Although there was a dramatic rise in value of imports between 1979 and the year of independence, 1980, strict import control is kept by Government through the allocation of foreign currency to firms. The expansion of trade during the period of sanctions indicates resilience of the economy which seemed to have suffered more from the war than from trade embargoes. Sanctions in fact led to diversification in the economy especially in manufacturing industry. Whereas in 1965 some 600 products were made, in 1980 over 6000 were manufactured.

Table 43 Destination of Zimbabwe's main exports for the period August–December 1980

	Value in Z$million	% of Total Exports
South Africa	59	17
West Germany	37	11
United Kingdom	18	5
Italy	16	4·5
Belgium	15	4
Botswana	12	3

What would you say were the principal features of the above table of destination of Zimbabwe's exports? Perhaps the dominance of South Africa impresses you, although as an industrial neighbour in need of manufactured goods of high quality South Africa is an obvious buyer. In fact, South Africa buys clothing and footwear, cigarettes, furniture and leather goods from Zimbabwe. A preferential trade agreement encourages trade between the two countries. Under this agreement Zimbabwean exports to South Africa are charged less duty than the same goods from other countries.

A second feature of the table is the industrial nature of our customers' economies apart from Botswana. Exports to other nearby African countries amounted to less than 4% of Zimbabwe total exports. Trade with these countries is desirable both politically and economically, and a major step has already been taken in this direction. In 1980, the Southern Africa Development Co-ordination Conference (SADCC) was established by Malawi, Mozambique, Angola, Zambia, Lesotho, Swaziland, Botswana, Tanzania and Zimbabwe with the aims of forging stronger links among members, reducing economic dependence on South Africa, securing international co-operation to assist with economic liberation and to mobilise resources on a national, inter-state and regional basis. Zimbabwe is a member of the second Lomé Convention which covers trade and aid in over 60 Africa, Caribbean and Pacific states as well as members of the European Economic Community (France, West Germany, Netherlands, Belgium, Luxembourg, Italy, Denmark, U.K., Irish Republic). In terms of the convention Zimbabwe has been granted a sugar and beef quota which are exempt from any levy imposed by the EEC on non-members.

Table 44 Origin of Zimbabwe's main imports for the period August–December 1980

	Value in Z$ million	% of Total Imports
South Africa	105	27
United Kingdom	32	8
West Germany	28	7
Japan	16	4
Zambia	12	3
France	8	2

Imports of Zimbabwe are listed above by origin and value with one chief exception – petroleum and allied products. This item amounted to the huge sum of Z$174 million in 1980 which is more than the value of all the imports from several countries in the table. Petroleum products are of unknown origin

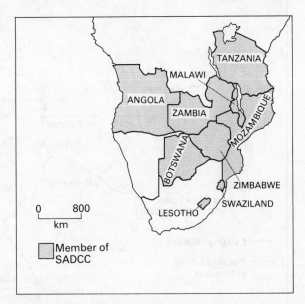

Fig. 60   Members of the Southern Africa Development Co-ordination Conference (SADCC)

141

and represent 21% or over one-fifth of the total value of imports. This great expense explains why the Government is anxious to conserve fuel to the utmost, why it supports research into ethanol, and why it is keen to obtain cheaper petroleum through the Beira–Feruka pipeline.

The dominance of South Africa is clear and the import–export trade of Zimbabwe cannot be halted quickly without serious adverse consequences to this country. Over 60% of Zimbabwe's imports and exports passed through South Africa in 1981. A long-term approach is necessary and this is likely to be adopted by SADCC.

A third feature of Table 44 is that most imports are supplied by the industrialised, or so-called developed countries, with the exception of Zambia. Given the history of Zimbabwe since its occupation by Europeans, the direction and nature of the trade are not surprising. Many African countries supply the more industrialised nations with raw material in return for manufactured goods. Zimbabwe, however, has a better developed infrastructure than most other countries south of the Sahara and exports some manufactured goods. This becomes

clear on examining the list of major exports and imports listed on Table 45.

Things to do

1 Describe the railway pattern in Zimbabwe noting the factors which have caused it.

2 What are the problems facing the traffic engineer in a large town like Bulawayo? Suggest realistic measures he might use to solve the problems.

3 When next you visit an airport, (a) observe the factors which appear to have influenced its siting, and (b) describe the facilities provided for passengers and the crews.

4 State the advantages of the Road Motor Services operated by Zimbabwe Railways.

5 Look at the map which shows possible future railway extensions. Which of these factors influence the extensions:

a) railways must be planned to meet a certain need such as carrying minerals;

b) the country along the line of rail should generate traffic;

c) railways have to meet strategic (military or political) needs?

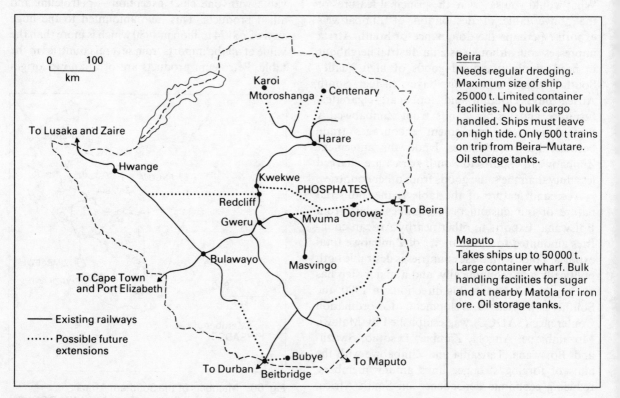

Beira
Needs regular dredging. Maximum size of ship 25 000 t. Limited container facilities. No bulk cargo handled. Ships must leave on high tide. Only 500 t trains on trip from Beira–Mutare. Oil storage tanks.

Maputo
Takes ships up to 50 000 t. Large container wharf. Bulk handling facilities for sugar and at nearby Matola for iron ore. Oil storage tanks.

Fig. 60.1 Possible future extensions of railway lines

Table 45 The top ten exports and imports of Zimbabwe (1980)

Exports	Value in Z$ million	Imports	Value in Z$ million
Tobacco unmanufactured	118	Petroleum and allied products	174
Gold	115	Steel plates and sheets	28
Iron and steel products	93	Textile piece goods	26
Ferro-alloys	88	Resins	21
Asbestos	80	Electricity	19
Cotton lint	57	Farming machinery	17
Nickel metal	53	Insecticides and disinfectants	16
Raw sugar	41	Buses and lorry chasses	16
Meats, fresh, frozen and chilled	14	Motor vehicle engine spares	16
		Motor car assembly kits	14

21 Population (Zimbabwe)

Historical outline

The Shona people have long been settled in the area between the Zambezi and Limpopo rivers. They came from the north bringing with them skills of cultivation, mining and trading. There is evidence that by 1000 AD the Shona were constructing dry stone buildings, that is, buildings without mortar, of which the largest was Great Zimbabwe. Such buildings were royal palaces and parts of them were reserved for the worship of Mwari (God). Over the centuries a big empire covering Zimbabwe and reaching to the Indian Ocean was created. This kingdom endured until 1500 and was ruled by the Mwanamutapa or Monomotapa.

The Rozwi Mambos who governed the second Shona empire forced the Monomotapa northwards to the Zambezi lowveld. The Rozwi conducted trade with India and prospered until invaded by the Nguni from the south in the 1890s. The Nguni were quickly followed by another Zulu invasion led by Mzilikazi whose people were called MATABELE. These trained warriors put the Mashona to flight or enslaved them and took their cattle. Stories of Matabele raids into what is now Mashonaland and the subsequent slaughter of whole kraals have been exaggerated.

European settlers began to arrive from the south after 1850. They included explorers, hunters, prospectors and missionaries. Many of these added to our geographical knowledge but it is David Livingstone who has given us the most comprehensive picture of the relief, flora, fauna and the people of this continent.

The pioneers of 1890–96 were attracted largely by the promise of gold and, to a lesser extent, by the allegedly fertile soils and hospitable climate of the highveld. Cecil John Rhodes gave the initial economic impetus for occupation of Zimbabwe by Europeans and three kinds of settlement resulted:

1 Gold-mining settlements. The gold mines were located on the gold belts (see Fig. 54) on and alongside the highveld stretching very generally from Bulawayo to Shamva.

2 Farms. The farmers depended for their markets and supplies on the nearby European villages. They were, therefore, clustered around places like Bulawayo, Harare, Chegutu and Masvingo.

3 Urban settlements. The materials needed by the farmers and miners encouraged the growth of retailing and small industries and the professions. The first settlements were clusters of buildings made from the veld materials of pole and dagga. Early photographs, interestingly enough, show such structures as square rather than round like the African's huts.

The land required for these settlements was not all occupied by Africans. The Africans, however, knew no clear-cut boundaries of ownership; they held land communally and each family cultivated a roughly defined patch. Cattle were grazed on communal land.

When crop returns became low because of suspected declining fertility of the soil, the people moved on to the other land. (See page 157.) Despite this, there was no population pressure on the land, because the estimated population was under half a million.

With the coming of the Europeans, the land position changed and as early as 1895 the first areas were set aside for the sole use of the African. Many Africans continued to live on European-owned farms, selling their labour in return for low wages and the right to cultivate so much land. In the towns, as demand grew for domestic servants and workers, there developed a drift of Africans from the rural areas to the new cash-oriented way of life.

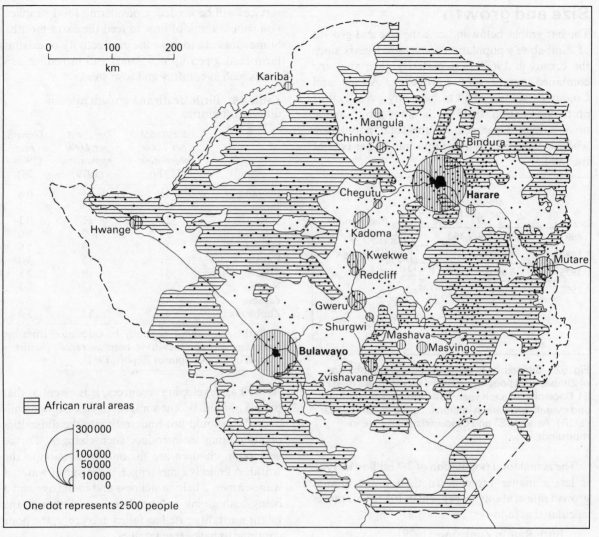

Fig. 61 Distribution of population in Zimbabwe

Distribution of population

Any analysis of population depends upon a sound knowledge of physical, economic and political factors which go to make up a region. For this reason, a population study is described at the end of a regional geography. The size and rate of growth of a population, its movements, birth and death rates, age–sex structure, ethnic composition and distribution are aspects of a population to be known by a geographer. The geographer can use the facts in many ways. For instance, he may employ them to give an explanation of the distribution of a population. In this case he would pose the questions 'Where do the people live?' 'Why do they live there?' 'Why not elsewhere?' Planning of a new resettlement scheme or a new business centre also requires population statistics. Think about the population data you would need to help you decide on the location of a new primary school or a bus route.

Population statistics are frequently estimates and they are usually based on a census taken some years before. A census itself may not be accurate because of problems in collecting the information e.g. dates of birth and occupations of each member of the family. In Zimbabwe a census was held in 1969 and one is planned for late 1982. Try to think of the questions which a census-taker would ask in a household.

Size and growth

The bar graphs below indicate the size and growth of Zimbabwe's population for selected years since the census in 1969. It is perfectly clear that the combined numbers of Europeans, Asians and Coloureds are too small to have any overall effect on the population. In 1981, the three groups made up just over 3 per cent of the total population whereas the Africans made up some 97 per cent of the total.

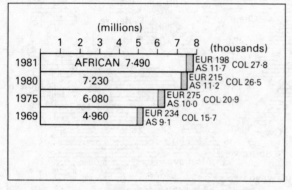

Fig. 62 Bar graphs to show the ethnic composition of Zimbabwe's population based on estimates made at 31 December of each year. Total African population and overall totals are in millions. Totals of Europeans (EUR), Asian (AS) and Coloureds (COL) are in thousands.

The actual total population of 7·7 million in 1981 is less a matter for concern than is the annual growth rate of about 3·4 per cent in 1981. This rate is calculated as follows:

Birth Rate in Zimbabwe (1979)
per 1 000 of population   = 47

Death Rate in Zimbabwe (1979)
per 1 000 of population   = 13

Growth Rate   34 per 1 000
               or 3·4 per 100
               or 3·4%

The next table compares growth rates of several countries. The top position of Zimbabwe and Kenya is clear and with a growth rate of 3·4 per cent per annum the population will double in 21 years. Put another way, the population of Zimbabwe is increasing at a daily rate of 600. To educate such a number of children will require one new primary school to be built every day of the year. Additional water supplies, food, fuel, housing and health services will be needed. Considering food supplies, you should think of how to feed the extra mouths. Some ideas are to raise the productivity of existing farm land, open up new lands and introduce new foods such as comfrey and soya steaks.

Table 46   Birth, death and growth rates of different countries

	Birth rate per 1 000 population (1979)	Death rate per 1 000 population (1979)	Growth rate (1970–79)
Bulgaria	15	11	0·6
Japan	15	7	1·1
U.K.	12	11	0·1
U.S.A.	17	9	1·0
U.S.S.R.	18	9	0·9
Kenya	51	13	3·4
Malawi	51	19	2·8
Nigeria	50	17	2·5
Zambia	49	17	3·0
Zimbabwe	47	13	3·4

Growth rates cannot generally be calculated from the given figures since they have been averaged. (Statistics from World Development Report, 1981).

As well as developing resources, it is essential that people should be encouraged to have fewer children. We should not underestimate the difficulties of attempting to introduce such changes. To the very poor, children are the only possession in the world. A child is a messenger, a drawer of water, a wage-earner, a help in sickness and in old age and a being both giving and needing love. Although the infant mortality rate has fallen markedly, the poor continue to have large families.

To convince people that parents should have two children means that there have to be widespread and effective child spacing clinics, an excellent advertising scheme and adequate social and health services to take care of the poor in sickness and in old age. Government is allocating funds for the increasing provision of clinics.

Rural–urban migration

This is a world-wide phenomenon and in the developed countries most people live in towns or cities. In 1980 it was estimated that in North America 66 per cent of the total population lived in urban centres while in Africa as a whole the comparable figure was only 24 per cent: for

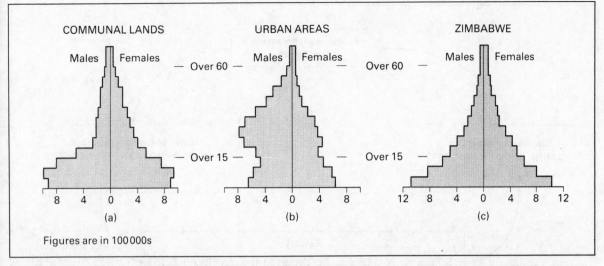

Fig. 63   Pyramids showing age and sex structure of African population in (a) communal lands, 1969; (b) urban centres, 1969; and (c) Zimbabwe, 1980. Diagrams (a) and (c) are adapted from Kay G (1969). Most Africans in the high density suburbs are not completely urbanised.

Zimbabwe the figure was 23 per cent. During the 1970s war caused havoc in many rural areas, and people flocked into the cities for security.

Land shortage in Zimbabwe combined with pressure on resources have encouraged the peasant farmer to seek work in towns. Drought years have also brought about movement to the towns. The town appears to offer a solution and men of working age move to it leaving behind children, women and old people. Families are therefore broken up and the communal lands are not farmed as they ought to be.

In the urban centres, shanty towns spring up but not on the same scale as in Lusaka where over one-third of the population live in makeshift centres. Epworth, Chirambahuyo and the Great Zimbabwe–Kyle area were some of the sites occupied by squatters most of whom have since been moved into ultra-low cost dwellings. While complete families sometimes become squatters and also live in the high density suburbs, there is a dominance of men.

This dominance is shown in the age–sex pyramids (Fig. 63). For comparison, an age–sex pyramid for Zimbabwe as a whole has been inserted. The balance between males and females in Zimbabwe should be contrasted with the imbalance in the communal lands and urban areas. In communal lands there is a majority of children under 15 years of age, and females outnumber males between the

ages of 15 and 60 years. In urban areas, young men dominate, with fewer children and females. You should attempt to explain these differences.

Most Africans in the high density suburbs are not completely urbanised. They have kept ties with their rural homes which they visit by bus at weekends and on public holidays. Frequently holidays are taken at harvest time. What do you think of the idea of living partly in the town and partly in the country?

Resettlement

At Independence in April 1980, it was recognised that relief of population pressure in the communal lands was a matter of priority. Many peasant farmers had no land at all while some land on commercial farms was under-utilised. Through the Zimbabwe Conference on Reconstruction and Development (ZIMCORD) international funds were made available in the form of loans and grants for the purchase of land for resettlement. Already part of this grant has been spent and by April 1982, some 12 200 people had been settled on 513 000 ha. Government plans to settle 900 000 people altogether. One of the major difficulties is the squatter, the landless peasant who in many cases cannot wait his turn. Selection of farmers is a careful process and those who are granted land, probably 5 ha in area, will be trained in the best farming techniques.

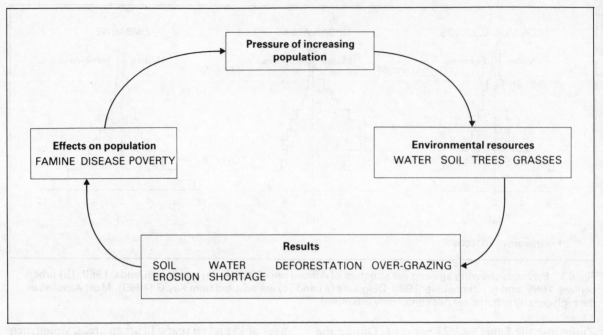

Fig. 64   Influence of an increasing population on environmental resources

Pressure of population on resources

Environmental resources suffer from population pressure as shown in Fig. 64. This cycle might be called the poverty cycle for obvious reasons.

As more people occupy an area, more maize is planted to yield more grain. Without adequate manure and nutrients, the crop returns become less and less. In a similar way, cattle can be grazed in an increasing number but when the carrying capacity of the land is exceeded, grazing will decrease. Water supplies are also likely to be a limiting factor.

Zimbabwe's rainfall is so erratic in almost all of the communal areas that dry years have to be allowed for by grain storage, making of silage and irrigation. The last is expensive and the peasant farmers usually find themselves dependent on aid in drought years.

The soil is naturally affected by overcropping and overgrazing. It becomes a dust that is easily blown away or washed downhill. Parts of Manicaland show only rock at the surface, the overlying soil having been carried off.

Trees have been felled on communal lands to provide fuel for cooking, building poles and warmth. Because of population pressure these lands are virtually treeless. Unfortunately, removal of trees exposes the soil to the full impact of rain drops, which erode the soil. Rain water which previously seeped through the soil to underground fissures and zones of crushed rock and later emerged as streams, now flows over the surface of the ground. Thus less water is stored.

Altogether a gloomy picture which requires intervention by Government. In Zimbabwe, resettlement schemes, planting of wood lots and more training for peasant farmers should alleviate the pressure of population on resources. From a longer term viewpoint, family planning or child spacing will have to be widely practised.

Things to do

1 From a 1:50 000 map sheet trace areas of woodland near to your home or school. Take your tracing to all or some of the areas, and try to work out the percentage of deforestation.

2 Referring to a 1:50 000 map sheet of part of a communal land area, decide on the best location of three primary schools and one secondary school. List the factors which helped you arrive at your decision.

22 Location, relief, climate, and water resources (Zambia)

The relief of Zambia is not as dissected as either that of Malaŵi or Zimbabwe. The plateau surface is level to gently undulating between 900 m and 1 500 m above sea level, but is broken occasionally by steep escarpments caused by faulting and by isolated hill ranges formed by volcanic intrusion in the ancient sedimentary layers.

The country can be divided broadly into three

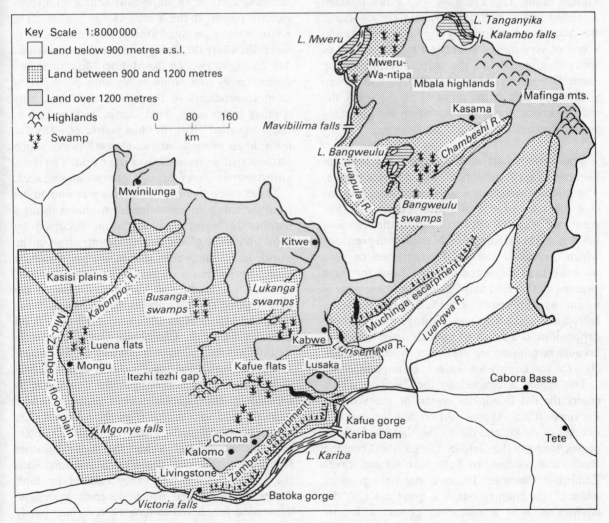

Fig. 65   Zambia relief map

Key Scale 1:8 000 000

☐ Land below 900 metres a.s.l.

▨ Land between 900 and 1200 metres

▨ Land over 1200 metres

🏔 Highlands

🌿 Swamp

0   80   160
km

L. Tanganyika
Kalambo falls
L. Mweru
Mweru-Wa-ntipa
Mbala highlands
Mafinga mts.
Kasama
Mavibilima falls
Chambeshi R.
L. Bangweulu
Luapula R.
Bangweulu swamps
Mwinilunga
Kitwe
Kasisi plains
Kabompo R.
Busanga swamps
Lukanga swamps
Muchinga escarpment
Luangwa R.
Luena flats
Mongu
Mid-Zambezi flood plain
Kabwe
Lunsemfwa R.
Kafue flats
Lusaka
Itezhi tezhi gap
Cabora Bassa
Mgonye falls
Zambezi escarpment
Kafue gorge
Kariba Dam
Choma
Kalomo
L. Kariba
Tete
Livingstone
Batoka gorge
Victoria falls

relief regions: (1) the southern areas drained by the Zambezi and its tributaries, (2) the northern areas drained by the Chambeshi-Luapula system and other headwaters of the Congo, and (3) a central watershed region separating the above two drainage basins.

Study the account of the Zambezi River on page 6 before you read this account. Turn to Fig. 6 on page 6 and study the basins and divides.

The southern Zambezi drainage area rises from about 600 m to about 1200 m above sea level near the edge of the watershed. A very large part of the country here is monotonously flat. Only in the east and the south is the relief very broken. Here relief has been influenced by faulting. The Zambezi flows eastwards below the Victoria Falls in a faulted basin. The Luangwa also flows through a faulted valley. Both these valleys are low-lying, flat-floored and enclosed by steep escarpments and a belt of very rugged country. Find the names of these escarpments on the map. Rivers entering these rift valleys from the plateau form deep gorges and falls at the point of entry. Study the map and name the gorges found on the following rivers: Zambezi, Kafue and Lunsemfwa.

The western part of this region has been influenced by earth movements of a different nature. The plateau surface has, in places, been warped (See diagram, page 4 of Introduction) and this, combined with the effects of differential erosion, has resulted in the formation of shallow depressions which, especially during the rainy season, are occupied by dambos and swamps. Look for these swamps on the relief map. Can you explain what is meant by 'differential erosion'? Page 5 of the Introduction will help you. Swamps form in these depressions as a result of poor drainage and also because large areas are underlain by impermeable clay. Do you know what is meant by impermeable?

This region is drained by the Zambezi which enters the flat floodplain region of the Western Province from Angola. After flowing over a number of rapids and finally the Victoria Falls, it passes through the Batoka Gorge, the Gwembe Basin (now occupied by Lake Kariba) and leaves Zambia at Luangwe. The river not only gives its name to the country but is a great asset to the country as it is a source of power, a tourist attraction, and has great potential for fishing. Can

you name two hydro-electric stations on the Zambezi? Name two centres near the river important for tourists and one stretch of the river important for fishing.

The two chief tributaries of the Zambezi are the Kafue and the Luangwa rivers. The Kafue which rises on the Zambezi-Zaire watershed to the north of Solwezi flows across the Copperbelt and is therefore a very important source of water for the population and industries of that area. It flows across the vast Kafue Flats where, when it is tamed, it will provide the necessary water for irrigating crops and supporting large herds of cattle. Can you name the stage of erosion the Kafue is in below the rail bridge? In what ways does the river in this section differ from the section above the bridge. It is an important source of hydro-electric power at the Kafue Gorge Station. The Kafue is also a potential fishery. Look at the map to ascertain where the Kafue joins the Zambezi River. The Luangwa rises on the Mafingi Mountains and drops steeply to a broad valley floor bordered by steep escarpments to the west and broken hilly country to the east. What are the escarpments in the west called? It is the chief source of water for the animals of the Luangwa Game Reserve which attracts visitors from all over the world. The river, unfortunately, flows through a tsetse-infested area.

The northern region is smaller in area and differs from the southern region mainly in that it forms a number of broad, shallow basins occupied by lakes and some of the largest swamp areas in the world. Lake Bangweulu and its swamps occupy a saucer-shaped basin warped by earth movements. The size of the swamps varies according to the discharge of the Chambeshi River, which flows from the Mbala Highlands across a broad flood plain known as the Chambeshi Flats. This Bangweulu-Chambeshi-Luapula system is the major source of water for the Northern and Luapula Provinces. The Lake Bangweulu depression is drained by the Luapula which meanders under papyrus sudd southwards from the lake and then west and northwards where it forms an international boundary. Name the two countries separated by this river. Below the Mavibilima Falls the Luapula flows in a valley marked by fault scarps. Lake Mweru which occupies a shallow depression is believed to have been formed partly by rifting and partly by warping. Lakes Bangweulu and Mweru have large fish populations. To the north-east of Lake Mweru is the Mweru-wa-ntipa Swamp of international importance because it is a breeding ground for the red locust, a pest.

Lake Tanganyika, part of which lies in the north-eastern end of Zambia, is about 64 km across at its greatest width, and about 700 km long. Can you explain in a few words how this lake was formed? What are the chief characteristics of such lakes? As the lake is enclosed by a steep and rugged escarpment zone, the Kalambo River which flows from the plateau into the lake has cut a narrow gorge by one of the highest falls in the world–the Kalambo Falls. The Kalambo Falls area has gained in importance because of the archaeological discoveries there, which give a continuous record of man's activities over a period of 60 000 years. What is archaeology?

The lake is an important source of fish and is also an important waterway connecting Zambia with the Zaire Republic, Tanzania and Burundi.

The central watershed region rises from 1200 m in the Central and Copperbelt Provinces to over 1 800 m above sea level in the Mafingi mountains in the north eastern part of the Northern Province. This is a continental divide separating the Zaire system which flows into the Atlantic Ocean from the Zambezi system which enters the Indian Ocean. It stretches from the Angola border, eastwards along the Zaire border and then across the Northern Province to form the Mbala Highlands in the north and southwards along the Malawi border to form the Luangwa-Malawi watershed. The plateau surface is flat to gently undulating except where broken by valleys, granite hills and ant hills.

Climate and water resources

Zambia's tropical continental position and its relief have a marked influence on its climate and water resources.

Although Zambia is relatively better watered than most tropical areas and has a number of lakes, swamps and perennial rivers, the all-year-round supply of water for domestic stock, agriculture and industrial purposes is a serious problem. This problem is caused by a number of factors, both natural and man-made.

Kalambo Falls, over 200 metres high, are the highest falls in Central Africa. What is the economic value of the falls?

1 variations in the seasonal rainfall;
2 the unequal distribution of this rainfall throughout the country;
3 fluctuations in the start of the rainy season;
4 excessive evaporation during the hot season.

By clearing the forests, especially in the catchment areas and by their system of shifting cultivation, people expose the land to the ravages of rain. Wet season run-off is increased and, as a result, the amount of seepage for perennial streams is decreased.

Rainfall is brought mainly by winds from the north-west which swing into northern Zambia

151

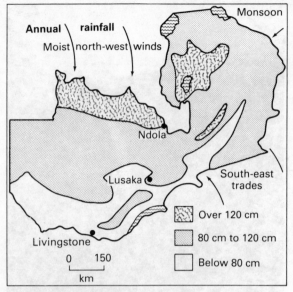

Fig 66   Zambia rainfall

from Zaire as the moist Congo air. The north-eastern part of Zambia receives a little rainfall from the north east Trade winds. (Look at Fig. 10, page 8, of the Introduction for the different airstreams). The rainfall distribution map (Fig. 66) shows clearly the uneven distribution of rain throughout the country. Rainfall decreases from about 1 250 mm in the north to about 400 mm in the south west. The rainfall statistics below are for

three towns, Ndola in the north, Lusaka in the centre and Livingstone in the south. Study the figures below carefully to find out:

1 in which direction the total rainfall decreases;
2 the months that receive less than 50 mm of rainfall;
3 the four months when most of the rainfall is received;
4 the number of months when each town receives more than 120 mm of rain.

Fluctuations in total rainfall and the length of the dry season increase in areas of low rainfall. A high rate of evaporation caused by the long duration of the hot, dry season further aggravates the water problem. A large percentage of the rain that falls on Zambia is lost by evaporation and it is estimated that only about 15% is made available for use by man. Can you suggest different ways in which water can be conserved in Central Africa?

The temperature distribution map, Fig. 67, shows that most of the country experiences relatively high temperatures. Annual temperatures are, however, influenced by altitude above sea level. The statistics below show this close relationship between relief and temperatures.

NOTE: The highest temperatures are recorded in the river basins (Livingstone and Chirundu) where the added effect of low rainfall causes grave water

Table 47   Mean monthly rainfall for these stations

Towns	July	Aug.	Sept.	Oct.	Nov.	Dec.	Jan.	Feb.	Mar.	April	May	June	Total
Ndola	0	1·0	·5	19·5	126·8	250·5	307	235	190	35·8	4·3	0	1 170·4
Lusaka	0	0·3	0·3	14·3	90·5	180·3	210·8	178	137·8	19·3	1·8	0	833·4
Livingstone	0	0·3	20	22·3	86·8	156	186·5	155·3	100	31	4·3	·05	763·0

(Figures in mm)

Table 48

Towns	Altitude in metres	Latitudes degrees south of equator	Mean temp. for hottest month °C	Mean temp. for coolest month °C	Mean annual temp. °C	Annual temp. range °C
Mbala	1 632	8° 45′	21·9°	17·6°	19·6°	4·3°
Mwinilunga	1 334	11° 45′	22·4°	15·8°	19·9°	6·6°
Kabwe	1 171	14° 30′	24·8°	16°	20·6°	18·8°
Livingstone	948	17° 45′	27°	16·2°	22·2°	10·8°
Chirundu	394	16°	30·4°	19·8°	23·9°	10·6°

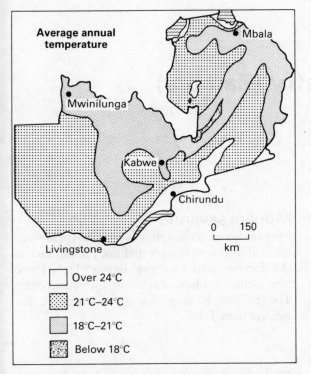

Average annual temperature

Mbala

Mwinilunga

Kabwe

Chirundu

0   150
km

Livingstone

☐ Over 24°C

▨ 21°C–24°C

▦ 18°C–21°C

▩ Below 18°C

Fig. 67 Zambia average annual temperature

shortage during the dry season. The river basins experience low rainfall because they lie in the rain shadow of the escarpments. Most streams that flow into the Zambezi and Luangwa are in spate during the short rainy season but soon dry out during the long dry season and therefore do not provide permanent sources of water. Can you account for the comparatively high mean temperature for the coolest month of Mbala?

Even on the upland plateau area all but the larger rivers and dambos dry out during the dry season. Dambos are shallow depressions into which run-off and seepage water collect to form small lakes during the rainy season and local areas of high water table during the dry season. The water resources of the country could be stabilised by conservation methods. Forests and catchment

areas should be protected from unnecessary destruction. Vegetation cover reduces the pounding effect of the rain drops on the soil and, by allowing evaporation of rain water from leaves, minimises the evaporation of soil water. This water which is slowly absorbed by the organic matter in the soil infiltrates the soil until the excess slowly drains away to give rise to springs and streams. Dams built across streams and rivers will store the summer flood for use during the dry season. Underground water could also be tapped by boreholes and wells. Can you name a town in Zambia which obtains its water supply from boreholes (see page 188)?

Things to do

1 Draw sketches to illustrate:
   a) rift valley;
   b) gorge;
   c) water divide.

2 Give examples of lakes in Zambia for each of the following ways in which lakes are normally formed:
   a) rift valley;
   b) depression formed by slight warping of the land surface;
   c) ox-bow;
   d) man-made.

3 a) What is a dambo?
   b) Of what economic importance is a dambo?

4 a) What is a flood plain? What are its characteristic features?
   b) Where does it normally occur?

5 Account for: a) the low annual temperature range at Mbala;
   b) the high mean annual temperatures at Chirundu.

6 a) Draw sketches to illustrate a rain shadow and convectional rainfall.
   b) Name two examples of rain shadows in Zambia.
   c) Draw a rainfall columnar graph to illustrate the seasonal nature of the rainfall at Lusaka.

153

23 Vegetation and forestry (Zambia)

The vegetation in Zambia is broadly classified as savanna but within this classification four distinct types may be recognised. Differences in the vegetation are due to differences in soil type, gradient, altitude and climate. (See diagram, page 10 of Introduction). Evaporation, relative humidities, distribution of rainfall and the total annual rainfall have an important influence on the distribution of particular tree-types in the country. The four broad types of vegetation found in Zambia include (a) tall grasslands; (b) deciduous savanna woodland; (c) mopani savanna and (d) chipya (a mixture of high grass and woodlands).

Tall grasslands

Grasslands are found on highland areas such as the Mbala Highlands and in dambos and swamp areas. Trees do not grow in dambos and swamps as these areas are water-logged for most of the year. Meadow-type grasslands on high altitude areas occur possibly because trees were destroyed by fire or cleared by local inhabitants and the areas then abandoned. In these areas very few trees are found.

Deciduous savanna woodland

The deciduous savanna woodland covers the greater part of the plateau and consists mostly of umbrella shaped trees. The density of the woodland area depends on the amount of water available for growth, either in the form of groundwater or rainfall. Some msasa found in this region are important for timber.

Mopani savanna

Mopane savanna vegetation is found in the lowland areas of high temperature and low rainfall such as the Zambezi and Luangwa Basins. Trees found here include baobab, acacia, euphorbia and palm. The baobab is normally an indicator of low relative humidities.

Chipya

Chipya vegetation is found on higher land such as around Lusaka and in the Western Province.

The natural woodlands are a great asset to the country. The many different types of trees are not only commercially important for timber but are also used in the refining process in the copper mines, for charcoal making and for domestic purposes. Do you know how and why tree trunks are used in the copper refining process? The woodland areas have further a very great influence on climate, soil and water. The trees break the force of heavy rain and, as the water drips slowly on to the ground, the fallen leaves act as a blanket over the soil. This allows the water to sink slowly into the soil instead of running off and causing soil erosion. The branches, by providing shade and breaking up strong wind currents, decrease the amount of evaporation. Soils of woodland areas of moderate rainfall are rich in humus where the fallen leaves have rotted slowly to form plant food.

The woodland areas are therefore useful in providing people with timber, preventing soil erosion and, by protecting the watershed or catchment areas, saving rivers and streams from drying up. It is also believed that Congo air moisture is replenished by transpiration from the leaves of the trees.

In consequence they need to be protected from forest fires as well as from large scale destruction caused by the chitemene system of cultivation. The excessive cutting down of trees for firewood also needs to be checked.

The country's forestry department is therefore concerned with:

1 protecting the land, especially catchment areas, from soil erosion;

2 setting aside as permanent forest land, under government control, areas of woodland in each province to supply forest produce for farms and local industries;

3 preserving, permanently, good forest land and opening timber plantations on a continuous yield basis so as to make the country self-supporting in timber;

4 conducting investigations and research in all the branches of forestry, with particular attention to the use of forests, and silviculture;

5 promoting by education and propaganda an understanding among the people of Zambia of the value of forests and training those engaged in forest work.

Although the natural woodland areas provide a wide variety of commercially important timbers, only very limited supplies of the better quality hardwoods are found, the most important of which is the teak or mukusi. The teak forests are found in the south-eastern part of the Western Province, growing in areas of Kalahari sands. Most of the timber exported from Zambia comes from this region. The timber is logged at present on a big scale at Kataba some 256 km north west of Livingstone. Logging is also carried on along the Zambezi to the east of Sesheke. Do you know how the logs from Kataba and the processed timber from the sawmills at Mulobezi are transported to Livingstone? If you don't, look for the answer on page 194.

The mukusi or teak which is reddish-brown, heavy and fine-textured, is widely used for railway sleepers and is also used in the copper mines, in building and for parquet flooring blocks and furniture.

The highland areas of the Copperbelt and North Western Province are covered with open forest which also yield hardwood for furniture, firewood and charcoal. Some of the trees found here include mubanga which is a popular carving wood, mupapa used for house and bridge building and dugout canoes, muwaka suitable for railway sleepers and heavy construction, kayimbi used on the Copperbelt and in the Luapula Province for parquet flooring, hut building and railway sleepers. Mukwa is the chief furniture wood in Zambia and it is also used for cabinet-making, plywood, veneers, coffins, boats and parquet flooring.

Conservation and plantations

The continued exploitation of timber in the woodlands will lead, if it is not checked, to the disappearance of these trees. The Forestry Department, however, practises forest conservation and most of the valuable timber-producing trees are protected. These can only be cut down under licence from the government. In order to make the country self-sufficient in both hardwood and softwood timber the department is opening up large timber plantations. Why does the Forestry Department choose mainly softwood trees such as eucalyptus and tropical pine for planting? Such plantations are found at Chati, Mufulira, Choma, Samfya, Kabwe, Chisamba, Lusaka, Chipata and many other areas. Look for these areas on a map of Zambia.

Before a plantation is begun, the area is surveyed and the soil is tested for suitability. A slightly sloping and easily drained area is chosen for a nursery, sheltered from winds and direct sunlight.

The area to be planted is divided into compartments, one of which is planted with trees each year. At Chichele, about 120 ha are planted each year. How is the plantation protected from fire sweeping across it? Seeds are planted in long beds in the nursery and when they are about 5 cm high the plants are removed from the beds and placed in boxes. Each box is placed in the shade and watered regularly. The shade is removed gradually and the plants get toughened by the sun. During the rainy season the seedlings are planted in rows in the prepared compartment, close together so that the trees will grow upright and tall. As the branches form a close canopy, ground vegetation is destroyed. The plantation is finally thinned out to allow the trunks to increase in circumference. When one compartment is logged another is planted and in this way there is a continuous supply of timber. Pines take a comparatively short time to grow and produce soft wood ideal for furniture.

Afforestation. Tropical pines near Lusaka.

Tropical pine nursery at Chichele

The timber industry

The industries based on the exploitation of forest products are the logging and treatment of poles by the Forestry Department, logging and sawmilling by two companies in the Sesheke and Senanga districts and the logging of local timbers in the Copperbelt Province by a company which supplies the mines with timber. Zambian timber products include railway sleepers, parquet flooring blocks and furniture. However Zambia imports temperate hardwood and softwood timber for the building industry, plywood boards, casks, boxes, paper and card products.

Things to do

1 From which regions in the world does Zambia import most of her timber? Why?

2 What particular qualities do indigenous Zambian timbers possess? For what purposes are these types useful?

3 Tabulate, the influence that vegetation has on:
  a) temperature;
  b) rainfall and run-off;
  c) soils.

4 a) What is meant by 'afforestation'?
  b) Why is afforestation necessary?

5 Suggest why conservation of forests and woodlands is in the national interest.

24 Agriculture (Zambia)

Although Zambia's surface area amounts to 752 000 km² only one third of it is suited to agriculture. Two thirds of the rest of Zambia is made up of tsetse fly-infested country (40%); forests, game reserves (15%); and areas permanently under water, rocky or otherwise agriculturally unsuitable (10%). Use the map (Fig. 69) to name the chief tsetse areas. Only about 3 to 5% of the land is under crops at any one time. Can you name the areas where most of the agricultural land is to be found? Look at the map for your answer. Most of the remainder is used as grazing land. Except in a few places, the soils are not of high inherent fertility, but good results can be obtained with the use of fertilisers and proper agricultural methods.

Over 75% of the Zambian population is engaged in farming. Most of these are subsistence farmers, growing just enough food for themselves and their relatives. The most prevalent method of subsistence farming is the Chitemene system, a type of shifting cultivation. Let us take a closer look at one of the areas where the Chitemene system is practised: the Bemba village of Chief Kasaka.

The village lies about 27 km from Shiwa Ngandu, and further from Mbala on the main road to Kabwe. You will not be able to find Kasaka's village on the map but look for Shiwa Ngandu

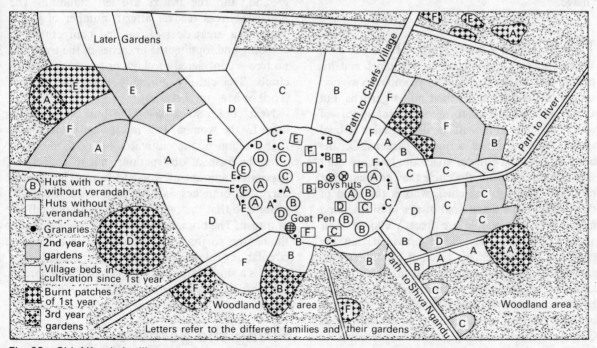

Fig. 68   Chief Kasaka's village

near Mpika. The village consists of twenty-nine huts and the community is composed mainly of four matrilocal family groups of which the male or female heads are near relatives of the headman. The adult population consists of nineteen men and twenty-three women.

The country where the village is found is an undulating area of gentle gradients forming a divide between the Luangwa in the south-east and the Chambeshi-Bangweulu depression in the north-west. It is a well-watered area drained by a number of streams flowing in opposite directions into their respective drainage systems. The savanna woodland vegetation which covers this plateau is broken only by dambos formed by the streams and is dotted here and there by clusters of huts forming villages and small circular patches marking their ash gardens.

Trees play an all-important part in the lives of the villagers. From trees they obtain all the material wealth for their daily living–huts, granaries, fences, beds, stools, drums, canoes, bark ropes used in making fishing nets and animal traps, medicines and most important of all trees provide the branches and leaves for burning the ground. The resultant ash is very necessary for the Chitemene system of millet cultivation as practised in this village.

The village (See Fig. 68)

When choosing the village site the chief and his people pick an area as near as possible to a good supply of trees to cut for their millet gardens, but at the same time close to a convenient supply of water. The huts in the village fill a circular or oval space in the middle of a ring of gardens. On the outer edge of the circular space the huts are built side by side but inside the circle they are spaced at random. Although the chief, who is the head of the village, is the traditional owner of all the land in his area, the people are free to choose their gardens wherever they please provided that the chief has first chosen the piece of ground for his garden. While no single person is allowed to own land, once an area is chosen and cleared by burning by an individual, no other person may lay claim to it unless the original cultivator has abandoned it. Only residents in the village are allowed to cultivate land controlled by the chief.

Gardens

The cultivated land is divided into:

1 'Mputa' or village mounds, a circular raised band, about 250 m across, round the village.

2 'Ifitemene' (singular–icitemene), the millet gardens which are cut in the wood land each year, at first near the village and then farther and farther out until they lie sometimes 12 or 16 km away. The word 'chitemene' is used by the Bemba-speaking tribes to mean a 'cut over area'. Once the garden has been sown it is known as 'Ubukula', and in its second and subsequent years under different crops it is called 'Icifwani'. The average size of an 'Ubukula' is about half a hectare and for this about 3 to 4 ha of woodland are cleared to provide enough branches and leaves to produce a thick layer of ash. The gardens, though of no exact shape, are roughly circular.

Tree cutting and burning

Once a suitable area for cultivation is selected the men of the village begin the dangerous operation of climbing to the crowns of the highest trees to lop off the branches. The trees are not fully cut from the trunks but lopped, with the exception of the smallest trees which are cut a metre or so from the ground, and the trunks are left standing. The pollarded trees recover after a number of years. There is a great deal of fun and competition in climbing and lopping the branches of the trees and no tree is considered too high or too dangerous to climb. Tree-cutting normally takes place from April or May until August.

Next comes stacking of the branches. This is done by the women. It is interesting to note here that the aim of the cultivator is not so much to clear the bush of obstructions, but to collect the maximum amount of wood to burn. The women carry the branches as high as possible from the ground so that the twigs and leaves do not fall off in transit. The branches are laid with their stems to the centre, so that they radiate out in a roughly circular or oval pile. Only one stack is made so that there is a single large circle, about half a hectare in size near the centre of the clearing.

Firing the gardens

This is an important and exciting event for the

villagers. No one is allowed to set his branches alight until the chief gives a special signal in case a blazing garden sets the whole bush alight and destroys the unstacked branches of other gardeners. The chief gives the signal to burn the stacks at the end of the dry season when the rains are about to break and the chief has to be exact in timing the signal. If the burning is done too early all the important ash will be blown away and lost, but if it is left too late the rains will come and soak the branches with the result that the branches do not burn well and the crop will be poor. The signal for the firing is the lighting of the chief's own pile.

Sowing

Once the bush has been burnt and the ash spread it becomes a garden, the 'ubukula'. Before the main millet crop is sown a quick-growing variety is sown in small patches just before the rain. The type of millet grown is 'finger millet'. Do you know of any other type of millet? The main crop is sown with the onset of the rains in the middle of December or January. The sower first marks out the garden with a stick into strips of about a metre wide so as to ensure that every part of the ground is covered. He walks up and down each strip casting the seeds broadcast. His wife walks behind him using a stick to cover the seeds with earth. Cucurbits, such as pumpkins, melons, etc. are planted round the edge of the garden at the beginning of the rains. Sorghum (kaffircorn) and cassava cuttings may also be planted in between the millet. Weeding or hoeing is not required during the first year of sowing because the burning destroys most weeds. The only attention the people pay to the crops after sowing is guarding against birds and wild animals as the crops ripen. They either build fences or pig pits with mounds between them, around the edge of the gardens.

Harvesting

The first millet crop ripens by April and the main millet crop by May or June. While the women reap the millet the men cut branches for new gardens. Work in the chief's garden is done by tribute labour—a number of women work and harvest the crop together. The grain from the millet crop is stored in temporary granaries out in

Name the crop shown in this photograph. Can you guess why the crop is grown on low ridges?

the fields and at the end of the harvest it is carried to the village by baskets to the permanent granaries.

Subsidiary crops

Subsidiary crops are planted either (a) with the main crop e.g. cucurbits, sorghum and cassava as already stated, (b) on old burnt gardens after the millet crop has been harvested or (c) on mounds round the village. Millet is the staple food and is used to make a thick 'porridge' called 'ubwali'. The subsidiary crops are grown to provide relish to be eaten with ubwali. Groundnuts form the chief 'relish' crop and are an important item in the diet of the people because they provide the necessary proteins. Groundnuts are sown in old millet gardens after the straw of the harvested millet crop is burnt. The soil is hoed roughly and the seeds are planted at the beginning of the rainy season. Crops such as cassava, sweet potatoes, legumes and maize are planted on mounds made in the older gardens. For cassava and sweet potatoes cuttings are used during the rainy season.

159

There is no regular harvest time for the subsidiary crops except sorghum and groundnuts. Crops such as maize, cucurbits and legumes are gathered as they ripen and root crops are dug up as required.

The last stage

The old millet gardens are used as many times as possible as long as the yield is satisfactory. Each garden goes through a sequence of crops e.g.

       1st year – millet;
       2nd year – groundnuts;
       3rd year – millet with cucurbits;
       4th year – sorghum or beans.

After four or five years when the soil is exhausted and the yields are too poor to warrant re-cultivation the garden is abandoned and it reverts to bush. By then, however, the owner has burnt a number of new gardens.

The disadvantages of the chitemene system outweigh any advantages it has. In its favour, it has been argued that it is the only method that is capable of providing enough food for the rural population. One must remember that the rural African is too poor to afford machinery to clear the woodland area, to buy fertilisers or to hire labour for growing his crops. Fire is the easiest and best possible means, under the circumstances, of clearing a large area of woodland. At the same time it destroys almost all the weeds, insect pests and also provides ash for fertilising the ground.

Burning destroys a great deal of organic matter which would be more profitable in the form of timber, firewood, leaf manure and other wood products. It is estimated that between 650 to 1000 kg of nitrogen per ha are lost to the atmosphere and the soluble mineral salts in the soil are leached by the first rains and all humus and bacteria, so necessary for decaying vegetable matter to enrich soil, are destroyed. Since all vegetation except the pollarded trees is destroyed, there is nothing left to protect the ground after the first crops from the process of erosion. There is a great deal of unnecessary waste of good woodland areas. In one area, for example, 3 to 4 ha of woodland are cleared and burnt to provide sufficient ash for a half hectare garden.

The difficulty in most rural areas today is that most of the males leave the village for work in the towns. As a result only the women and old men are left to raise crops. This shortage of labour results in haphazard methods and poor crop yields.

The government, however, in its development plans, is placing a new emphasis on rural agricultural development. The government's aim is to help the vast majority of traditional tillers of the soil to grow more by advice and assistance. Particular attention, however, is being paid to the new 'emergent farmers' who, largely through their own efforts, have developed into commercial farmers instead of continuing with their subsistence type of farming. A number of agricultural training centres, for example at Kasama and Mporokoso in the Northern Province, have been opened to train farmers in commercial farming. Attention is also being focused on the formation of co-operatives and agricultural settlements, such as that at Chombwa (near Mumbwa), where all the farmers belong to a co-operative, which looks after such things as buying seed, fertilisers and running the scheme's tractors. In these new settlement schemes the government participates directly by providing full facilities for modern mechanised agriculture, for organised pest control and fertilisers to newly cleared areas of land, where large groups of farmers are settled and professionally managed. At Chombwa after the land was prepared for agriculture by bush clearing equipment and tractors, each farmer was given 8 ha of land. The whole layout of the scheme and the cropping pattern was so organised as to simplify mechanisation at every stage. All plots along a particular strip were planted with the same crops and followed the same rotation in any one year, so that there was a line of identical plots for ploughing, fertilising or spraying.

At the end of 1967 there were 466 producer farming and settlement co-operative societies in the country.

In 1967, apart from a number of crops of minor importance, the following were marketed co-operatively:

Table 49

Crop	Production – t	Value – K
Maize	125 400	1 328 000
Groundnuts	13 500	1 220 000
Cotton	62·7	34 000
Millet	560	30 000

Checking the quality of newly introduced vegetables at the Chapula training centre

Mechanisation at the Chapula training centre for vegetable cultivation

Picking cabbages at the Chapula training centre

Individual farmers are also being given the benefit of mechanisation in the form of a rural tractor service.

Small numbers of tractors grouped in units of four to six machines work from a base where servicing facilities are available. The farmers pay for the hire of the tractor and operator.

At Chapula (near Kitwe), the Food and Agriculture Organization of the United Nations is assisting the government with a project designed to establish a small-scale irrigation, development and training centre for vegetable cultivation. The plan is to introduce common vegetables which have a high nutritional value. The farmers are also assisted in marketing the vegetables wholesale.

Commercial agriculture

What are the factors that influence farming? Read Chapter 3, page 13 of the Introduction before you read this account.

About 90% of the maize marketed comes from a belt stretching from Choma to Kabwe. Name the chief centres of cultivation in this belt. Can you state the reasons for the concentration of farming along this belt? Large quantities of maize are also produced in the Mkushi and Chipata areas. Maize yields in the country vary according to the soils

Table 50 Production figures for chief commercial crops – 1979/80

Crop	Production
Maize	336 000
Tobacco:	
flue-cured	4 100
burley	380
Sugar cane	900 000
Seed cotton	15 000
Sunflower	12 000
Groundnuts	2 800

and amount of fertilisers used. Where are nitrogenous fertilisers produced in Zambia? If you do

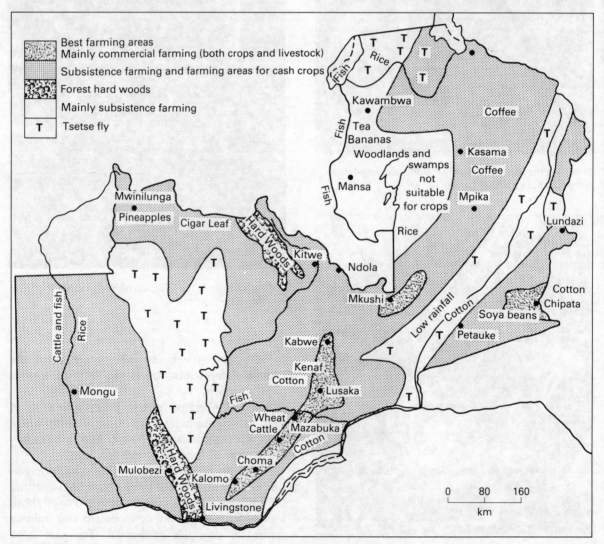

Fig. 69 Zambia farming regions and tsetse areas

162

not know, look at the chapter on Industries. Since most of the country's soils are poor, large quantities of nitrogenous fertilisers are used to increase production. Harvesting machines are increasingly used, especially on the Mkushi Block. The average yield per ha on commercial farms is about 3·3 tonnes per hectare while that obtained by traditional farmers is lower because of old-fashioned methods of cultivation. During years of surplus production maize is exported, e.g. to China in 1968, but during years of poor yields maize is imported, as in 1980 from Zimbabwe and South Africa. There are five grain elevators in the country. Do you know these centres? Look up Monze, Lusaka, Kitwe, Natuseko and Ndola in the atlas. Most of the maize produced is used by the people as their staple food.

Tobacco being weighed

Tobacco is the most important cash crop after maize. Of the three types, Virginia, Burley and Turkish, Virginia is by far the most important. Most of the main producers are found in the belt along the rail line from Kalomo, Choma and Lusaka to Kabwe. The Chipata and Mkushi areas also produce tobacco.

Burley and Turkish tobacco are cultivated largely by African farmers. The production of Virginia flue-cured is in the hands of white farmers mainly. Some Africans and Asians have taken over, with government aid, farms abandoned by a number of white farmers who left the country after independence. Production on these farms is on a large scale with over 20 ha per farm under tobacco, yielding on an average of 814 kg per ha. Tobacco is also cultivated on government training schemes, e.g. Mukonchi, 48 km east of Kabwe, which produces about 10% of Zambia's Virginia flue-cured tobacco.

The chief buyer of Zambian tobacco is the United Kingdom. A tobacco factory in Lusaka manufactures popular brands of cigarettes.

Experiments in the cultivation of cigar leaf are being carried out in the Copperbelt Province. As there is a growing demand for cigar leaf in the Western countries, its cultivation should prove profitable.

Groundnuts are grown throughout the country as a subsistence crop. The chief areas where it is cultivated as a cash crop are: an area stretching from Petauke to Chipata and Lundazi (this is the chief area); Zambezi and Kabompo districts of the North Western Province; and the areas along the line of rail.

Most of the production is exported overseas.

Cotton is cultivated near Gwembe and Magoye in the Southern Province, along the Luangwa Valley in the Eastern Province and near Mumbwa in the Central Province. Over half of the cotton produced is cultivated by Africans. The seed cotton is sent to the Lusaka Ginnery which has a ginning capacity of about 6·4 million kg of cotton a season. A textile mill to spin and weave cotton into cloth is in operation at Kafue. This mill has a capacity to turn out about 14 million m of cloth a year. Since Zambia produces only one quarter of the cotton required by this mill, most of the raw cotton has to be imported from Tanzania.

Sugar is cultivated on the Nakambala Estates

in the Kafue Flats region near Mazabuka. In 1969 the estate cultivated 2 584 ha of cane under surface irrigation. This cane produced 34 109 t of raw sugar. A mill on the estate crushes the cane. Sugar is sent to Ndola for refining. In 1978 there were over 8 000 hectares under cane cultivation throughout Zambia. Much of this was refined in Zambia itself, 15 % of the refined quantity passing through the Nakambala works, the other 85 % going to Ndola. It is expected that the optimum area under cane, 10 000 hectares will be reached by 1981.

Coffee is grown in small quantities near Mbala. Coffee is also cultivated in the Kawambwa area. Tea, too, is being tried in this area. Can you guess why this area may be suitable for tea and coffee?

A cannery in Mwinilunga uses the pineapples and vegetables produced in that area. The cultivation of citrus fruits in the Central and Southern Provinces and bananas in the Luapula Province are becoming increasingly important.

Kenaf and fodder crops were tried in the Chisamba area, the former failing to grow well and being discontinued. Rice is grown on the mid-Zambezi Flood Plain in the Western Province and experiments in rice cultivation are being carried out in the Bangweulu Swamp area.

Things to do

1 The above diagram shows the share of items in the gross value of marketed produce for 1968.

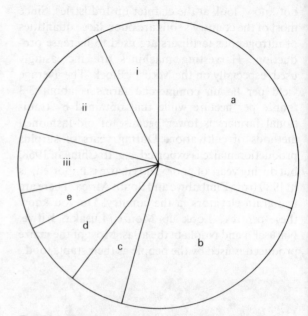

Fig. 70 The share of items in the gross value of marketed produce, 1968

The letters and numbers refer as follows: (a) maize, (b) tobacco, (c) cotton, (d) sugar, (e) other crops; (i) dairy produce, (ii) livestock slaughters, (iii) poultry products and others.

a) Copy neatly and shade your diagram in different colours and draw up a suitable key to indicate the different items.

Mechanical harvesting of wheat on the Kafue Polder near Mazabuka. Suggest one factor which favours mechanical harvesting in this area

164

b) Calculate the percentage of the marketed produce formed by:
  i) crops;
  ii) animal products.
c) What percentage of the marketed crops was made up by:
  i) maize?
  ii) tobacco?
d) What, in order of importance, were the three chief marketed agricultural products of Zambia in 1968?
2 What are the advantages and disadvantages of the Chitemene system of cultivation?
3 a) Why is it necessary that Zambia should strive towards an improvement in her agricultural production?
b) Name some of the factors favouring and those hindering agricultural development of the country?
c) What is the government doing towards increasing agricultural production?

Stock-raising and wild life

In 1968 livestock slaughter, dairy, poultry and other animal products made up 29·3% of the gross value of marketed products.

The table below gives the composition of commercial livestock for 1978.

Beef cattle	300 000
Dairy cattle	7 000
Pigs	8 000
Goats	800
Sheep	12 000
Poultry	14 000 000

Beef cattle

The country has about 2 300 000 head of cattle. Of these over 1½ million are owned by 'traditional' cattle owners.

What are the factors that control stock raising? Look at Chapter 3, pages 15 to 18 of the Introduction.

Large areas of the country are infested with tsetse fly which spreads the fatal cattle disease called trypanosomiasis. (Study the photograph of a tsetse fly on page 17). These areas are shown on the map (Fig. 69) on page 162. Note that there are three main areas. Describe the locations of these areas. Now look at Fig. 73 (page 170) for the location of the game parks. What relationship do you see between the location of the game parks and the tsetse fly areas? If cattle cannot be reared how do wild animals survive here?

The 'traditional' cattle owners produce only a very small percentage of beasts for commercial use. Most of these people keep cattle for prestige purposes–cattle to them are a symbol of wealth and an insurance–and therefore they are very reluctant to sell their cattle. Further, since they are more interested in numbers, the quality of their animals is very poor. Through very inadequate and haphazard management, only a third of the cows calve and there is a very large number of deaths among those born. Since they use cattle for work in the fields and for drawing carts, the bigger and fitter bulls are neutered for this purpose, while the weaker ones are allowed to breed. Furthermore, their cattle are under-nourished as they are kept chiefly in the woodland areas that have little grass. There is no supplementary feeding during the long dry winters.

The chief breeds of 'traditionally' owned cattle include the Tonga, Lozi and Angoni. These cattle are found in three main areas, namely, the lower Kafue basin and the surrounding region, the mid-Zambezi plain and the smaller valleys of the Western Province, and the plateau region of the Eastern Province.

Of the local breeds the Angoni cattle are best as they are able to produce more beef per head than imported breeds under Zambian conditions. These cattle are allowed to graze on the open land and during the dry season they graze on the flood plains and dambos where the pasture is better. This type of grazing, on the plateau in the wet season and on the plains in the dry season, is practised especially by the Lozi on the Mid-Zambezi plain and by the Ila on the Kafue Flats.

The most popular commercial breeds are the Afrikander, Boran and Angoni; all hardy types which are able to withstand high temperatures and poor winter feeding. Imported breeds such as Hereford and Aberdeen Angus are used for cross-breeding as these are not suited to the high temperatures of these parts of Zambia. These breeds are reared successfully on the Zimbabwean highveld.

Most of the commercial cattle are found along the 'line of rail' areas stretching from Monze in the south-west to Kabwe in the north and also in the Mkushi area.

To encourage an increase in beef production the Zambian government has taken a number of measures. The first of these is the establishment of a number of state ranches, e.g. Mkushi, Chisamba, Mbala, Chishinga and Solwezi. The purpose of these state ranches is:

1 to open up new undeveloped areas;
2 to teach local African cattle farmers animal husbandry;
3 to produce breeding stock for distribution to the commercial farmers;
4 to produce beef for sale in the rural areas.

Let us take a closer look at one such state ranch. Study the map (Fig. 71) and find out the following:
1 Between which two towns does the ranch lie?
2 Use the scale given to calculate the approximate distance to
  a) the nearest trunk road;
  b) the railway siding of Chisamba.
3 What is the approximate latitudinal and longitudinal position of the ranch?
4 How far from Lusaka is the ranch?

5 What is the average height of the land above sea level?
6 In what directions does the land around the ranch slope? How do you know this?

The Chisamba State Ranch is an interesting case to study. The manager studied cattle management at the Natural Resources Development College in Lusaka and also took a special course in artificial insemination of cattle at the research centre at Mazabùka.

This ranch, the manager informed us, was 15 004 ha and therefore one of the smaller state ranches in the country. Some of the larger ranches were as big as 40 000 ha. In September, 1978, the ranch had 3 049 head of cattle.

The cattle were made up as follows:

cows for breeding purposes	1 665
bulls for breeding purposes	93
heifers	954
calves of varying months	61

Now look at the map of the ranch (Fig. 72). Notice that the ranch is divided into three sections and each section is further sub-divided into paddocks by wire fence. Each section is managed by a 'stockman' who is directly responsible to the manager. Under each 'stockman' are three herdsmen who look after the cattle. Each stockman is responsible for about 1 000 head of cattle. Each of the three sections has its own compound for the servants, and its own cattle handling unit. The unit consists of facilities for cattle dipping and spraying, treatment for diseases and for castrating. The stockman is responsible for the cattle in his section.

The paddocks vary in size from about 300 to 500 ha. These paddocks are used in rotation to avoid over-grazing. At any one time three paddocks are in use in each of the sections. This means that approximately 300 head of cattle graze in one paddock. The length of time they remain in a paddock depends on the quality of the grass and leaves which in turn vary according to the seasons. During the wet season a paddock may be used continuously for three months but during the dry season cattle are allowed to remain only for about a month. Fodder crops are not cultivated at the ranch. The only supplementary feed during the winter months is a high protein meal and a regular supply of salt blocks purchased in Lusaka. To improve the natural grazing an area of 400 ha

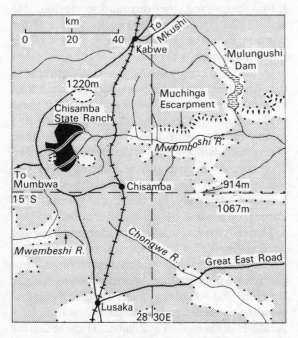

Fig. 71   Chisamba State Ranch – location

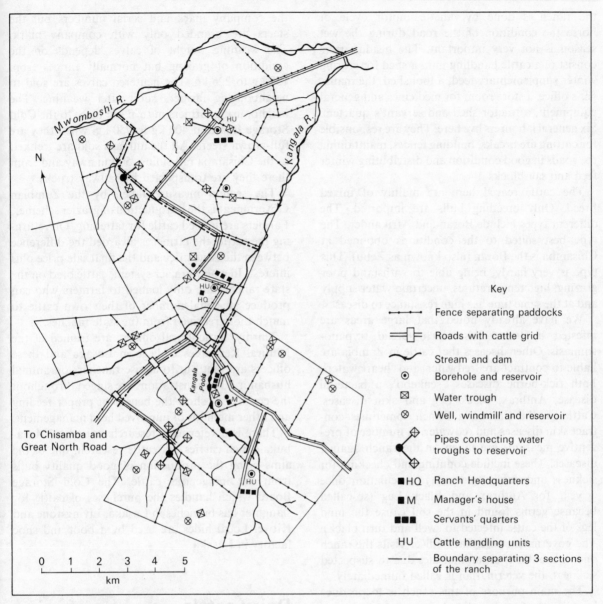

Fig. 72 Chisamba State Ranch – land use

Key

•┼•┼•	Fence separating paddocks
▭	Roads with cattle grid
～	Stream and dam
⊙	Borehole and reservoir
⊠	Water trough
⊗	Well, windmill and reservoir
⊕	Pipes connecting water troughs to reservoir
■ HQ	Ranch Headquarters
■ M	Manager's house
■■■	Servants' quarters
HU	Cattle handling units
—·—·—	Boundary separating 3 sections of the ranch

(to be increased later), is to be planted with star grass. This grass has high feeding value, establishes itself very fast and at the same time is fire-resistant.

Since the Mwomboshi river flows along the northern boundary of the ranch and its tributary the Kangala crosses the greater part of the ranch there is no real water problem. During the dry season the Kangala is very low and sometimes dries up but wells and windmills supplement the natural supply. The map (Fig. 72) indicates clearly that the ranch occupies part of a watershed. Every

paddock has a water trough or a dam, and wells and boreholes worked by windmills are well distributed throughout the ranch.

The paddocks are separated by wire fence and a 'fire break'. Why do you think a fire break is so necessary on a ranch of this type? Note also that cattle grids are found along the road at paddock boundaries. What is the function of these grids?

The headquarters of the ranch is centrally situated and connected to all sections of the ranch by a good, dry-weather road. Since travel through the ranch is done by vanette, motor cycle or horse the condition of the road during the wet season is not very important. The headquarters consist of a cattle handling unit, a shed for storing winter supplementary feed, a tool shed, the manager's office, a store room for medicines and general equipment, a tractor shed and servant's quarters. Six general labourers live here. They are responsible for cutting fire breaks, building fences, maintaining the roads in good condition and distributing winter feed and salt blocks.

The cattle reared here are mainly of mixed breed. Only breeding bulls are imported. The different types include Boran and Afrikander. The type best suited to the conditions obtained at Chisamba is the Boran (also known as Zebu). This type is very hardy, being able to withstand poor grazing, high temperatures, uncertain water supply and at the same time has high resistance to diseases.

We have already noted that large areas are infested by tsetse flies which spread trypanosomiasis. Other diseases that cattle in Zambia are liable to contract are 'redwater' and 'heart water', both tick-borne diseases, 'senkebo', a bacterial disease, Anthrax, Black Leg and skin diseases. Cattle on the Chisamba Ranch sometimes contract skin diseases and redwater. A number of preventive measures are taken on the ranch against diseases. These include counting and checking for sickness and deaths every day, inoculation once a year for Anthrax and Black Leg (so-called because germs found in the soil cause the hind legs of the cattle infected to swell and turn black). The government veterinary officer visits the ranch once a month. If an animal dies due to suspected sickness, the veterinarian is called immediately.

The main purpose of this ranch is to produce breeding heifers for distribution to other state ranches and neighbouring farms. The breeding stock has approximately 60% calving rate. At birth the calves are ear-marked with the month and year of birth. This helps to keep a check on their weight and to decide the most profitable breeds. All bull calves are neutered at three weeks. The calves are weaned at six to seven months depending on the condition of the mother. If, as a result of poor grazing and management, the cows are in poor condition the calves are weaned early. The calves are separated according to sex on weaning. On weaning, heifers are branded with the company mark and serial numbers but the steers are branded only with company mark. The weaning weight of calves depends on the condition of grazing but normally ranges from 150 kg to 225 kg. The neutered calves are sold to neighbouring farmers soon after weaning. The neighbouring farmers in turn sell these to the Cold Storage Board at 400 kg to 750 kg, when they are full-grown steers. All the animals sold are trekked to the Chisamba rail siding, 50 km away and from there they are transported by railway trucks.

The second measure taken by the Zambian Government is the introduction of grazier schemes. Farmers are loaned cattle for fattening. On returning the cattle, the farmer is awarded the difference between the issue price and the final sale price plus interest. In a new grazier system, cattle bred on the state ranches are only loaned to farmers who can produce an equal number of their own cattle to match those received from the state ranches.

Thirdly, agricultural officers are trained at the Natural Resources College in Lusaka and these officers are sent out to advise ranchers on animal husbandry. Demonstrations are staged throughout the country to show the benefit of proper feeding and other methods of improved herd management.

There is a veterinary research station at Mazabuka which carries out cattle research, one of the aims being the production of good quality bulls from the indigenous cattle. The Cold Storage Board which handles the purchases of cattle for slaughter has branches in Lusaka, Livingstone and Kitwe. Local hides are used by a boot and shoe factory in Lusaka.

Dairy cattle

Dairying is carried on near the main urban centres along the line of rail. The chief centres of the dairy industry are the Lusaka-Chisamba area, Mazabuka, Kabwe and the Copperbelt. Imported European breeds such as Friesians, Jerseys and Ayrshires are the chief dairy cattle reared. Now look at the photos of Friesians and Jerseys shown on page 20. Have you seen such cattle around your area? These cattle depend on natural pastures for about four months in the year during the rainy season and on artificial feeding during the rest of the year. Fodder crops cultivated for this purpose include cowpeas, lucerne, velvet beans and maize.

Milk is normally available during the rainy season but in very short supply during the dry season. Therefore, to supplement fresh milk during this season, reconstituted milk is produced. Milk production is handled by the Dairy Produce Board. Cheese, butter and other dairy products are imported in the form of butter fat or powdered milk.

Poultry, sheep, goats and pigs

Very few sheep are reared commercially in the country. Most of the mutton and lamb consumed is imported from Australia and New Zealand.

Goats are kept chiefly as part of the subsistence economy by Africans.

A large number of pigs are reared by maize farmers. Pigs are fattened on maize and skimmed milk. (See page 20.) What do the pigs contribute towards maize cultivation on the farms? Do you know what skimmed milk is? There is a large pork-processing factory at Lusaka and several smaller ones in the main copper producing regions.

Poultry farming is carried on, like dairy farming, near the main urban centres where there is a ready market for its products. These products are eggs, broilers, day-old chicks, ducks and turkeys. A large part of the poultry industry is in the hands of co-operative societies. The table below gives the value of commercially produced poultry products for 1978.

Table 51 Poultry data for Zambia

Products	Number	Value in Kwacha
Eggs	172·3 m	K10·3 m
Dressed poultry	5·3 m	K13·1 m
Live poultry	7·9 m	K19·6 m
Day old chicks	14·3 m	K 4·4 m
Pullets	1·1 m	K 0·65 m

Day-old chicks are exported to neighbouring countries, e.g. Zaire, Kenya, Uganda, Tanzania and Malawi.

Wild life

The savanna region with its open woodlands and tall grasses is the natural home of many types of wild animals. Some of these animals which used to roam vast areas of Central Africa are (1) the herbivores which include elephants, hippopotami, buffalo, giraffe, wildebeeste, many species of antelopes, zebras and rhinoceros and (2) carnivores which include lions, leopards, cheetahs, hyenas and foxes and crocodiles in the rivers.

Today, however, due to poaching, a direct result of the development of rural areas, a large number of animals are killed by people who practise hunting for sport and also by people who kill animals to trade in meat, ivory or skins. The animals killed chiefly for these purposes are elephants for their ivory and crocodiles for their skins.

To prevent the complete disappearance of many species of wild animals the government has set aside large areas in which animals are protected. The chief National Parks are shown on the map (Fig. 73). Others include Mweru Marsh, Lunga, Lukusuzi and Lusenga Flats Game Reserve. Did you know that the Kafue National Park is reputed to be the largest game reserve in the world?

As a result of protection some animals, especially those such as elephants, hippopotami and buffaloes, not controlled by natural predators, began to increase very rapidly. When an area becomes over-populated with animals the vegetation begins to suffer. There is an excessive removal of edible plants over wide areas which, as a result, suffer from greatly increased erosion during the rainy season and therefore their productivity becomes greatly reduced. If this carries on unchecked the land becomes devastated and the animals die of starvation. To prevent over-grazing, the number of animals has to be controlled to maintain a healthy balance between animals and vegetation. The animal numbers are controlled by a practice called 'game cropping' which also serves a second purpose of providing in some measure much-needed protein in the areas near the game parks.

In 1966, a total of 1·4 million kg of meat was shot by hunting area residents on free licences. It is estimated that with proper management about 4·5 million kg of meat could be harvested every year from all the game parks.

Wild life viewing and hunting safaris could become a major tourist industry for Zambia. Revenue is derived from the issue of hunting

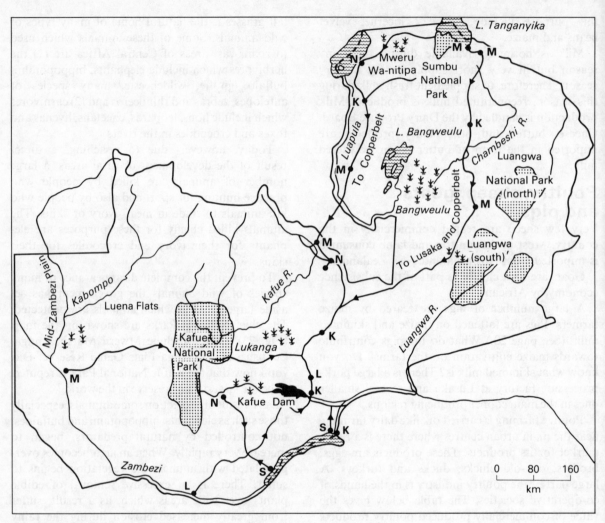

Fig. 73 Zambia game reserves

licences, park entrance and camp accommodation fees, hotel accommodation and from the sale of curios. In 1966 a total of K46 000 was received for controlled hunting area licences and safari concessions. The development of wild life as an important source of meat and as an important tourist industry is, however, still in its infancy.

Things to do

1 'Traditional' cattle number about five times those on commercial farms and yet they produce only about a quarter the number of cattle for slaughter as commercial farms. Why is this so?

2 a) What is re-constituted milk?

 b) When does it normally appear on the market? Why?

3 Why are poultry farms only located close to urban areas?

4 a) What are the different ways in which wild life could be used to attract tourists?

 b) Name another African country where wild life viewing and hunting safaris are big business?

5 The production of beef in the country falls far short of the demand. This is a significant problem in some ways. What type of benefit does meat provide to a diet? What steps do you suggest the government could take to increase beef production to at least the level of the present demand?

6 Account for the distribution of beef cattle in Zambia.

25 Fisheries (Zambia)

Fish, which supplies much-needed protein and is at the same time the staple relish food for large numbers of people, is an important natural resource of the country. Landlocked Zambia has a number of lakes, swamps, rivers and dams which in 1968 produced 28 960 t of fish. Study the map (Fig. 73) and name (1) the lakes; (2) the swamps; and (3) the chief rivers that form the chief fisheries of the country. Which of these is the most recently developed fishery? Can you name the fisheries that supply the following areas with fresh fish:

a) Kabwe;
b) Copperbelt;
c) Lusaka.

There are over 300 different kinds of fish found in Zambia. These range in weight from a few grammes to over 100 kg. Some of the more important species caught in these fisheries include the tiger fish, catfish, squeaker, snout fish, gorge fish, mud fish, butter fish, barbel, small-mouthed bream, large-mouthed bream, Lake Tanganyika whitebait (Kapenta) and Nile perch.

Fishing methods

Fishing methods in Zambia can be divided into two main groups:

Subsistence fishing using dugout canoe and net. Can you identify the type of net being used? Today subsistence fishermen and farmers need cash. What has this fisherman bought?

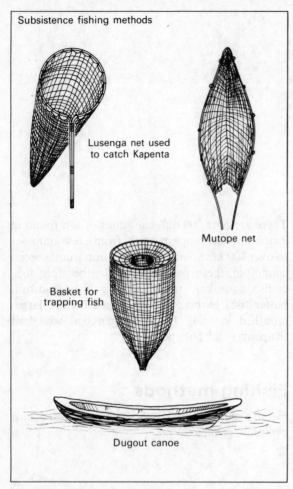

Fig. 74   Small scale fishing equipment

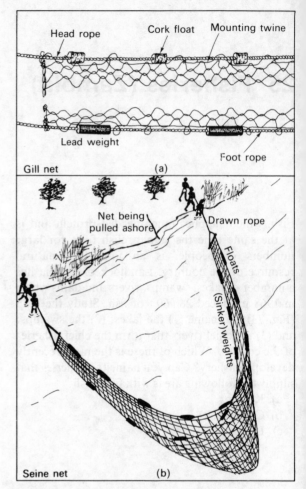

Fig. 75   Small scale fishing methods

1 The small-scale fishing methods used mainly by subsistence fishermen. These methods include the use of traps, hand lines, baskets, hand nets and spears. Dugout canoes are used to transport fish caught to the villages along the shores. See Fig. 74.

2 Commercial fishing methods: for commercial purposes two main types of nets are used. These are the seine net and gill net. See Figs. 74 and 75 for diagrams of these nets.

Fisheries

About one-eighth of Lake Tanganyika falls within Zambia's boundaries. This fishery is important for two main types of fish, namely, kapenta or sardines and pamba (Nile perch). The main types of net used are the purse seine variety. (See fig. 75). This is the same type as used in many Mediterranean waters; indeed Greek fishermen are to be found on the lake. Pamba are caught with gill nets, set at the bottom at about 15 to 90 m below the surface. Two commercial firms, based at Mpulungu, operate on the lake with the use of modern equipment.

The Lake Mweru-Luapula fishery is on the Zaire-Zambia border and lies in one of the most densely populated areas of Africa. The most common method of fishing here is gill netting. Variations of gill netting include 'Kutumpula' used on the Luapula and southern areas of Lake Mweru where the fish are driven into the net by splashing water, and 'Kansenswa' where nets are set across a swiftly flowing river and fish are trapped as the net drifts with the stream. Most of the fish caught here is marketed fresh in the Copperbelt.

The Lake Bangweulu area consists of patches of shallow water separated by reed-covered areas which gradually merge into pure swamp to the east. The swamps are fed by a number of rivers, the largest being the Chambeshi. There are a number of canals, channels and lagoons which act as waterways for boats and canoes.

Although gill netting is the main method of commercial fishing, seine nets, lines and baskets are also used. Some of the catch in this fishery is smoke-dried for local consumption.

The Kafue Flood Plain Fishery extends from the Itezhi-Tezhi gap to the Kafue gorge, a distance of 392 km. The river meanders through a large, flat grassland plain from 24 to 64 km wide. There are a number of depressions on the plain which form isolated lakes when the water level has gone down, leaving the rest of the plain dry. During the dry season this is a grazing ground for lechwe (a kind of antelope) and cattle. The droppings of these animals provide rich food for the fish which come here during the flood season.

Gill netting is the most common method of fishing here. Since the fishery is quite close to the main markets there is a great demand for fresh fish. A large part of the catch during the wet season is smoke-dried. Can you think of a reason for this? Note the Mid-Zambezi Flood Plain, somewhat similar to the Kafue Plain in its physical characteristics, is an important source of fish for the local people. Can you suggest why this Plain has not developed into an important commercial fishery.

During the construction of the dam wall at Kariba an area of about 48 000 ha was cleared of trees to allow fishermen to use nets later. The fish population of the new lake was built up by the introduction into the lake of about 9 000 kg of fingerlings (baby bream) from the Chilanga fish farm near Lusaka. The area of the Lake Kariba used to be inhabited by the Gwembe Valley Tonga who lived by cultivating along the river banks. In 1955, when work was begun on the dam, it was decided that the Tonga would have to be moved from the valley. The Tonga had therefore to adapt themselves to a life of fishing. They had to be

taught the latest methods of fishing and, as a result, a fisheries training centre was opened at Sinazongwe, 192 km from the dam wall. The centre teaches the Tonga how to make and repair nets, to dry fish and prepare them for the market. They are also taught boat-building, the servicing of marine engines, fishing regulations and the financial management of the fish trade.

Gill netting is the chief method of fishing. A number of landing jetties have been built along the lake to facilitate fish trade. These landing places include Chipepo, which has a modern harbour and a covered market; Sinazongwe which also has, besides the Fisheries Training Centre, a covered market; plant; Siavonga, which is near the dam wall, also has a fish jetty and fish market. See page 110 Zimbabwe: Commercial Fisheries.

Trade

Fish is sold fresh (frozen if it is to be carried long distances), sun-dried and smoked or salted and dried. About 60% of the fish that comes to the market is dried. Large fish are gutted and split open and laid out in mats on the roofs of huts to dry. Larger fish are smoked as this process is quicker. These fish are split open, gutted, sun-dried for a short time and then smoked over a fire on racks either in the open or inside a hut. The fires are usually made in pits, with wood, reeds or whatever is available used as fuel. In the Lake Mweru Fishery fish are also salted and sun-dried.

Almost all the fish from the Zambian Fisheries is sold within the country but a small amount of dried fish is exported to Zaire.

Things to do
1 List:
  a) the fisheries that are shared with the neighbouring countries;
  b) the fisheries found wholly within Zambia.
2 In the spaces provided, state briefly how each of the fishing methods named below is used:

Method	*How it is used*
Gill Net	
Seine Net	
Kutumpula	
Kansenswa	

Sun-drying Kapenta at Mpulungu

3 Describe briefly the different ways in which the fish caught in the Zambian fisheries are prepared for the local market.

4 The table below gives the 1977 fish production figures in t for the different fisheries in Zambia.

　a) Show the above production figures in a pie graph (use a radius of 4 cm). Divide the circle into sectors to represent the different fisheries.

　b) Which were the two most productive fisheries in 1968?

5 Describe the importance of fisheries to Zambia.

6 On the map (Fig. 73) settlements are shown by the first letter only. Name all the settlements.

Table 52 Fish production in tonnes

Upper Zambezi	River Kafue	Lake Bangweulu	Lake Mweru-Luapula	Lake Mweru-wantipa	Lake Tanganyika
3 490	9 830	9 496	9 533	12 513	7 866

26 Mining (Zambia)

Zambia's economy is based almost totally on mining. Study the table of the chief minerals and their provisional production figures given for 1979 and then answer the questions that follow:

Table 53

Minerals	Production in t	Value in kwacha
Coal	598 000	15 200 000
Copper (electrolytic)	564 000	796 000 000
Copper (blister)	20 000	29 000 000
Zinc	38 200	20 600 000
Lead	12 800	11 100 000
Cobalt	3 270	139 000 000

1 Arrange the minerals in descending order of importance by value.

2 What was the total copper production in 1979
  a) in tonnes?
  b) in millions of kwacha?

3 a) What percentage of the total value of mineral production shown in the table above was made up by copper?
  b) Turn to Fig. 87 page 192 to find out what percentage of the total value of all exports was made up by copper in 1979.

4 Can you name the mineral that fetches (a) the highest price; (b) the lowest price per tonne on the market?

Geology and the distribution of minerals

Geologically Zambia is not much different from most parts of Central and East Africa. The country consists of a complex of ancient sediments in which rocks of volcanic origin are to be found. As a result of such intrusion much folding and distortion of the sedimentary rocks has occurred. These rocks are generally described as a 'basement series' and are found mainly in the eastern and south eastern parts of the country. These series which form the oldest rocks in the country are divided into a lower and upper series known as the Basement Complex and the Muva Group respectively.

On these basement series four groups of sedimentary layers lie unconformably. Try to find out from your teacher what this means. They are found mainly in the central and north western parts of the country.

The first group which is the oldest and most extensive is known as the Katanga System and is the group which contains all the important mineral deposits. Look at the map (Fig. 76) and name all the minerals that occur in this system. Does the Katanga System cover the whole of the Copperbelt region?

The second group which also consists of sediments is called the Karroo System. Rocks of this system are found in several places but are especially extensive in the Western Province where they are found beneath the Kalahari sands. They appear at the surface only in the middle Zambezi and Luangwa valleys where, as a result of faulting, they have been lowered many hundred metres. Volcanic lava intrusions appear above these rocks in the Zambezi valley above and below the Victoria Falls.

Look at the map (Fig. 76) again to find out which mineral is associated with the Karroo System.

The third group, which is known as the Kalahari

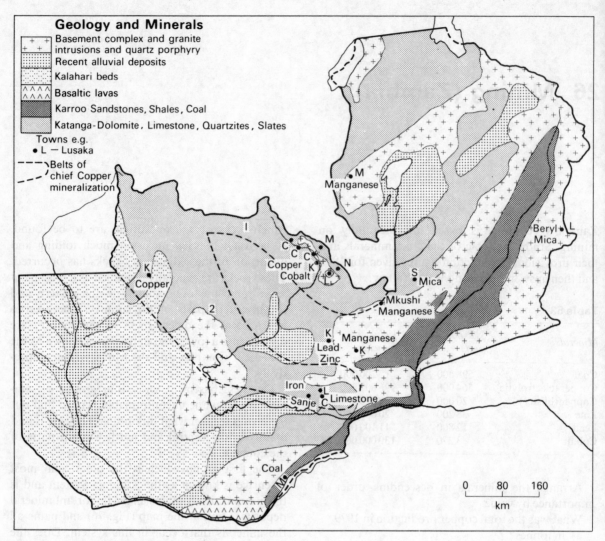

Geology and Minerals

- + + Basement complex and granite intrusions and quartz porphyry
- Recent alluvial deposits
- Kalahari beds
- ∧∧∧∧ Basaltic lavas
- Karroo Sandstones, Shales, Coal
- Katanga-Dolomite, Limestone, Quartzites, Slates

Towns e.g.
- ● L — Lusaka

Belts of chief Copper mineralization

Fig. 76 Zambia geological map

System, is found mainly in the western part of the country. It consists of a layer of unconsolidated wind blown sands, loosely cemented red and white sandstones, gravels and thin limestones. In most areas the ancient rock formations are concealed by recent deposits of residual soil, alluvium and in dissected areas, talus (rocks and pebbles which have been carried to the foot of a slope).

The main copper mineralisation occurs in the Katanga series in two belts:

1 An arc-like belt extending roughly from east of Kapiri Mposhi, through the Copperbelt to Solwezi and Mwinilunga;

2 A belt extending in a west north-westerly

direction from the south-east of Lusaka through Mumbwa and thence westwards through Kasempa to Mwinilunga.

1 The Copperbelt forms part of the first belt while a number of prospects such as King Edward mine, the Sable Antelope group of mines and the new Kalengwa open pit mine occur in the second belt.

To take a closer look at the Copperbelt let us study the map (Fig. 77).

a) In which province is this region located?

b) Which international boundary runs close to this region?

c) Do you know whether the copper-bearing rocks extend into the neighbouring country?

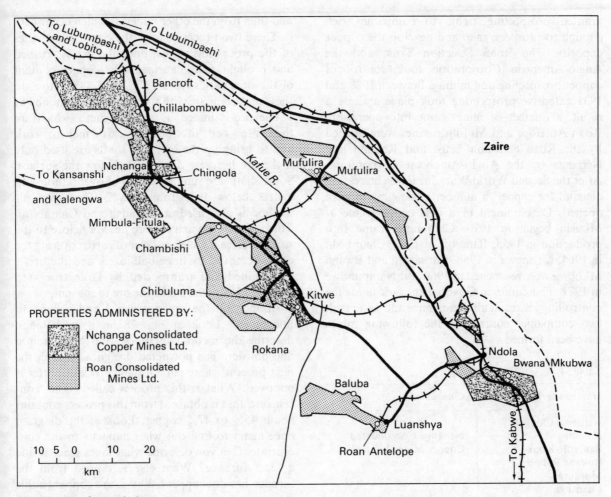

Fig. 77   The Copperbelt

2 To get an idea of the size of the Copperbelt use
the scale given on the map to get the approximate
distances between:

    a) the southern end of copper occurrence at
Bwana Mkubwa and the northern end of copper
occurrence at Chililabombwe;

    b) the western extent of Chibuluma occurrence
and the eastern limit of the Mufulira deposits.

3 Name the mines located near the following
towns:

Chililabombwe, Chingola, Kitwe and Luanshya.

4 Does the railway line to Lubumbashi and Lobito
run through the Copperbelt of Zambia?

    The actual date of the discovery of copper in
the Copperbelt region is unknown as the local
people were mining copper by primitive methods
and using it for ornaments, long before the Euro-

peans made their own discovery. The first white man
to discover copper was George Grey who found
copper at Kansanshi as leader of an expedition in
1899. From 1900 onwards a number of companies
were formed to prospect for copper deposits. In
1902 William Collier discovered deposits at Bwana
Mkubwa and Luanshya. Mining operations did
not begin until 1909. Can you guess why? If you
cannot then look for the answer on page 190.
Bwana Mkubwa was the only mine producing
copper in Zambia until 1931 and even here there
were several stoppages in production. In April,
1931, the mine was closed because the deposits
were not rich enough to be worth mining. In 1969,
however, the mine was re-opened due to high
copper prices.

    In 1923, the British South Africa Company

granted prospecting rights to companies rich enough to prospect, map and develop the copper deposits. The Roan Selection Trust and the Anglo-American Corporation took control of copper prospecting and mining. Between 1928 and 1931 extensive prospecting took place and, as a result, a number of mines came into operation. Roan Antelope and Mufulira mines were opened by the Roan Selection Trust and Rokana and Nchanga by the Anglo-American Corporation. After the Second World War, due to the increasing demand for copper, a number of new mines were opened. Development of a new copper mine at Mkushi began in 1970. Chibuluma came into production in 1955, Bancroft in 1957, Chambishi in 1964, Kalengwa in 1968, Kansanshi and Bwana Mkubwa were re-opened in 1969 and Nampundwe in 1971. The Zambian Government now holds the controlling shares in all these mines and as a result two companies controlling the following mines have been formed:

Table 54

Mines and refineries	Companies
Nchanga-Chingola Rokana Bancroft-Konkola Rokana Refinery	Nchanga Consolidated Copper Mines Limited
Mufulira Luanshya Chibuluma Chambishi Kalengwa Ndola Copper Refinery	Roan Consolidated Mines Limited

Production

Copper is normally found in chemical combination with a number of other minerals. These combinations include chalcopyrite, a sulphide of copper and iron; bornite, also a copper iron sulphide; chalcocite, a copper sulphide; malachite, a hydrated copper carbonate; cuprite, a copper oxide; and tenorite, a black oxide of copper. Try to collect samples of these ores if you live close to a copper mine.

The copper ores in Zambia occur in rocks of varying kinds, the most important of which are shales. To extract copper metal, therefore, the copper ore has first to be separated from the shales

and then from the other minerals which occur with it. These two processes form the essential activities of the processing plants, once the ore is crushed and brought to the surface. The copper content of the ores varies from 1·73% to 5·44%. How do these ores compare with those found in Zimbabwe?

The ore is mined by sinking shafts which are then fitted with lifts both to carry men to work and to bring up the ore. The shafts are used only if the ore lies very deep down below the surface. Some shafts are sunk to depths of over a thousand metres below the ground level. The open pit method is also used at Nchanga and Chambishi. This is possible when the ore lies very close to the surface. Here the surface layer of earth covering the ore is removed by huge bulldozers and the ore is then mined and transported by large trucks to conveyor belts which take the ore to the mill.

At the mill the ore is crushed and ground to fine power. Look at Fig. 78 on page 179 and describe the method used to grind the ore into fine powder. The powdered ore goes through the next process where part of the worthless matter is removed. What is this process called? The 'concentrate' that is obtained from this process contains about 45% to 47% copper. Look at the diagram once again to find out what happens to the concentrate. Can you describe what takes place inside a blast furnace? What else is tapped from the furnace besides copper? Why is the copper at this stage sent to a converter? In what form is copper from a converter cast? How is this copper different from anodes? Note the chief impurities found in the copper that is tapped from the converter are the minerals silver, bismuth, nickel and traces of gold. The anodes are sent to refineries where they are refined by an electrical process. They are placed in tanks filled with a solution of copper sulphate and diluted sulphuric acid. Cathode sheets of pure copper, weighing some 5 kg each, are suspended in these tanks.

When an electrical current is introduced the anodes gradually dissolve in the solution and copper is deposited on the cathode sheets which as a result grow in thickness to a weight of about 100 kg. This takes about two weeks. The cathodes are melted in a furnace and cast in various shapes, the commonest being wire bars each weighing 160 kg. You understand, therefore, why this is called electrolytic copper. It is 99·98% pure, the

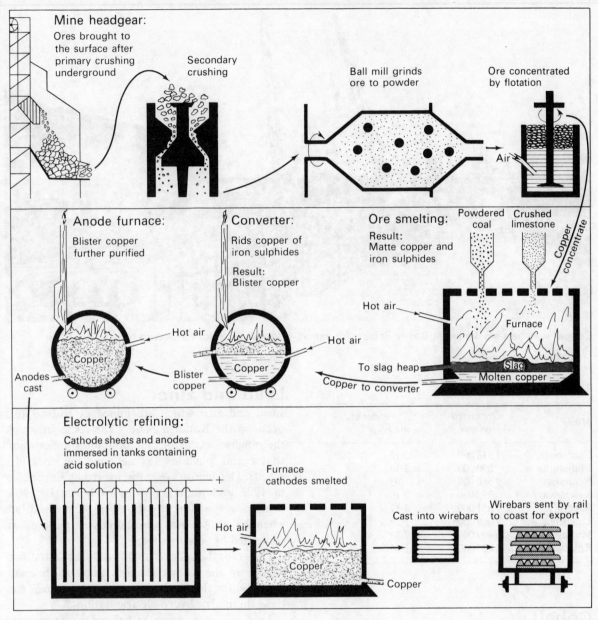

Fig. 78 Production of copper

chief impurity being oxygen. Note that green tree trunks are burnt in the furnace at this stage to extract oxygen from the molten copper. Gold and silver are extracted as by-products of the electrolytic refining process. Look at the map of the Copperbelt (Fig. 77 page 177) and name all the centres that have electrolytic refineries.

The 1977 production figures are given below for each of the mines.

The first column of figures shows the total amount of ore mined in 1977. The second column shows the percentage of copper within the ore.

1 Arrange these into order of amounts of ore mined.

2 Which mines are producing the highest concentrate of copper in the ore?

Copper wire bars stockpiled at Dar es Salaam for export. Suggest a use for these wire bars

Table 55

Mine	Ore mined (tonnes)	% copper in ore milled
Chambishi	1 915 000	2·15
Chibuluma	590 000	3·13
Nchanga	9 510 000	3·43
Kalengwa	352 000	7·19
Bancroft	1 651 000	3·17
Luanshya	7 069 000	1·58
Mufulira	6 409 000	2·39
Rokana	5 427 000	1·66

Cobalt

Mining and processing of cobalt is increasing to keep pace with rising world demand. Production of cobalt is expected to reach 4 000 tonnes by 1981. It is processed at Rokana for the Nchanga group of mines and at Chambishi for Roan. Zambia is the world's second largest producer of cobalt after Zaire.

Cobalt is important for its magnetic properties and its ability to withstand high temperatures. It is used in magnets, cutting tools and diesel and jet engines.

Lead and zinc

Lead and zinc which are mined at Kabwe also occur in the Katanga Series. The rocks in which the minerals occur include dolomites, limestones, shales and phyllites (a metamorphic rock-like schist). The deposits were discovered by Europeans in 1902 and mining operations began in 1904. Mining was, at first, by the open pit method but when the surface ores were exhausted, mining was continued by sinking shafts.

Power for the mines is obtained from two stations located in the Kabwe Region. Look at the map (Fig. 79) for the names of these two stations. Are these thermal or hydro-electric stations?

Lead is a soft, dense and therefore heavy grey metal which is able to withstand weathering. It is malleable and has a low melting point. Nearly a third of the world's lead is used in making the plates of electric storage batteries. Because of its great density it is used as a protective shield against radiation. It is also used in covering cables, in white lead oxide for paint, in bullets and for roofing material. Since it resists corrosion it is used in the chemical industry as a lining for tanks containing acid. It is also used in alloys. It is mixed with tin to make solder and as an alloy,

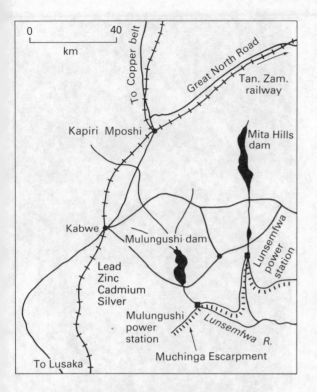

Fig. 79   Kabwe hydro electric power schemes

lead, with tin and antimony, is used for making type for the printing industry.

Zinc, which resists rust, is a soft white malleable metal. As already noted zinc is used in the manufacture of brass. It is also used in galvanising; that is, a process of covering sheets of iron or steel with a thin coating of zinc which, since it resists rust, protects the iron or steel from rusting due to weather. A large part of the world's zinc is used in the manufacture of galvanised corrugated iron which is used as roofing material. Zinc is also used in making collapsible tubes (e.g. toothpaste tubes) and containers for dry batteries. Many types of pipes and paints and antiseptic ointments contain zinc.

Manganese

Manganese is an important mineral used as an alloy and as a 'cleanser' in the iron and steel industry: in the manufacture of steel it is used to remove sulphur and oxygen and is mixed with steel to produce the alloy called manganese steel. Since manganese steel is hard, tough and resistant to rust, it is used for steel rails and for heavy duty

Pouring molten zinc into moulds at the Broken Hill lead and zinc mine at Kabwe. What are some of the uses of zinc?

181

machinery such as is employed in mining, rock crushing and road working.

The ores occur mainly in granite intrusions and quartz porphyry in the basement complex. There were six producing mines in the country, Kampumba, in the Kabwe District, Chiwefwe and Arieus in the Mkushi District, Mashimba, Bahati and Bunda mines in the Mansa District. The Kampumba deposits consist of solid ore deposits and rubble deposits spread along slopes of the three hills known as East, Middle and West Hills. The ore has an average metal content of 50% and occurs in places in combination with iron ore. The ore bodies in the Mansa District have a metal content of 50–57% and occur in seams of increasing thickness–from a few centimetres to three to four metres, running horizontal to the surface.

Much of the manganese mined comes from Luapula and Mansa. It is also mined at Luano in the Copperbelt for use in copper refining.

Coal

Coal seams are found in sediments of the Lower Karroo Series and therefore occur in Zambia in

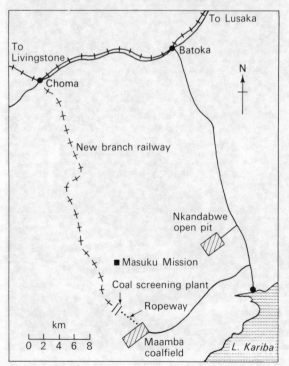

Fig. 80   Zambia coal in Zambezi escarpment

Nkandabwe open pit coal mine, now closed due to the poor quality coal and flooding. Open pit mining is cheaper than underground mining, why?

the Zambezi and Luangwa valleys. The Gwembe coal formation in which the Nkandabwe and Maamba coal seams occur is covered by a thick layer of gravel and sands and is exposed only in the Ntole and Kandabwe river valleys.

Coal deposits were first discovered in the Gwembe valley in 1952 but no attempt was made to mine them then as the Hwange Colliery in Zimbabwe supplied cheap coal for Zambia. In 1965, due to strained relations between Zambia and Zimbabwe, the deposits were re-surveyed and mining began in 1966 at Nkandabwe. The coal was mined by the open pit method and transported by road to the railhead at Batoka, 67 km away. New deposits were discovered in November, 1965, at Siankandobo, 36 km to the south-west of Nkandabwe (see Fig. 80). These deposits have a high ash content compared with Hwange coal. In 1968, when as a result of flooding, the Nkandabwe mine was closed down, Maamba, the mine at Siankandobo, became the chief producer. The ropeway, indicated in Fig. 80, carries buckets of coal up this part of the Zambezi Escarpment. What do you think is the function of the coal screening plant?

Other minerals

Small quantities of gold, silver and selenium are found as by-products of the copper mines. Selenium is used in sound film apparatus, for automatic street lighting, burglar alarms and photographic exposure meters. The lead and zinc mine at Kabwe also produces a small amount of silver.

Cadmium which is used as a protective coating for iron and steel, is produced by the Broken Hill mine at Kabwe.

Small quantities of beryl, tin and mica are also mined.

Limestone is mined at Shimabula near Lusaka. Gypsum is mined in the Kafue Basin near Monze. Limestone and gypsum are used in the manufacture of cement by the Chilanga Cement Factory which supplied the cement for the Kariba and Kafue dams.

The majority of the iron ore deposits lie within a radius of 144 km of Lusaka. Iron ore occurs in country underlain by sediments of Katanga series. A few of the more important occurrences are at Sanje, 42 km west-south-west of Lusaka, the Cheta River which is 40 km south-west of Lusaka, the Pemba Hills, 30 km west of Lusaka and Nambala-Sonkwe Ridge, 136 km west of Lusaka. The metal content of the ores, in some cases, is over 60% and reserves are sufficient to maintain an iron and steel industry in the country for some time. Iron-ore deposits have also been discovered in the Solwezi District. These deposits are not, as yet, mined commercially.

Things to do
1 Name the minerals that are recovered as by-products from:
  a) the copper mines
  b) lead and zinc mines
in Zambia.
2 Which mineral mined in the country is used in the extraction process of other minerals e.g. copper, zinc and lead?
3 Name the different ways in which copper mining has encouraged a concentration of population in the Copperbelt.
4 What do you think are the long-term growth prospects of an iron and steel industry based on local ores in Zambia?
5 a) Draw a map of the Copperbelt, inserting the mines and the copper refineries.
  b) Describe the processing of the copper ores.
6 Examine specimens of the minerals mined in Zambia. Learn how to distinguish between these.

27 Power (Zambia)

Electricity in the country is generated both by thermal and hydro-electric stations (see Fig. 81). At first the country relied mainly on thermal stations most of which were on the Copperbelt, a region which is the largest consumer of power in the country. Coal, fuel oil and wood were used as fuel for the thermal stations producing power for the copper mines. Each mine had its own power station until 1948 when it was decided to connect the main thermal stations and supply power to the different mines from a central area, Kitwe. To operate this scheme a company known as the Rhodesia Congo Border Power Corporation was formed. As a result of the rapidly increasing demand for electricity, another thermal station, which became the corporation's chief power station, was built at Nchanga. When the Chibuluma and Bancroft mines were opened power had to be imported from the hydro-electric station at Le Marinel in the Zaire. Kariba began supplying power to the Copperbelt on 28 December, 1959. In 1969 over 70% of all the power requirement of the Copperbelt was supplied by Kariba.

There are a number of hydro-electric stations in the country built to cope with the ever-increasing demand for electricity, a demand created by the rapid growth of industries in the country. The first hydro-electric station to operate in Zambia was Mulungushi which began supplying power to the lead and zinc mines at Kabwe in 1925.

Another hydro-electric station on the Lunsemfwa River supplements power produced by the Mulungushi station. Power is carried about 45 km to Mulungushi and thence another 58 km to Kabwe. A hydro-electric station built at the junction of the third and fourth gorges just below the Victoria Falls in 1938 supplied power to Livingstone until a new underground power station next to the old one was built to increase the power supply to Livingstone and also to supply power to areas as far north as Mazabuka. This station also exports power to Zimbabwe.

Smaller hydro-electric stations are found also at Kasama (Luombe River), Mansa (Luongo River), Mbala (Lunzuwa River), Serenje (Lusiwasi River) and Musonda Falls (Luapula).

A new multi-million kwacha hydro-electric scheme has been constructed at the Kafue Gorge, 25 km to the south-east of the town of Kafue (see Fig. 81). The project consists of a dam and power station at Kafue Gorge and storage and regulation dam at Itezhi Tezhi. Zambia now has both the north bank power station at Kariba or the Kafue Gorge Power Station in operation. The country decided to go ahead with both power stations as the industrial demand for electricity in the near future would not

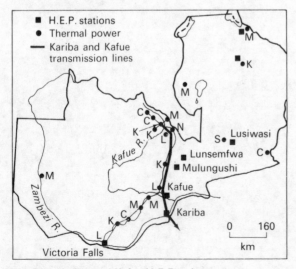

Fig. 81   Kariba and Kafue H.E.P. schemes

The new underground power station at Victoria Falls. Write down the advantages of hydro electric power generation over thermal power generating plants

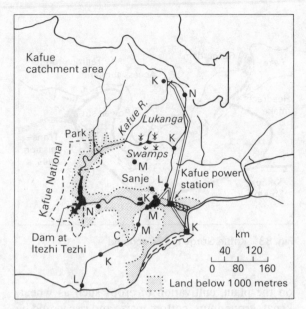

Fig. 82 Kafue scheme

be met if only one of the projects was developed. Zambia, however, decided to develop the Kafue Gorge hydro-electric station first for a number of reasons.

The Kafue Station is closer to the industrial areas and thus would reduce the cost of electricity transmission especially to the new industrial centre at Kafue itself, where industries such as textile milling, chemicals and fertilisers have sprung up. The dam at Itezhi Tezhi Gap not only provides an important fishery close to Kafue and Lusaka, but also provides all year round irrigation water for the Kafue Flats. Sugar cane is the chief crop cultivated here and its expansion will make Zambia self-sufficient in sugar. By controlling the flood waters

Kafue Gorge

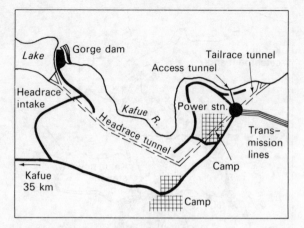

Fig. 83   Kafue Gorge H.E.P. scheme

360 m. The water is led out to the river by the tail-race tunnel about 1 300 m long (see diagram 84). The underground power house contains six turbo-generators which produce 150 MW each, a transformer and operation room. Only four of the generators are commissioned. The other two will come into operation when the demand for electricity increases.

As already indicated (page 126), work on the north bank power station at Kariba began in 1970 while work on a second hydro-electric station at Victoria Falls will bring installed capacity here up to 100 MW. The government plans to bring electricity to the more densely populated rural areas, and link small diesel generating units with the larger hydro-electric schemes at a later stage.

on the plain, cultivation of crops such as wheat, kenaf, groundnuts, cotton, maize and rice would be increased. The new lake will also provide all the water required for industrial and domestic purposes by the Lusaka and Kafue areas. Since the lake is close to a tarred highway from the Copperbelt and Lusaka it could be developed as an important holiday attraction.

The site for the underground power house 450 m below the rock surface is on the south bank of the Kafue below the Chinonkomene hill. The dam wall is 45 m high from the valley floor. The water is led to the power house by the head-race tunnel about 10 km in length. The water flows gently at first but near the power house six pen-stocks take the water down a vertical drop of

Things to do
1 How is a thermal power station different from a hydro-electric station?
2 With reference to hydro-electric power stations, what is meant by 'head of water'? Give examples of two hydro-electric stations having a natural 'head of water' in Zambia.
3 What impact will the Kafue hydro-electric and irrigation scheme have on Zambia when it is fully completed?
4 In what ways is the Kafue hydro-electric scheme different from, and similar to, the Kariba Scheme?

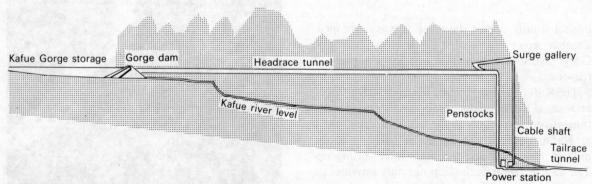

Fig. 84   Kafue – the underground power house

28 Industry and towns (Zambia)

Industrial growth

In the industrial field Zambia has progressed very rapidly since independence. The index of industrial production rose from 100 in 1961 to 262·8 in June, 1968. The contribution of the manufacturing industries to the country's wealth rose from 4·6% in 1954 to 10·7% in 1967. The government is striving to make the country's economy less dependent on copper because of market price changes and the risk of a slump on the market. To implement its policy of encouraging industrial development, the Industrial Development Corporation was formed. This corporation has been handed the task of diversifying the economy and, at the same time, by encouraging a wide range of other industries within the country, to reduce the reliance on imports for the supply of consumer goods. The government also wants industries to be distributed more evenly throughout the country. By developing industries in the rural areas the government is trying to curb the migration of population to urban areas. These rural industries will also lead to an increasing demand for agricultural products, thus encouraging the development of the agricultural industry.

The Industrial Development Corporation, a government body, participates directly in industry by holding shares ranging from 100% to 2% in interests that include mining, explosives, oil, road services, textiles, sugar, hotels, tobacco, business houses, grain-milling, chemicals and many others.

In spite of the government's decentralising policy, access to markets, ease of communications, power supply and location of raw materials have resulted in the location of most of the country's industries in the urban areas along the line of rail. The Copperbelt, however, has the lion's share in the industries of the country. The reasons for this are:

1 There is a concentration of population here, which not only supplies the necessary labour force but also creates a ready market for manufactured articles.

2 Power is easily available from thermal stations operated by the copper mines and from Kafue and Kariba.

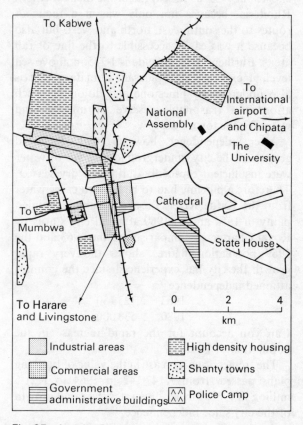

To Kabwe

To International airport and Chipata

National Assembly

The University

Cathedral

To Mumbwa

State House

To Harare and Livingstone

0 2 4
km

Industrial areas

High density housing

Commercial areas

Shanty towns

Government administrative buildings

Police Camp

Fig. 85 Lusaka City

3 The region has a good network of both tarred roads and railways.

4 A number of industries were established to produce goods such as explosives and ventilation equipment for use in the mines.

The chief urban centres

Lusaka

Lusaka began, in 1905, as a siding of the railway line built from Livingstone northwards to Broken Hill. It was named after Chief Lusaaka of the Lenje Village where it was built. Since the siding was built on the eastern edge of a flat area underlain by limestone and dolomite it was to suffer from serious water problems; there is hardly any surface drainage and therefore during the dry season there is a serious water problem and because the land rises gently to the north, east and south it becomes water-logged during the rainy season.

In spite of the drainage problems, Lusaka was chosen, in 1935, as the capital of the then Northern Rhodesia, because not only was it a focus of routes to the south, east, north and west, but also because it was easily accessible to the line of rail areas. Further, as its altitude is 1 245 m above sea level, it experiences a pleasant climate and it is also underlain by limestone and dolomite which afforded a reasonable reserve of underground water for the town's use.

After independence, however, with the rapid growth of the city, underground reserves of water were insufficient especially during the dry season. Therefore a pipeline had to be built to carry water from the Kafue River. Lusaka became a municipality in 1954 and in 1960 attained city status by Royal Charter. A comparison of the 1963 and the 1969 population figures shows the very rapid growth the city has experienced since the country attained independence:

1963 . . 123 150

1980 . . 538 000

Can you account for the rapid increase in the population of Lusaka?

The tremendous increase in the value of building plans passed, from K147 142 in 1964 to K21·5 million in 1967, further illustrates the rapid growth of the city since independence.

A look at the map of the city (Fig. 85) shows that it has no clearly defined centre. The chief commercial area is along that part of the Great North Road, known here as Cairo Road, which passes through the city; the government administrative buildings and low density residential areas occupy the eastern ridges, while the industrial and high density residential areas are found on the western flat land.

Lusaka is not only the most important urban area but is also the legislative, judicial and administrative capital of Zambia. It is, moreover, an important education centre boasting such institutions as the country's only university, a College of Further Education and a College of Natural Resources. Study the map (Fig. 85) and name the two important institutions that are located along the road to Chipata.

The city's industries are closely related to the surrounding farm produce, e.g. tobacco auctioning, tobacco-manufacturing, cotton-ginning, dairy products, grain-milling and meat-processing. Other industries include furniture, assembly of commercial trucks, steel-galvanising, pottery and distilling and brewing. In which part of the city is the chief industrial area located?

Lusaka is also an important route centre. Study the map (Fig. 85, page 187) to find out how many road routes converge on Lusaka. Roads from three different countries meet here. Which are these countries? It has a modern international airport capable of handling the most modern aircraft. In which direction is this airport from the city?

The city's water supply comes from boreholes and via a pipeline from the Kafue River, and electricity comes from the Kafue and Kariba hydro-electric stations. Its own thermal station is only operated in an emergency.

Kitwe

Kitwe, which is the largest urban area and the chief commercial and industrial centre on the Copperbelt, was made a city in 1966. Its population was 315 000 in 1980. It is an important copper mining location; it is the centre of Nchanga Consolidated Copper Mines' Copper Refinery and also has a new plant named TORCO for the treatment of refactory ores that could not be treated by the normal processes. It is also the distribution centre for electricity on the Copperbelt. It has a

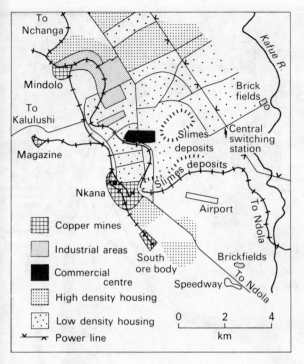

Fig. 86   Kitwe

number of industries manufacturing products for use in the mines (e.g. plastic helmets and buckets) batteries and acid accumulators, electrical equipment and glazed bricks and pipes. Other industries include iron foundries, maize milling, brewing, food and drink processing and the manufacture of matches. Study the map (Fig. 86, above) and answer the following questions:

1 Which river flows to the east of the city?
2 What are slimes deposits?
3 What is meant by the Central Switching Station on the map? You may find the answer on page 181.

Ndola

Ndola is the gateway to the Copperbelt for the commercial and agricultural areas of the Southern and Central Provinces. A city with an estimated population of 229 000 in 1974, it is a focal point of land communications. It is a railway junction for lines going to the south, to Mufulira, Kitwe and Chingola, to Luanshya and to the north via Lubumbashi to Lobito. It is served by an international airport. It is the administrative headquarters of the Copperbelt Province and also an important commercial, industrial and marketing centre

Industries include printing, a truck assembly plant, a Dunlop tyre factory, manufacturing of plastics, cement, soaps and vegetable oils, furniture and tyres, a sugar refinery, the Roan Consolidated Mines' Copper Refinery, breweries, sawmills and a factory producing acetylene and oxygen. It is the terminus for the oil pipeline from Dar es Salaam and the siting of the oil refinery here will greatly boost the importance of the city.

Mufulira

Mufulira, with an estimated population in 1974 of 136 000, has one of the largest copper mines in the world. Its industries include a copper refinery, explosives factory at Kafironda, light engineering and printing.

Luanshya

Luanshya, with a population just over 100 000, is the commercial centre for the Roan Antelope Mine. It has a number of industries which include the manufacture of sulphuric acid, a copper fabrication plant producing copper wires and cables, a factory producing ventilation equipment, glazed pipes and tiles, plastic articles, clothing and a new welding electrode factory.

Other towns in the Copperbelt include Chingola, Kalulushi and Chililabombwe, the commercial centres for Nchanga, Chibuluma and Bancroft mines respectively.

Livingstone

Livingstone, the administrative headquarters of the Southern Province was the country's capital from 1911 to 1935. An important communications centre today, it began as a bridge town and developed, because of its situation 11 km from the famous Victoria Falls, as the country's chief tourist centre. It had a population of about 50 000 in 1974.

It is the chief point of entry for railway-borne goods from the south and the collecting and distribution centre for goods destined for the Western Province. Its industries include the assembly of motor vehicles, assembly of radios, manufacture of blankets, hardboards and candles, flour-milling and tobacco-grading.

Radio assembly at Livingstone. Why is this type of industry located in a town with easy access to other towns? Pay particular attention to the word *assembly*

Its chief attractions, besides the Victoria Falls, include the national museum which contains a collection of African weapons, tools, arts and crafts, old maps and many other things connected with the life and times of David Livingstone and Cecil John Rhodes. It also offers to the visitors an enclosed game park, an African handicraft village and boat trips on the Zambezi.

The town is served by an international airport. Do you know from where the town obtains its power supply?

Kabwe

Kabwe is a mining town half-way between the Copperbelt and Lusaka with an estimated population of 98 000 in 1974. Can you name the minerals mined here? It is the administrative headquarters of the Central Province and also the headquarters of Zambia Railways. The railways have new workshops to maintain and service their locomotives and a training centre for their staff.

The town's industries include light engineering, brewing, milling, dairy products and the manufacture of jute grain bags. Do you know where most of the world's jute is cultivated? Is the jute plant similar to the sisal plant? Note that kenaf, a plant somewhat similar to jute, is also used in the manufacture of grain bags. Zambia is now experimenting in the cultivation of kenaf at Chisamba and Kafue.

The town gets its power supply from the Kariba-Kafue Grid while the mine uses Mulungushi power.

Kafue

About 45 km to the south of Lusaka, Kafue is developing into an important industrial centre in Zambia. A number of factors favour the development of this small town. These include:
1 Ease of communications—it is at the meeting point of trunk roads from Livingstone, Salisbury, Lusaka and the Copperbelt, and also on the main north–south railway line;
2 Ample supplies of hydro-electric power from the Kafue hydro-electric scheme;
3 As it is very close to the Kafue River it has ample

supplies of water for domestic and industrial requirements;

4 It lies close to a rich farming hinterland—the area near Mazabuka on the Kafue flats is a potentially rich agricultural area and the region to the north towards· Lusaka and Mumbwa is important for cotton, tobacco, maize and cattle. This area is comparatively densely populated and is therefore able to supply all the necessary labour force. Its industries include a textile mill, nitrogenous fertiliser and chemical factory.

Other sizeable urban centres in the country include Kasama, Chipata, Mazabuka, Mongu and Mbala. Kasama, Chipata and Mongu are also provincial administrative headquarters. Do you know of which provinces these are headquarters?

Things to do
1 Livingstone was the old capital and Lusaka is the present capital of Zambia. Compare and contrast the location and functions of these two urban centres. Draw sketch maps to show their locations.
2 What is the aim of the government in decentralising industries in the country? Note the difficulties.

3 If you live in a town draw a simple sketch map of your town to show
a) the street pattern;
b) the location of
 i) the civic centre;
 ii) trading centre;
 iii) industrial areas;
 iv) main residential areas;
c) the main highways
 i) railway—if any;
 ii) roads;
 iii) airport—if any.

4 Make a list of the different industries found in your town. You could list them under the following groups:
 Using agricultural raw materials; heavy industries; light industries; mining; others.

5 Assume you are an industrialist who wants to build a copper fabrication plant in Zambia. You have two places in mind, Kafue and Luanshya, for the location of the factory. Describe all the factors that would influence your decision. Read Chapter 4 (page 22) of Lands and Peoples of Central Africa before you tackle this question.

29 Communications and Trade (Zambia)

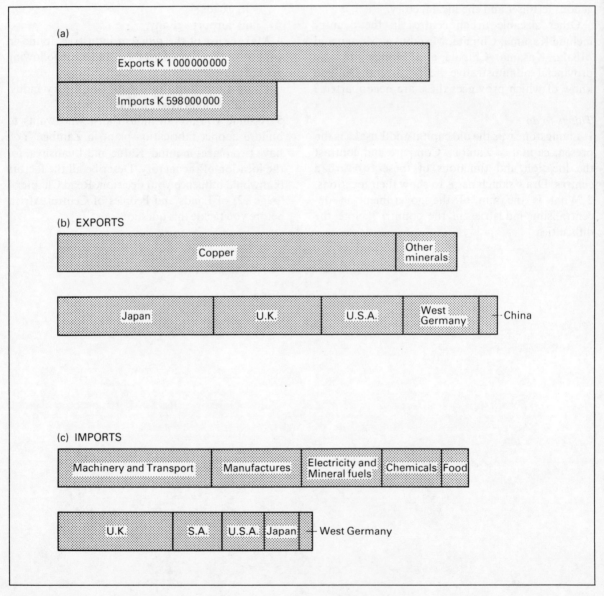

Fig. 87 Zambia's trade in 1979. (a) Value in Kwacha of total exports and imports; (b) Major exports and selected customers; (c) Major imports and selected suppliers. Scales in (b) and (c) differ so the bar graphs are not comparable

Trade

The total value of Zambian exports for the year 1979 was K1 000 000 000. Study Fig. 87 which shows the chief exports and their relative importance. Minerals accounted for over 97% of the exports in 1979.

1 Can you name the chief exports?

2 Which two minerals make up the bulk of the exports in the column headed 'other minerals' in Fig. 87(b).

3 In 1979, which country was Zambia's most important customer?

The total value of imports in 1979 was K598 000 000. Fig. 87 gives the relative importance of the chief commodities imported into the country in 1979.

It also shows Zambia's chief trading partners and the relative value of their trade in 1979.

1 Attempt to explain why machinery and transport equipment form such a large proportion of the imports.

2 Fig 87(c) shows that about two-thirds of the imports are made up by machinery and transport equipment and manufactured articles. What does this tell you about the extent to which the country is industrialised?

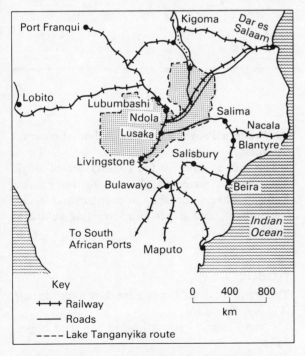

Fig. 88 Zambia transportation map—external

Trade routes

Since Zambia is a landlocked country her imports and exports have to travel through the neighbouring countries of Zimbabwe, Mozambique, Malaŵi, Tanzania, Zaire and Angola. The chief outlets, besides the South Africa ports include three ports on the East Coast and one on the West Coast. Look at the map (Figure 88) to find the names of these ports. Since 1965 Zambia has developed a number of alternative routes to the coast, some of them new particularly through Tanzania and Malaŵi, so that she may be less dependent on South African ports. These include:

1 the Tanzam railway line from Kapiri Mposhi to Dar es Salaam;

2 the Lake Tanganyika route from Mpulungu to Kigoma and thence by rail to Dar es Salaam;

3 the rail route from Ndola to Kalemie on Lake Tanganyika, by steamer to Kigoma and from there by rail to Dar es Salaam;

4 the road route to Salima in Malaŵi and from there by rail to Beira or Nacala;

5 the road route from Kapiri Mposhi to Dar es Salaam;

6 the rail route from Ndola to Benguela, and

7 the direct air route from Ndola to Dar es Salaam.

See the diagram (Fig. 89) for these trade routes.

Communications
Railways

The railways in Zambia were once part of Zimbabwe Railways, an integrated system serving both Zimbabwe and Zambia. When Zambia gained independence the railways in Zambia broke away from Zimbabwe Railways to become Zambia Railways, a government undertaking, with its headquarters at Kabwe.

The railway line was extended north from Bulawayo in Zimbabwe to tap the minerals that were discovered in Zambia. The route taken by the line, therefore, was influenced by the presence of these minerals. The line from Hwange reached Victoria Falls in 1904 and the Broken Hill mines at Kabwe in 1905 and was extended to the Copperbelt and the Zaire border in 1909. The line is now linked up with the Benguela Railway which gives the country access to the port of Lobito Bay and also with the Zaire rail system which provides a steamer connection across Lake Tanganyika with the East African

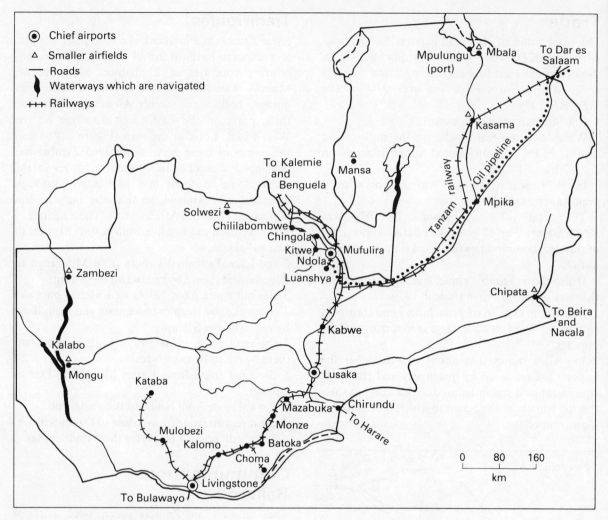

Fig. 89   Zambia transportation map

Railways. A further connection with the East African Railways was made with the completion of the line from Kapiri Mposhi to Dar es Salaam. This line will help to open up the relatively under-developed area of the Northern Province and has added a new route for the copper exports of the country. Mpika will be the chief servicing centre for this railway.

Besides the 832 km main line from Livingstone to Ndola there are a number of branch lines connecting all the copper mines to Ndola, which, as a result, has become an important railway junction. The Zambezi sawmills line runs from the logging camp at Kataba to Livinstone. This line was built to transport timber from the teak forests of

the Western Province. A branch line also serves the Maamba colliery.

The railway lines in the country are of single track with a guage of about a metre. Zambia Railways have a workshop to maintain and service locomotives, and a personnel training centre at Kabwe.

Roads

The trunk roads in Zambia are shown on the map (Fig. 89). These are:

1 From Victoria Falls to Lusaka and the Copperbelt;

2 the Great North Road from Chirundu via

Kapiri Mposhi and to Mpika and East Africa;
3 from Lusaka to Chipata and Malawi;
4 from Lusaka to Mongu.

All the trunk roads, which have a total length of over 3 800 km, have a bituminous surface.

Most areas in Zambia have a regular passenger bus service and goods transport service.

Airways

There are three international airports and a number of smaller airports for internal passenger and goods services. From the map (Fig. 89, page 194) name the centres with international airports. The new airport at Lusaka is capable of handling the largest aircraft. Lusaka is the base for Zambia Airways which operates regular domestic and international flights

Waterways

Zambia's waterways include Lakes Tanganyika, Bangweulu and Mweru and parts of the Zambezi and Luapula Rivers. Some of the goods imported through Dar es Salaam are transhipped from Kigoma to Mpulungu, Zambia's only port. There are a number of small harbours on the other lakes, used mainly by fishing crafts. Mongu has its own harbour Maramba on the mid-Zambezi flood plain. Boats transport goods to such places as Kalabo from here. Sections of the Zambezi above the Victoria Falls are used for transporting timber from the Senanga teak forests. Which other river in Zambia, besides the Zambezi, has stretches used as internal waterways? Look for the answer on the map (Fig. 89).

Things to do
1 Name three routes by which copper is exported from Zambia.
 a) What are Zambia's chief exports other than minerals?
 b) Name three of Zambia's chief customers in order of importance.
 c) Name three of the chief imports.
 d) Name the chief suppliers of Zambian imports.
3 What impact will the new railway line from Kapiri Mposhi to Dar es Salaam have on the Northern Province in particular and Zambia in general?
4 Describe briefly the immediate and long-term advantages and disadvantages to Zambia of her trade break with Zimbabwe, 1970–1980.

Aerial view of Mpulungu. Identify the features lettered on the photograph

30 Population (Zambia)

The population of Zambia is made up of Africans, Europeans, Asians and Coloureds. The non-African population in 1969 was approximately 90 000.

Study table 56 below which gives the 1980 distribution of population by provinces and also shows the percentage change in the population since the census of 1974 and calculate the total population in 1974 and 1980.

Table 56

Province	August 1980 census	1974 Sample census	% change since the 1974 census
Central	513 000	919 000	−57
Copperbelt	1 248 000	1 046 145	+24
Eastern	656 000	570 000	+17
Luapula	413 000	321 000	+27
North western	302 000	242 000	+20
Northern	678 000	584 000	+14
Southern	686 000	534 000	+30
Western	488 000	460 000	+ 6

The actual distribution of population varies from place to place (see Fig. 90). Numerous factors, often inter-related, determine this uneven distribution.

Some of the more discernible factors include:
1 physical influences, e.g. relief features, water supplies, soils, etc.:
2 historical influences—tribal warfare and settlement;
3 disease and pests, e.g. tsetse fly;
4 human influences e.g. mining and other industries, bomas, co-operatives.

A study of the population density map brings out the following distribution pattern:
1 The line of rail area extending from Livingstone in the south to the Copperbelt in the north forms a belt with population concentrations mainly around the urban and peri-urban areas. A number of factors, many of them inter-related, determine the high density of population along this belt. The copper and cobalt mines of the Copperbelt and the lead and zinc mines at Kabwe attracted a good network of communications and these two factors in turn attracted a number of industries, all of which together attracted a large rural migrant population in search of wage-earning jobs.

Besides having mineral and being close to good lines of communication to facilitate transport, this belt lies on the plateau and therefore with an average annual rainfall of over 750 mm, it is better watered than most areas in the country, and with temperatures moderated by altitude the climate is very favourable not only for settlement but also for crop production. The inherently fertile soils of this belt combined with the other factors described above have made it the chief area for commercial crop production and stock farming.
2 The eastern plateau region extending from Petauke in the south to Lundazi in the north was settled by the Ngoni who migrated northwards from southern Africa. This plateau also has relatively fertile soils and a climate suited to the cultivation of groundnuts, maize and tobacco, and cattle rearing. It is, therefore, able to support a large population.
3 The mid-Zambezi floodplain in the Western Province settled by the Lozi also has a relatively high density of population. The Zambezi Floodplain is a fertile area well suited for pastoral and crop farming. Fishing is also important here.
4 Fishing appears to have attracted a concentration of population along the lower Luapula Basin. This area, ruled by Chief Kazembe during

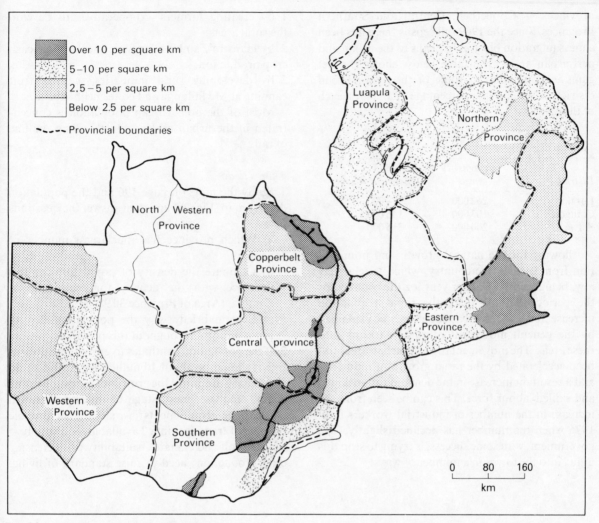

Fig. 90   Zambia population distribution

the eighteenth century, thrived as a meeting point of a number of trade routes and therefore attracted a large population. Many smaller tribes which came to Kazembe for protection against the advance of the more warlike tribes also settled here.

5 Separating the relatively high density areas of the mid-Zambezi Basin and those along the rail line is a region of very sparse population. A large part of this region which is infected by tsetse fly and therefore not suitable for cattle rearing is taken up by the Kafue National Park.

6 Another area of low population density is the Luangwa Basin, also infested with tsetse fly. The Luangwa Game Park occupies a large part of this area. The Muchinga escarpment forming the

western wall of the Luangwa Basin has a very sparse population because of the hilly and broken nature of the land.

Over most of the plateau and the Zambezi and Luangwa Basins local concentrations of population are determined by the availability of water during the dry season. This is especially so on the Kalahari sands area in the south western part of the Western Province and the escarpment zones of the Zambezi and Luangwa basins where due to steep slopes surface run-off is rapid and therefore there is little surface water during the dry season.

In 1980 slightly over 50% of the country's total population was located in the three line of rail provinces — Copperbelt, Central and Southern Provinces. Since the 1969 full census there has been a mass migration of rural Africans to the urban and peri-urban areas. The table below shows the net gains in population of some of the major urban districts. Calculate the percentage change for each of the districts.

Table 57

District	August 1969 census	1980 census
Lusaka	262 000	538 000
Chingola	103 000	146 000
Kitwe	200 000	315 000

Allowing for the natural growth and immigration from outside the country, which is relatively low, being below 5 000 per year for the country for the period 1977 to 1980, the rapid population increase in the urban areas could only be explained by the general movement of rural Africans into these areas. The movement towards urban areas has been accelerated by the rapid growth of industries and a resultant increase in the demand for unskilled and skilled labour force. This can be seen from the increase in the number of industrial workers until 1975 when the number has declined slightly. The government, with some success, is trying to stop this influx into the towns in a number of ways:

1 by creating farmers' co-operatives to develop the rural areas;
2 by loans to Zambian farmers to encourage cash crop production;
3 by developing rural industries such as fruit canning at Mwinilunga and coffee near Mbala.

Most of the non-African population is concentrated in the urban centres, chiefly along the line of rail.

Things to do
1 Study the table on page 196 and the population density map (Fig. 90) and then answer the questions below:
   a) Which province has the largest number of people?
   b) Compare the density of population for this province with the density for the whole of Zambia. (Area of Province 30 980 km².)
   c) Explain briefly why the population density is not uniform throughout this province.
2 If the population continues to grow at the present rate it should be about 10 million by 1990. Should Zambia try to control the growth of her population? Think on these lines: Stage of industrial growth and labour requirements; would the favourable balance of trade continue? available food supply— types of soil and climate—suitability for increasing crop production; need to raise standard of living.

Epilogue

Since the last edition of this book in 1981, many economic steps have been taken by the new Zimbabwean Government and statistics for the 1970s have become available. An overview of the major Government economic plans is given below.

In March 1981, the Government organised the Zimbabwe Conference on Reconstruction and Development (ZIMCORD) in order to seek international aid for post-war reconstruction, land settlement and rural development. Nations of the world contributed generously and the grants and loans exceeded the amount requested. A large percentage of ZIMCORD resources was channelled into the rural sector. The communal lands (formerly known as Tribal Trust Lands) suffered the ravages of war. Kraals, dip tanks, wells, schools, clinics and bridges were destroyed in many areas. Repair of these and rehabilitation of the peasants are to be combined with the provision of such services as better access to markets, fuller extension services, credit facilities, electricity and the development of small towns. With an improved infrastructure, the people are less likely to move to towns in the high density suburbs which are already overcrowded. Government is also committed to assisting the commercial sector and the former African Purchase Areas, now known as large-scale and small-scale commercial sectors respectively.

A large sum of money has been set aside for resettlement schemes, some of which have already been implemented. Such projects will relieve population pressure in the communal lands and increase productivity by using the under-utilised land purchased from the commercial farmers (those who wished to sell). Co-operatives will be set up in agriculture and in other sectors of the economy. The *Ujamaa* villages of Tanzania are based on collective farming. What are the advantages of farming co-operatives?

Mining continues to play a vital role as an earner of foreign exchange but it is still too dependent on world market price fluctuations. A mineral such as copper is mined in Zimbabwe, exported abroad, made into tubing which is then imported by Zimbabwe. How can this circle be broken?

Manufacturing is expected to contribute more to import substitution in fields such as fertilisers and steel production. At the same time, labour intensive industries should be established. Why? The shortage of skilled labour is a problem affecting not only manufacturing, but also transport and power. What are the short and middle term solutions to provision of skilled manpower?

Substitution of oil imports by domestic sources continues, and Government is encouraging expansion of renewable resources such as ethanol and hydro-power. Electrification of the railway system has started and afforestation schemes are in hand.

Zambia, Malaŵi and Zimbabwe are all members of the Southern Africa Development Co-ordination Conference (SADCC) which will be a most meaningful organisation if the variety of projects under consideration are implemented. The projects cover the fields of trade, transport, power, farming, health and education, to state but a few. To achieve the aims of SADCC will demand the closest co-operation from the nine countries involved.

All three countries considered in this book are treated by the World Bank and others as third world countries. 'Third World' is a convenient term to indicate those countries which are developing. The first world is the group of industrialised nations of the capitalist system and the second world is made up of the communist countries. In global discussions the first and second worlds have become known as the North, while the developing countries are called the South.

Some third world countries are very rich, namely the oil producers of the Middle East like Kuwait, Qatar and Iraq. Most, however, are poor and the gap between them and the rich is widening. Part of the reason for this increasing gap is that third world countries are the producers of raw materials which are largely processed and consumed in the countries of the North. The diagram below clarifies this ideas:

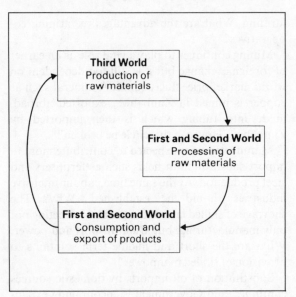

The countries of the North make the greater profit in this type of economic cycle. A solution to this problem which is partially practised is to process raw materials in the producing country. Such a step is costly in terms of establishing industrial plant and training of local personnel. Multinational companies show a natural reluctance to invest capital in countries which lack political stability and a suitable infrastructure. For these reasons and others, industrialisation in third world countries has been a very slow process.

Of all problems facing developing countries, the population explosion is by far the greatest. Zambia and Zimbabwe have a growth rate of 3·4% per annum, which means an increase of 29 children per hour every hour of the day. Malaŵi's growth rate of 2·8% is considerably lower but is still high compared with industrialised countries. In Chapter 21 the effects of population on resources are described and the necessity of research into all aspects of peasant society are emphasised. In the economic sphere alone, much research work has to be tackled. Some of the questions to be answered are: 'What are the most suitable crops for peasant farmers in areas of low rainfall and low fertility?' 'What are the cheapest and most effective means of conservation?'

A plan which is likely to help stem both the rapid growth of population and the movement of people to urban centres is the creation of small towns in the rural areas. A town serves many purposes. It has commercial, industrial, financial, residential, social and technical services. In addition, it has an infrastructure of transport, electricity, water supply and sewage disposal. Every town has close ties with the area surrounding it and each benefits from the other. The catchment area of a town is a source of goods like milk and vegetables as well as the source of many customers. The town offers agricultural extension services, grain depots, bus services and a range of manufactured products.

Much research has to be undertaken to determine both the location of towns in rural areas and their relative size. Clearly, some kind of hierarchy has to be established. It is important that the emphasis of development in the three countries should be on the rural sector where the great majority of the people live.

Index